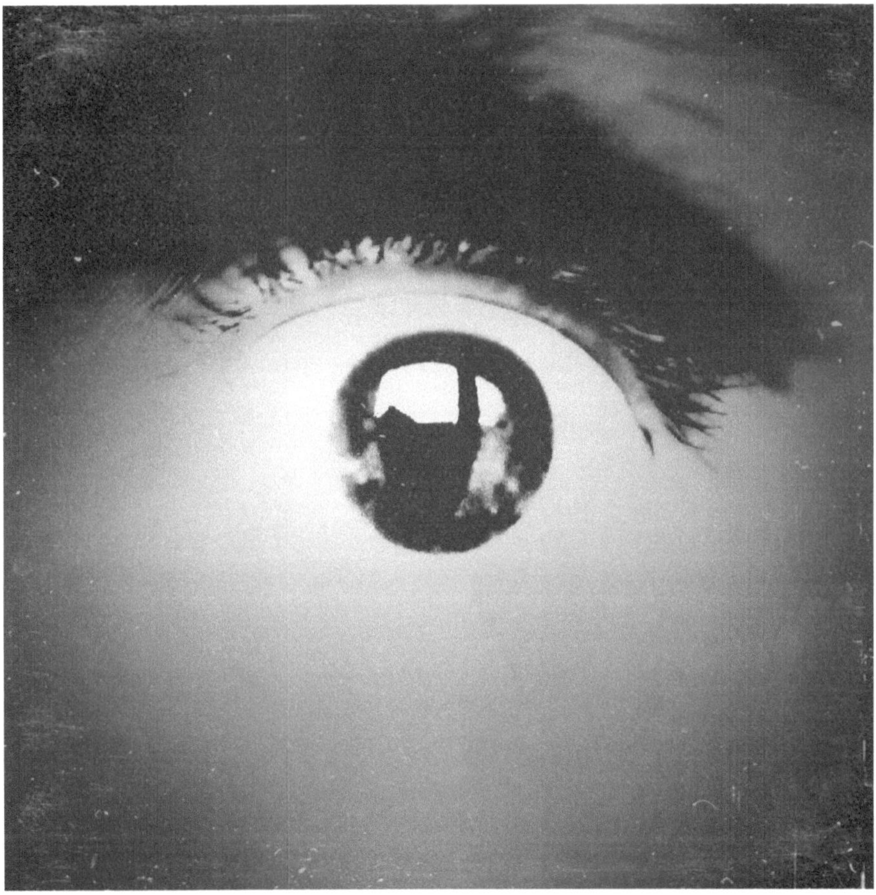

ISBN 9798860498808
Title: The inner light of migrants
Author: Alessandro Chiodo

First published in 2023
Edited by Alessandro Chiodo, Münster

Front cover: artwork by Alessandro Chiodo
© VG Bild-Kunst, Bonn 2023

Find out more about the author:
www.alessandrochiodo.net

The inner light of MIGRANTS

by
Alessandro Chiodo

PONDERA VERBORUM ART PROJECT

ANNO MMXXIII

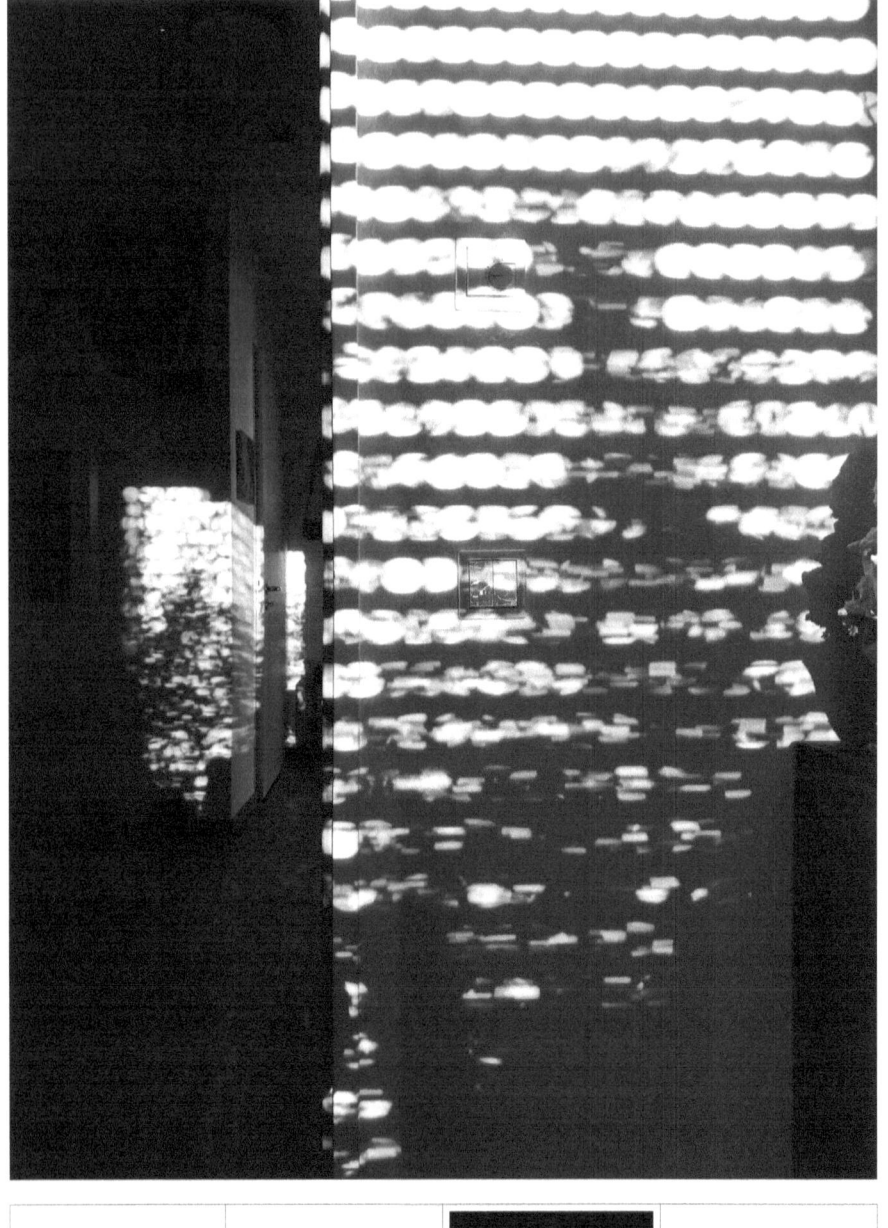

The inner light of MIGRANTS

by
Alessandro Chiodo

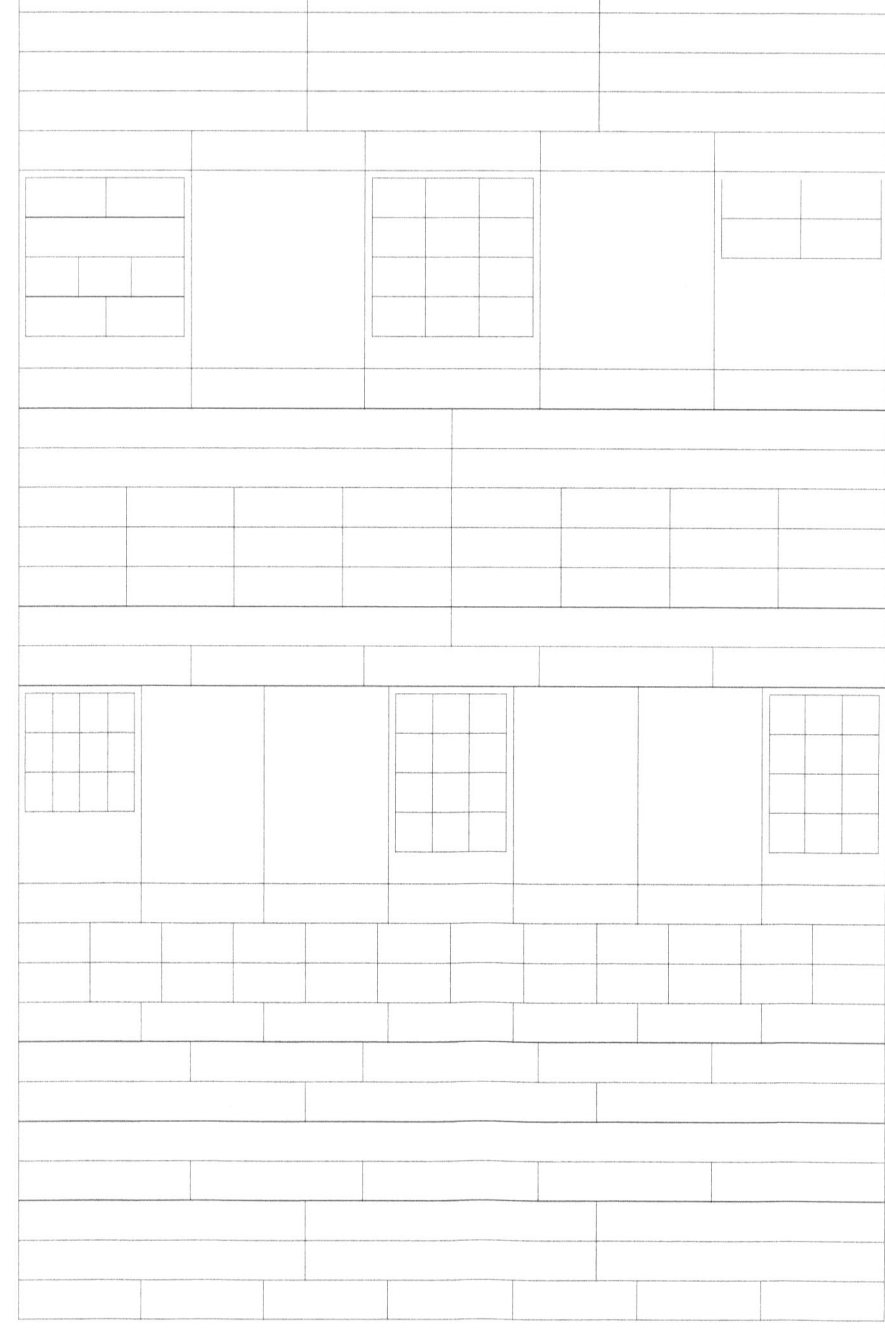

to L. E. C.

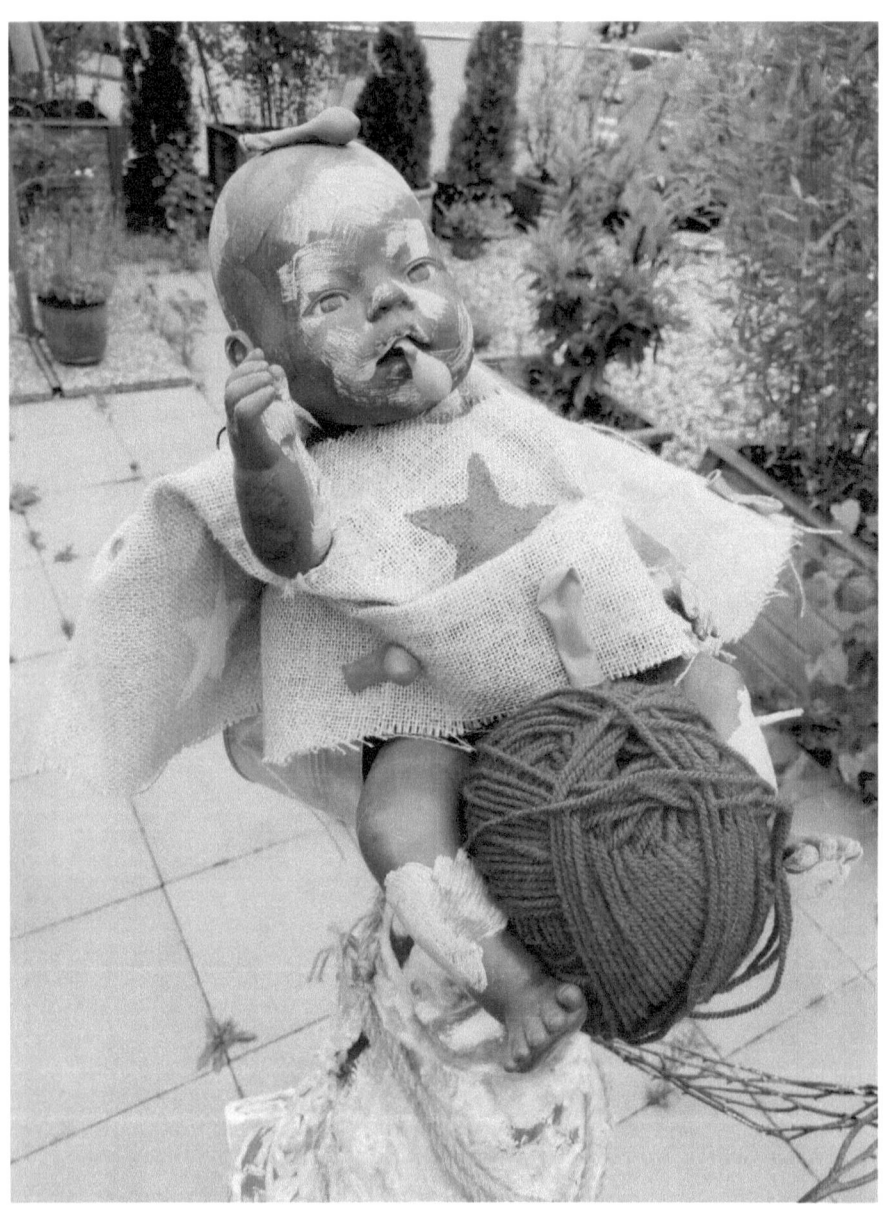

Inner light Inner light Inner light Inner light Inner light Inner light
Inner light Inner light Inner light Inner light Inner light Inner light
Inner light Inner light Inner light Inner light Inner light Inner light
Inner light Inner light Inner light Inner light Inner light Inner light
Inner light Inner light Inner light Inner light Inner light Inner light
Inner light Inner light Inner light Inner light Inner light Inner light
Inner light Inner light Inner light Inner light Inner light Inner light
Inner light Inner light Inner light Inner light Inner light Inner light
Inner light Inner light Inner light Inner light Inner light Inner light

MiGraNT POwER S

Inner light Inner light Inner light Inner light Inner light Inner light
Inner light Inner light Inner light Inner light Inner light Inner light
Inner light Inner light Inner light Inner light Inner light Inner light
Inner light Inner light Inner light Inner light Inner light Inner light
Inner light Inner light Inner light Inner light Inner light Inner light
Inner light Inner light Inner light Inner light Inner light Inner light
Inner light Inner light Inner light Inner light Inner light Inner light
Inner light Inner light Inner light Inner light Inner light Inner light
Inner light Inner light Inner light Inner light Inner light Inner light
Inner light Inner light Inner light Inner light Inner light Inner light
Inner light Inner light Inner light Inner light Inner light Inner light
Inner light Inner light Inner light Inner light Inner light Inner light
Inner light Inner light Inner light Inner light Inner light Inner light
Inner light Inner light Inner light Inner light Inner light Inner light
Inner light Inner light Inner light Inner light Inner light Inner light
Inner light Inner light Inner light Inner light Inner light Inner light

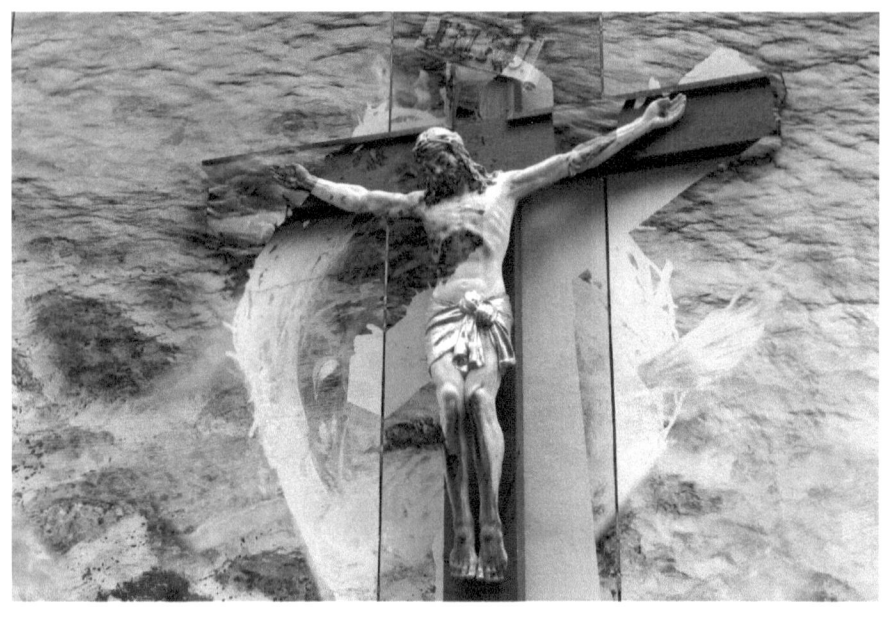

The racist chap says:
«Not a step! Go home!»

The migrant replies:
«No! We carry on!»

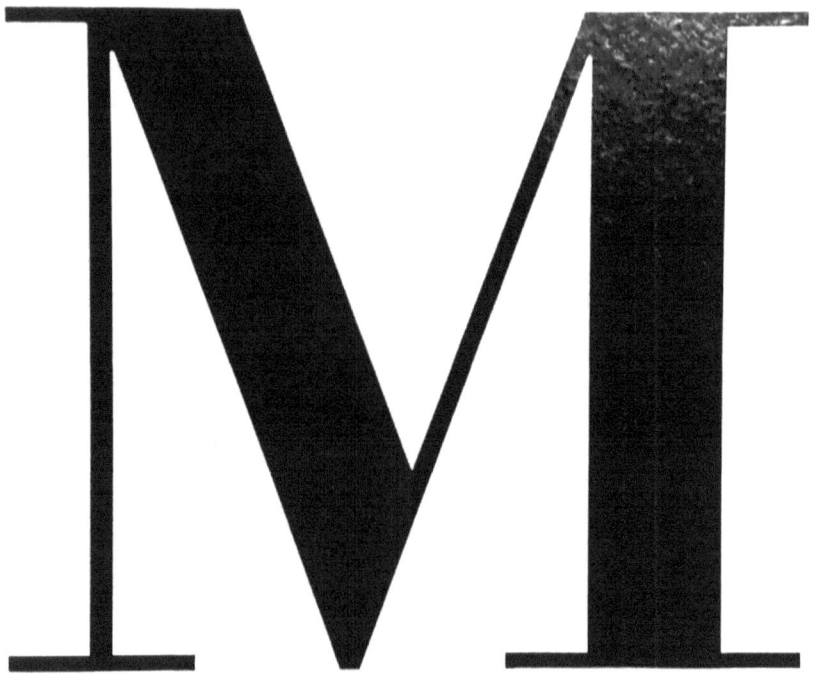

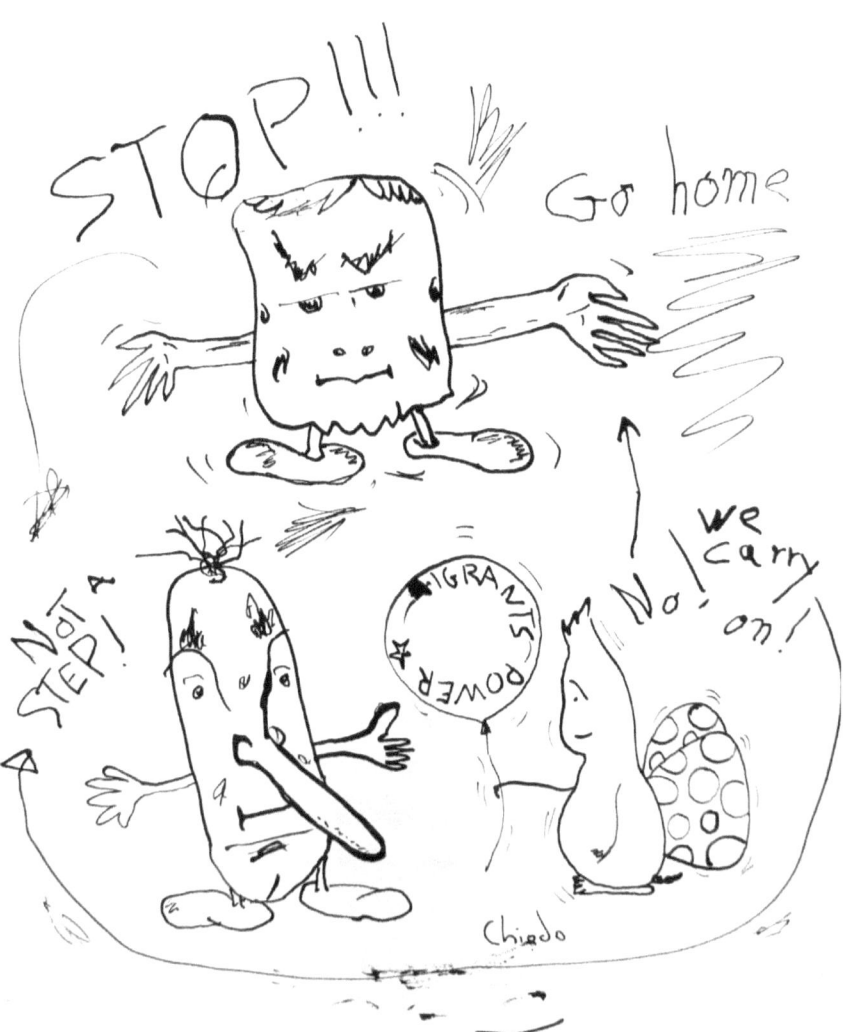

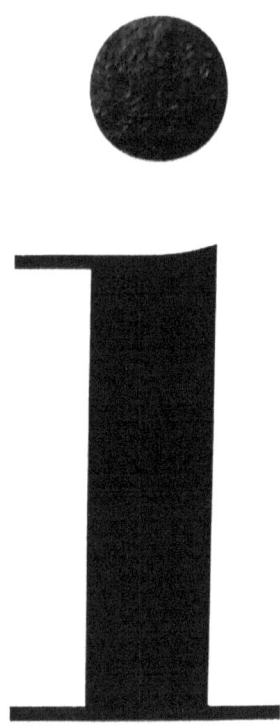

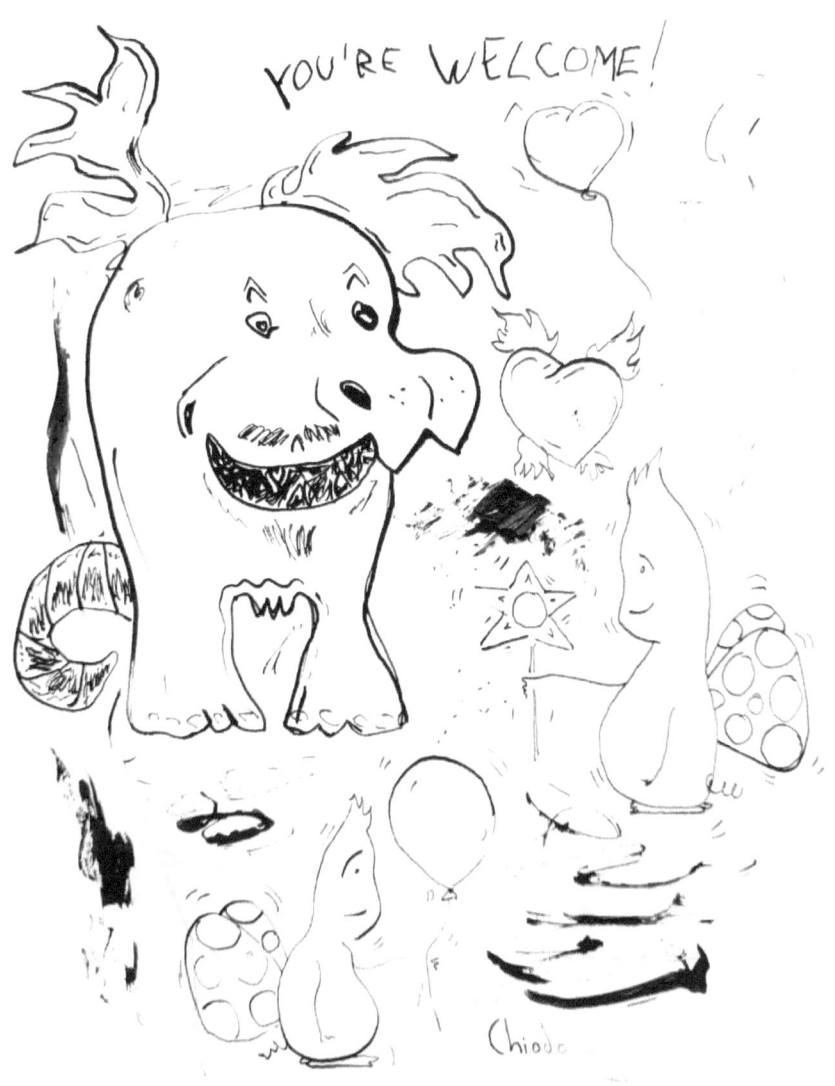

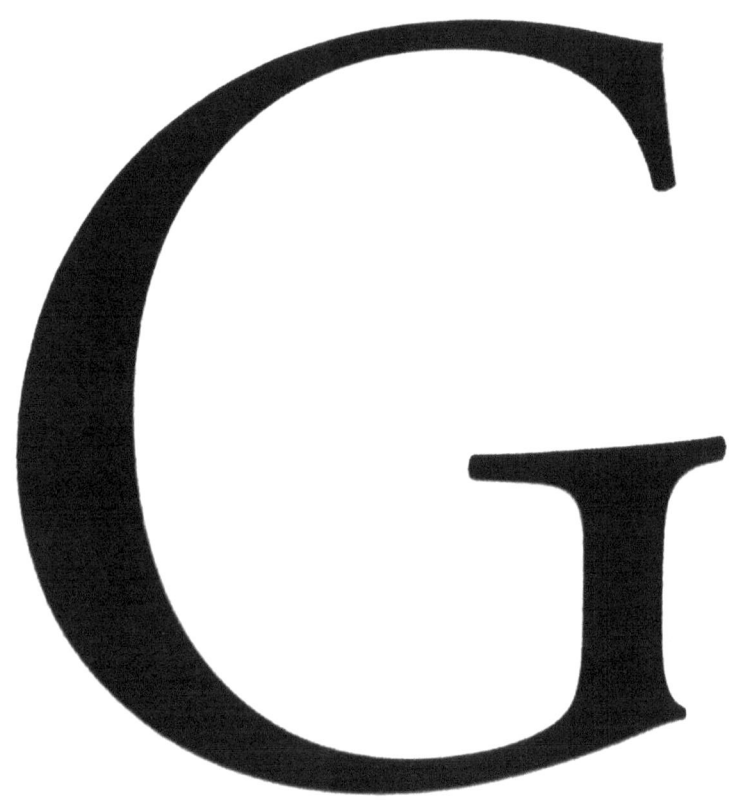

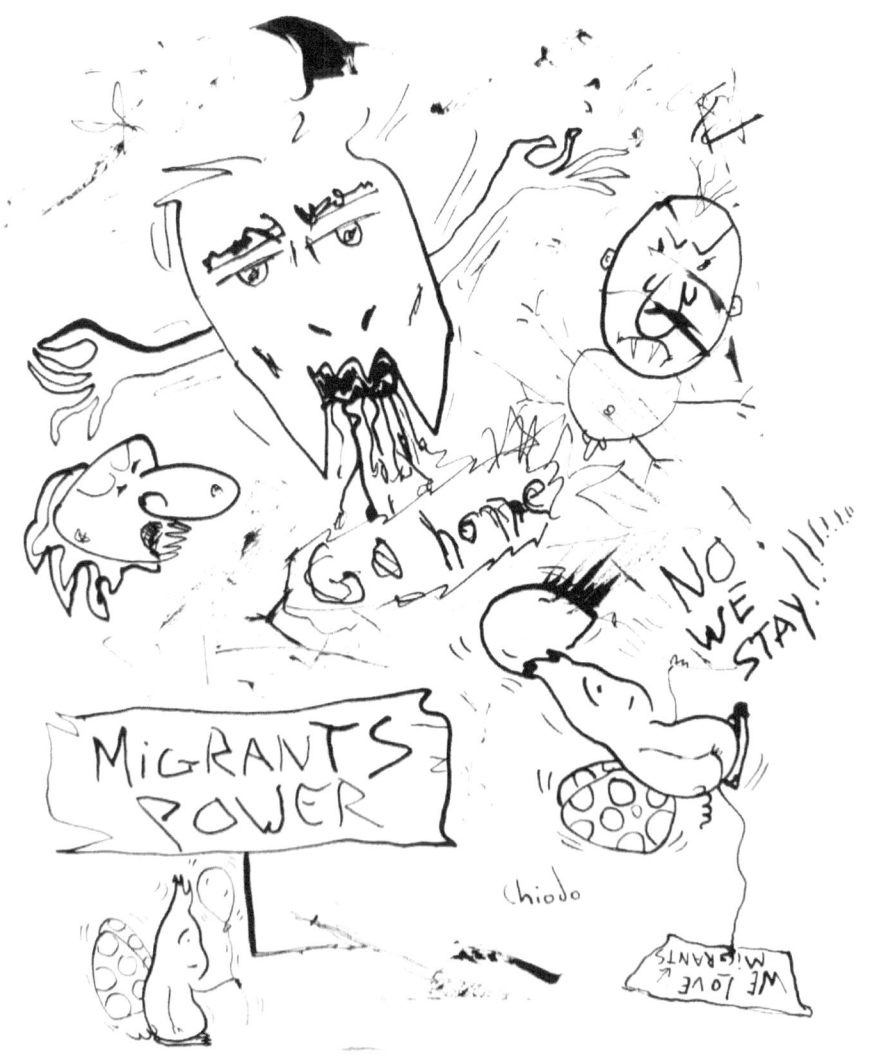

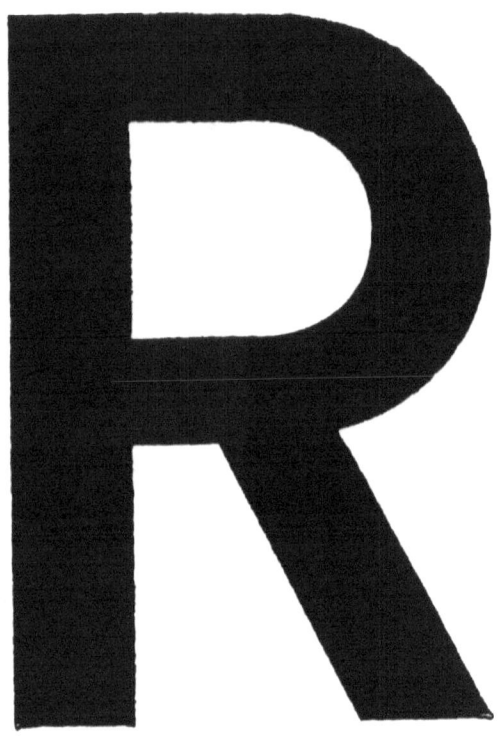

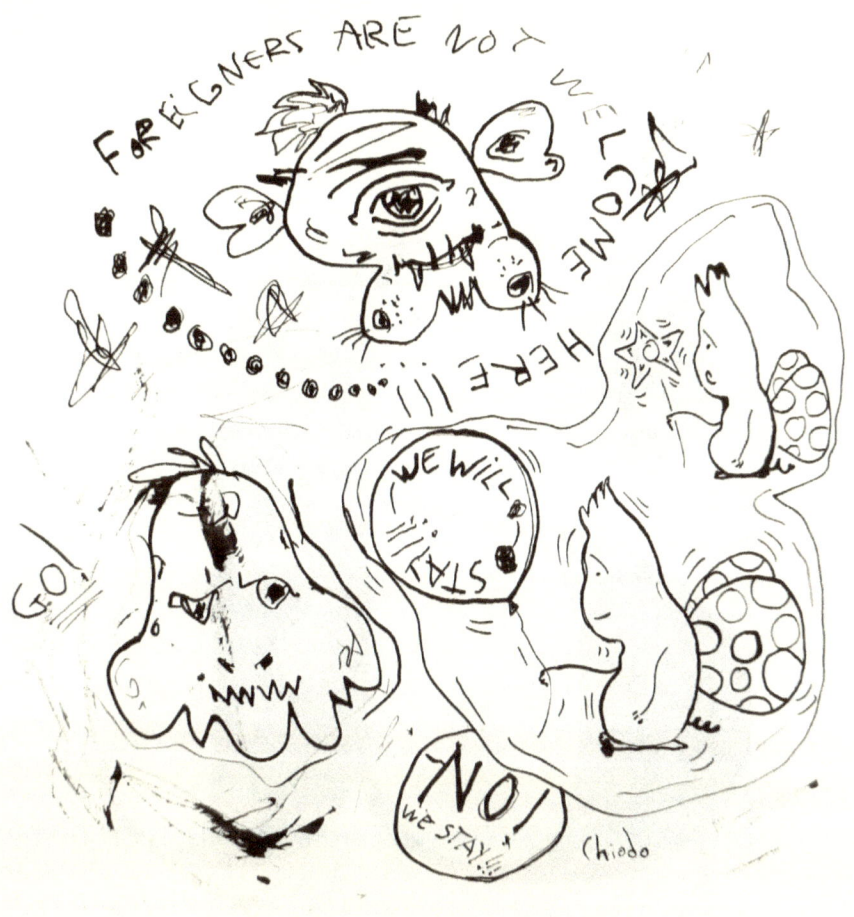

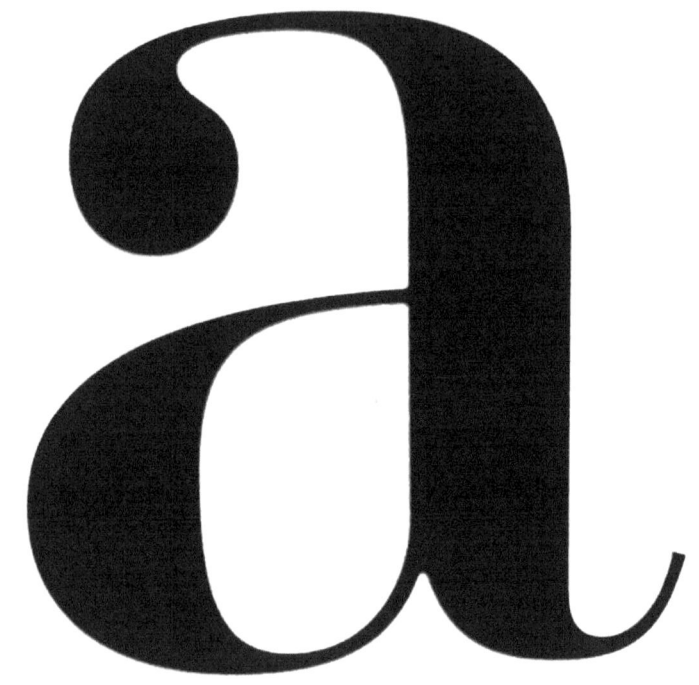

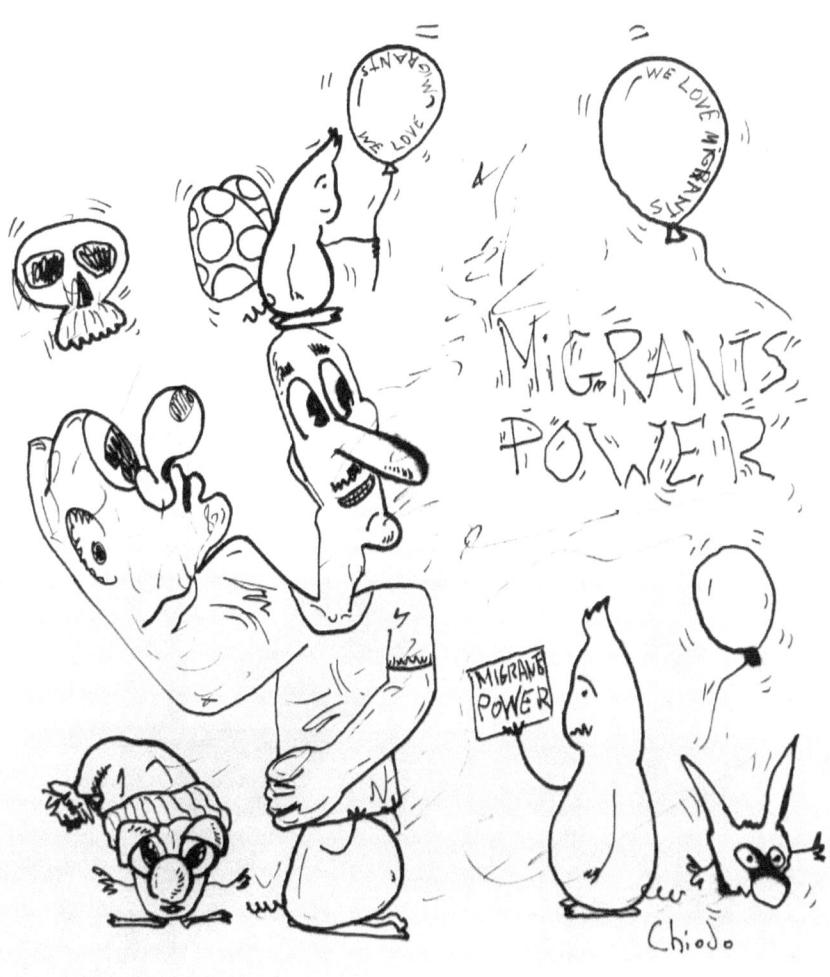

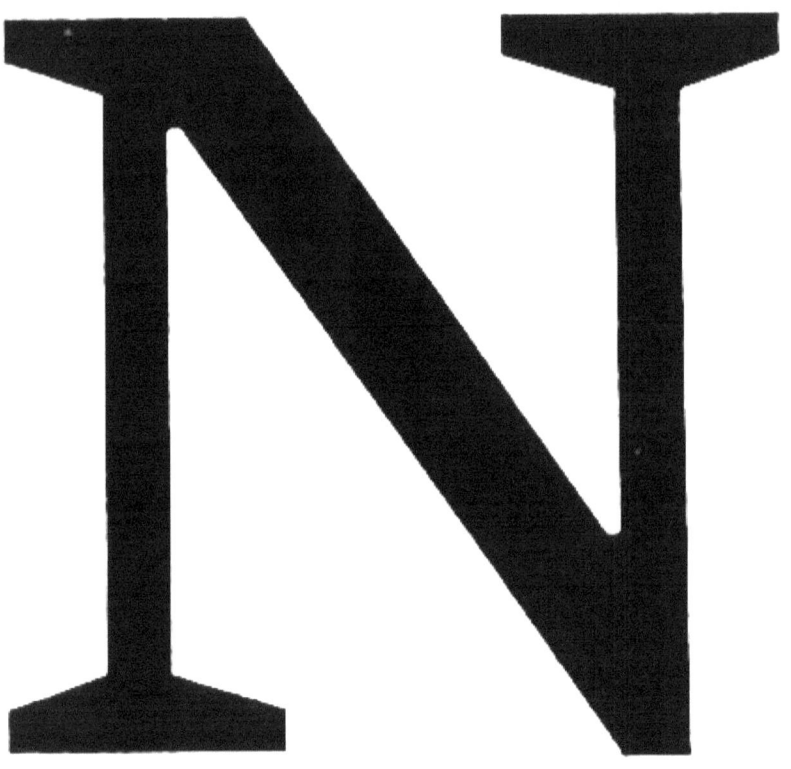

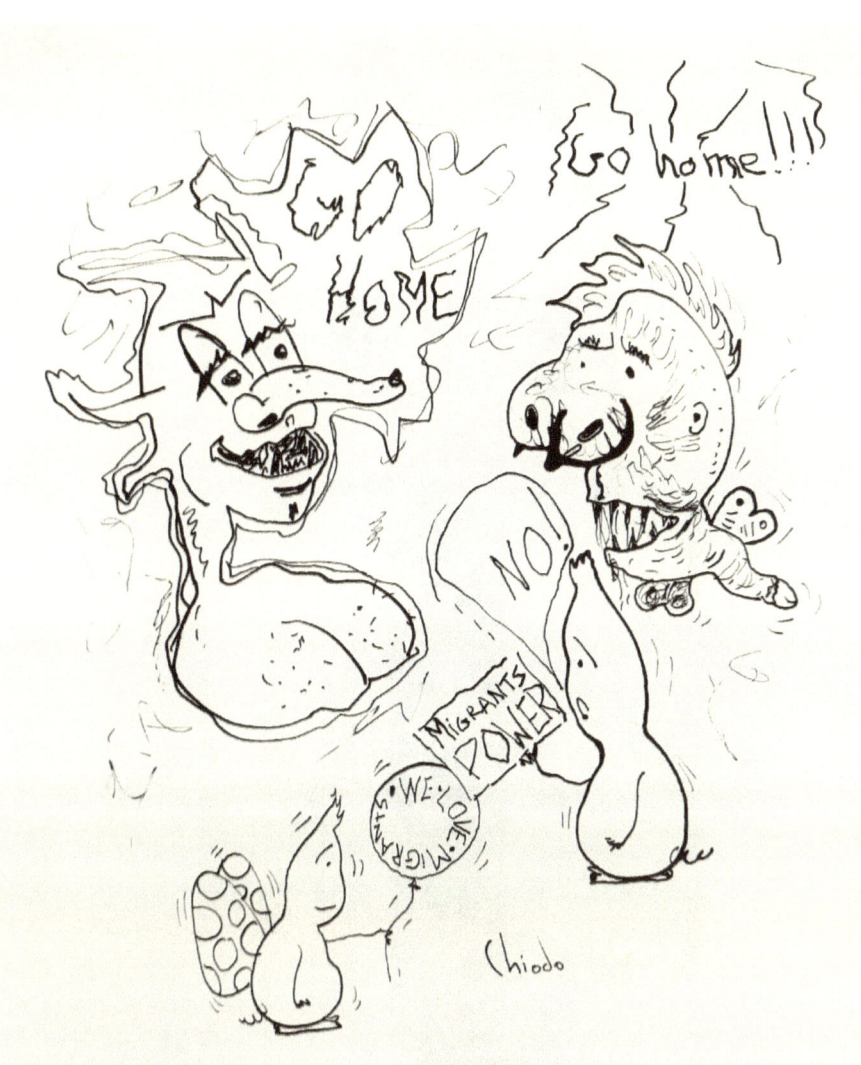

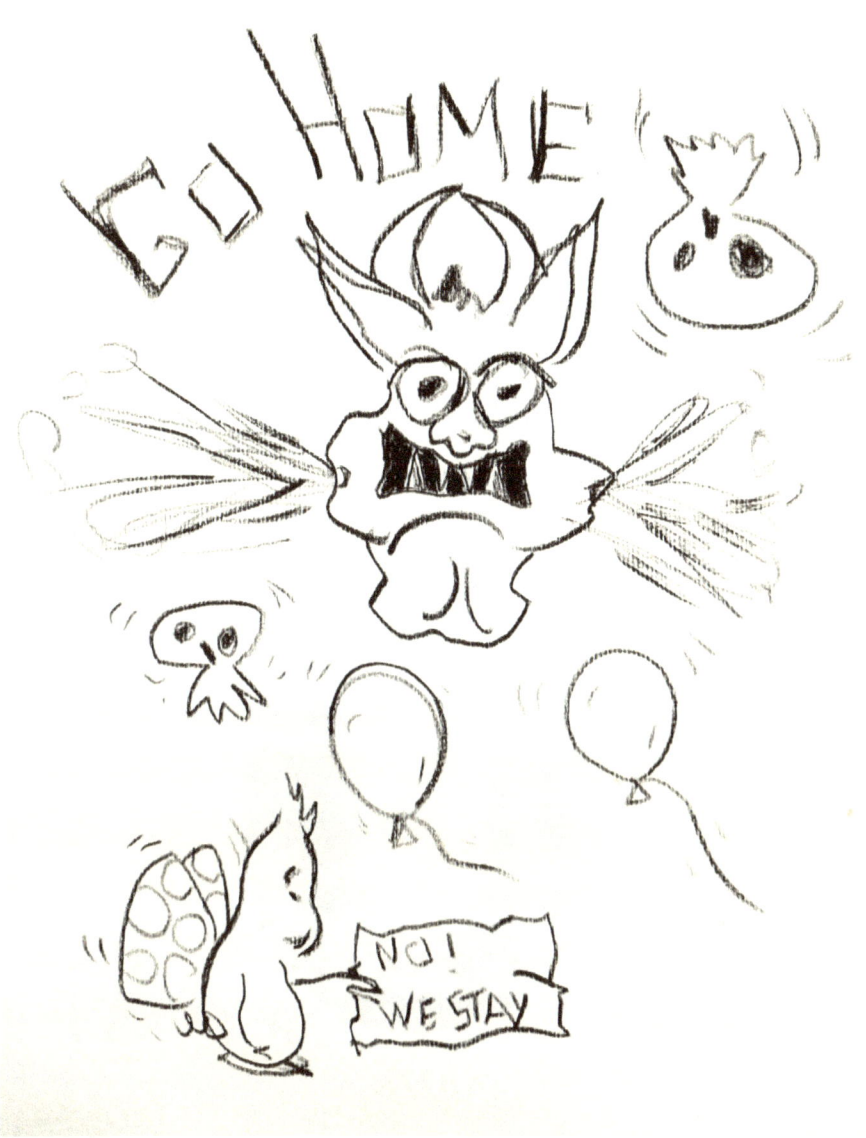

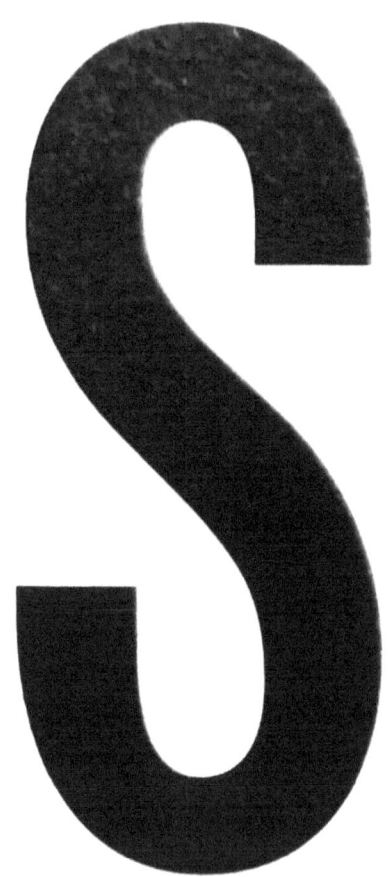

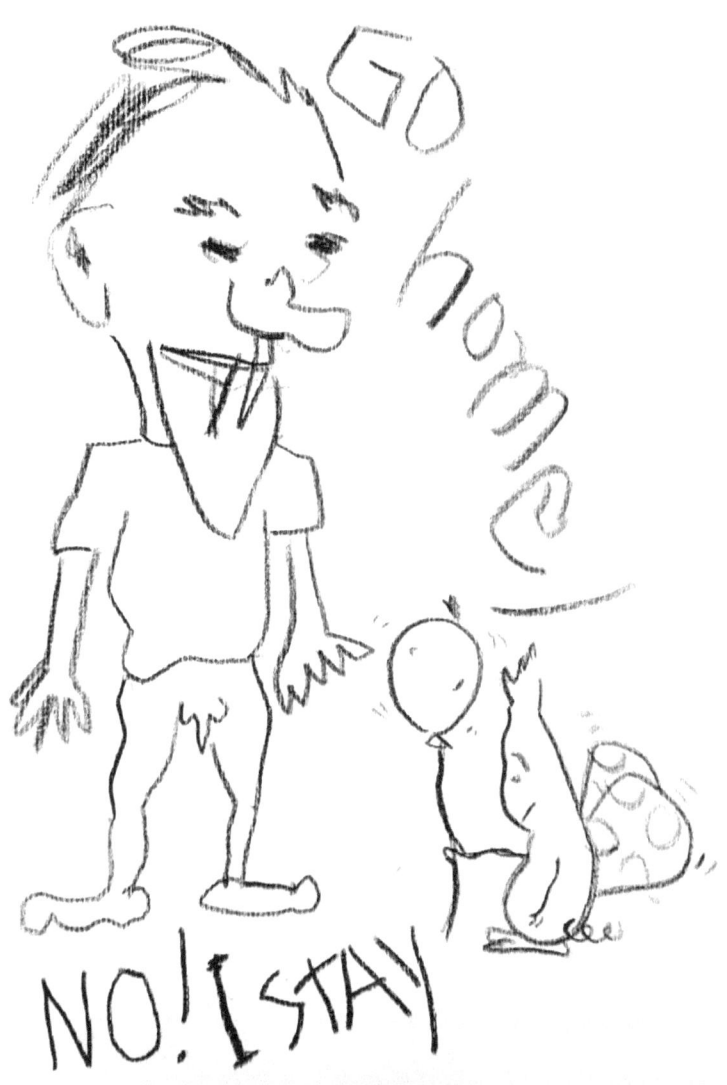

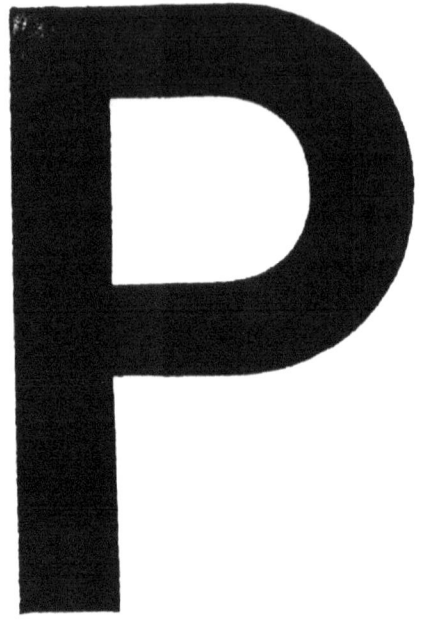

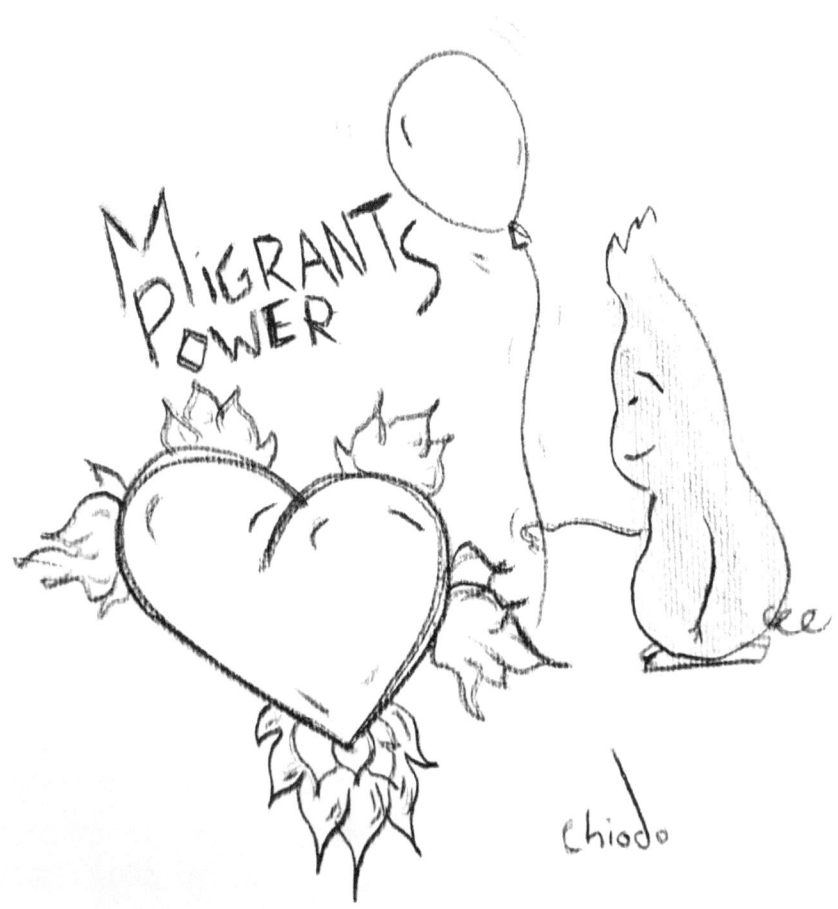

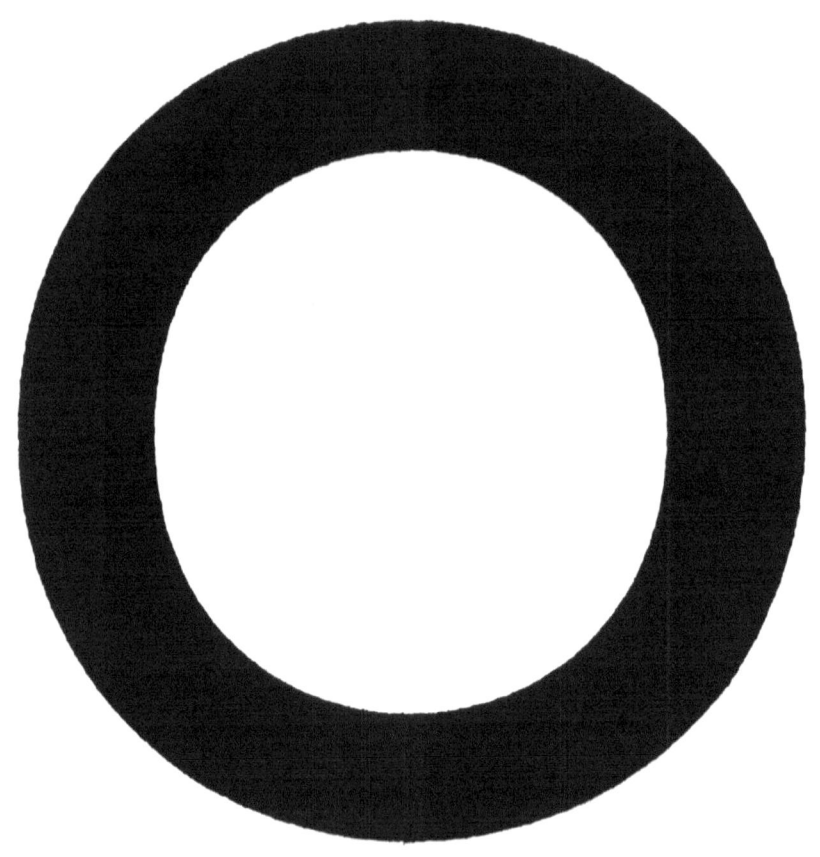

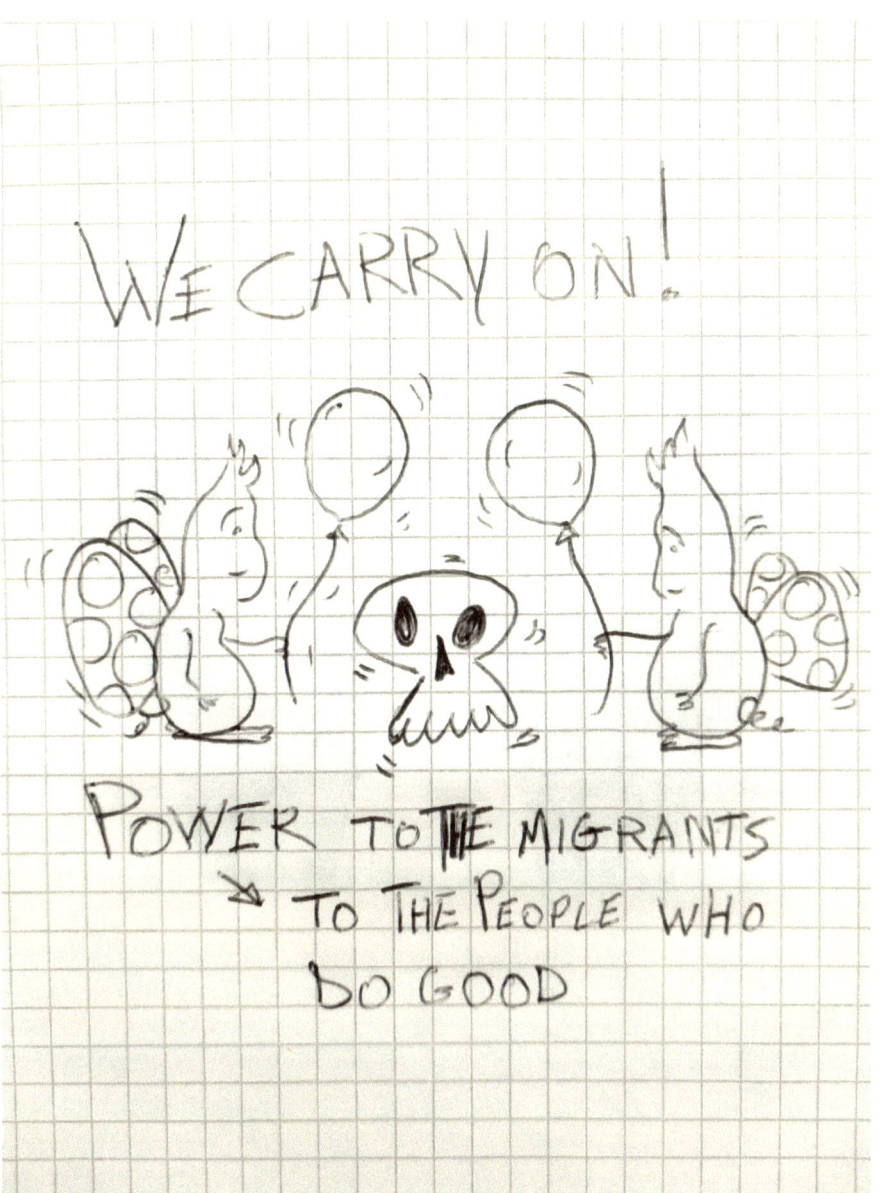

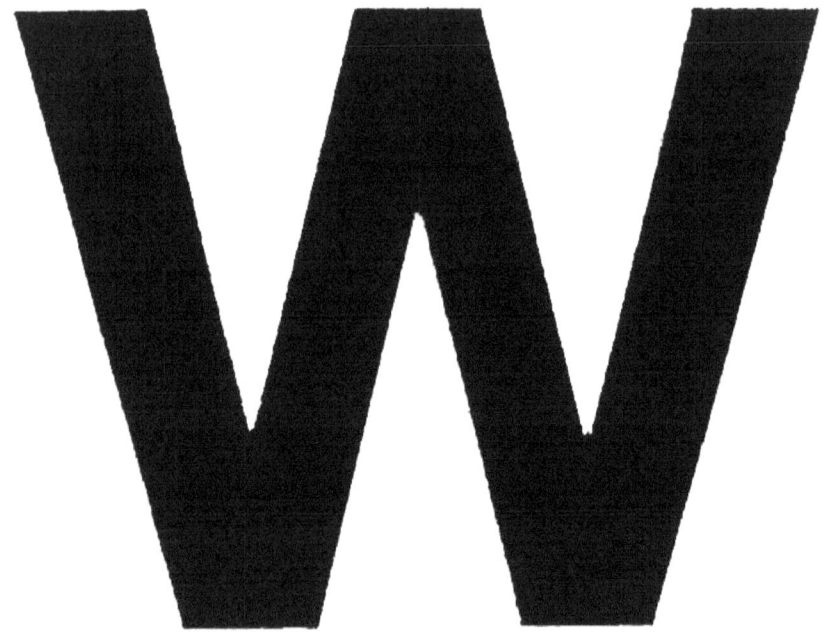

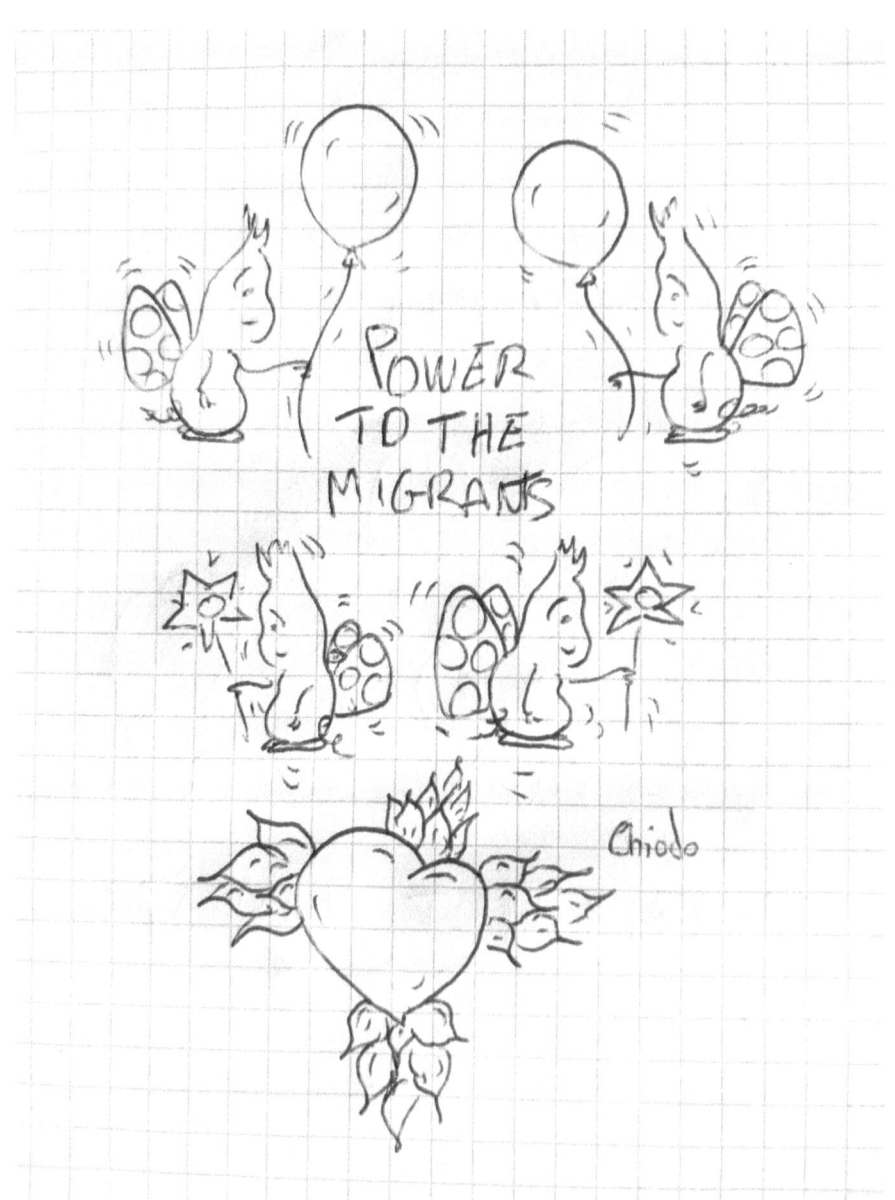

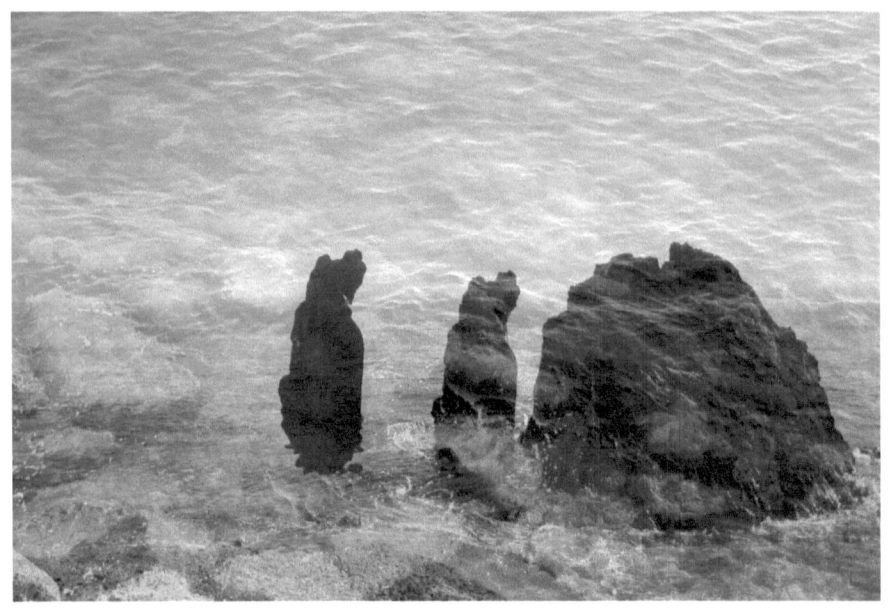

Racist and xenophobic chaps

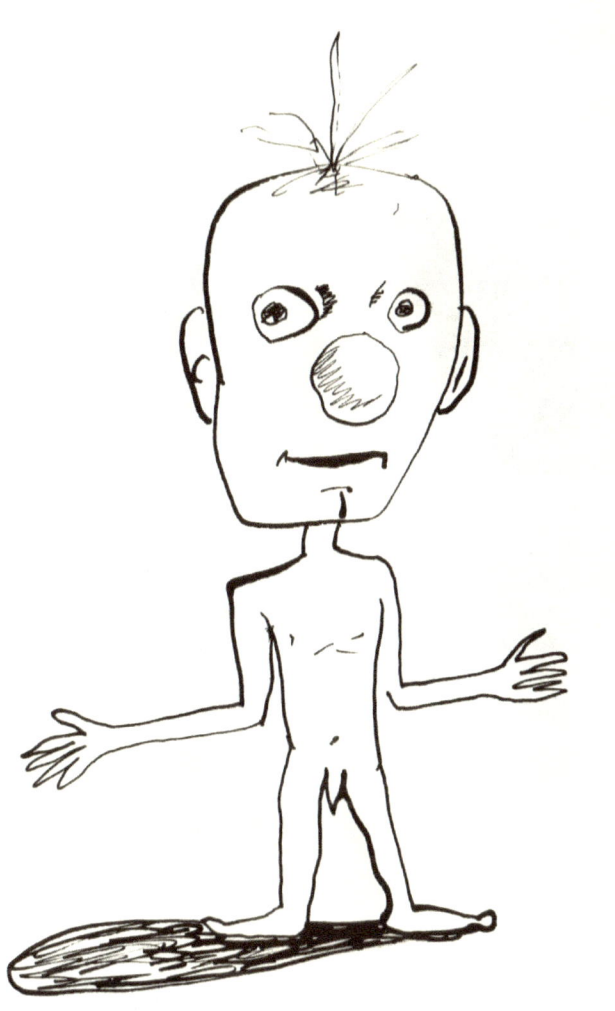

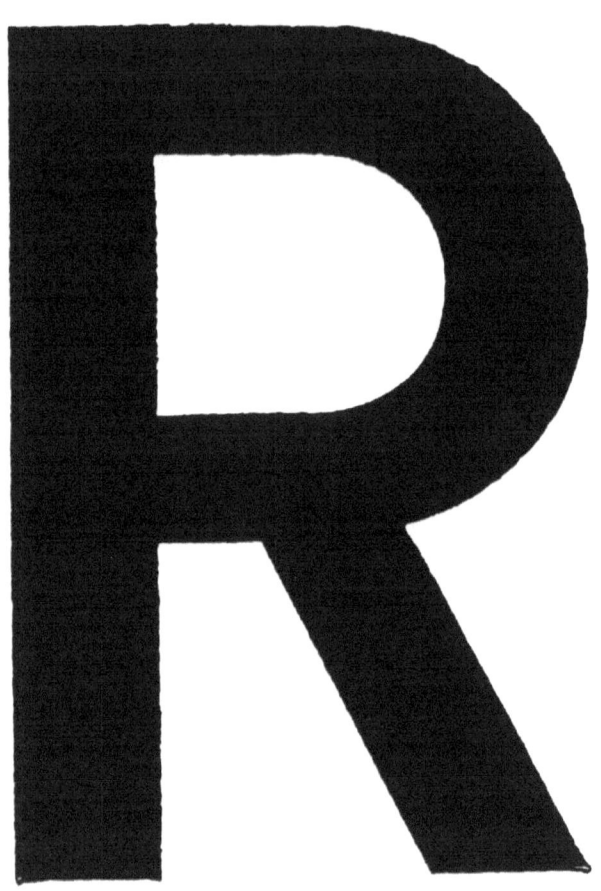

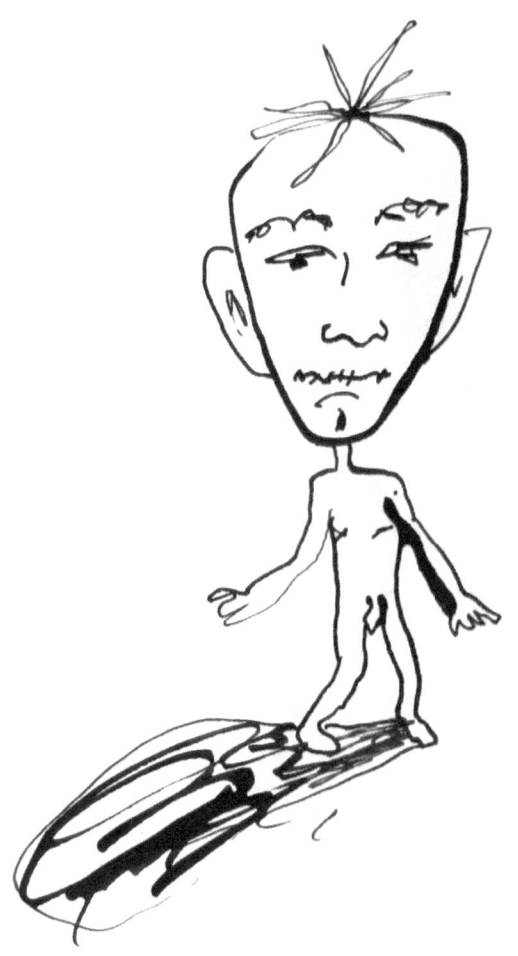

Migrants Power

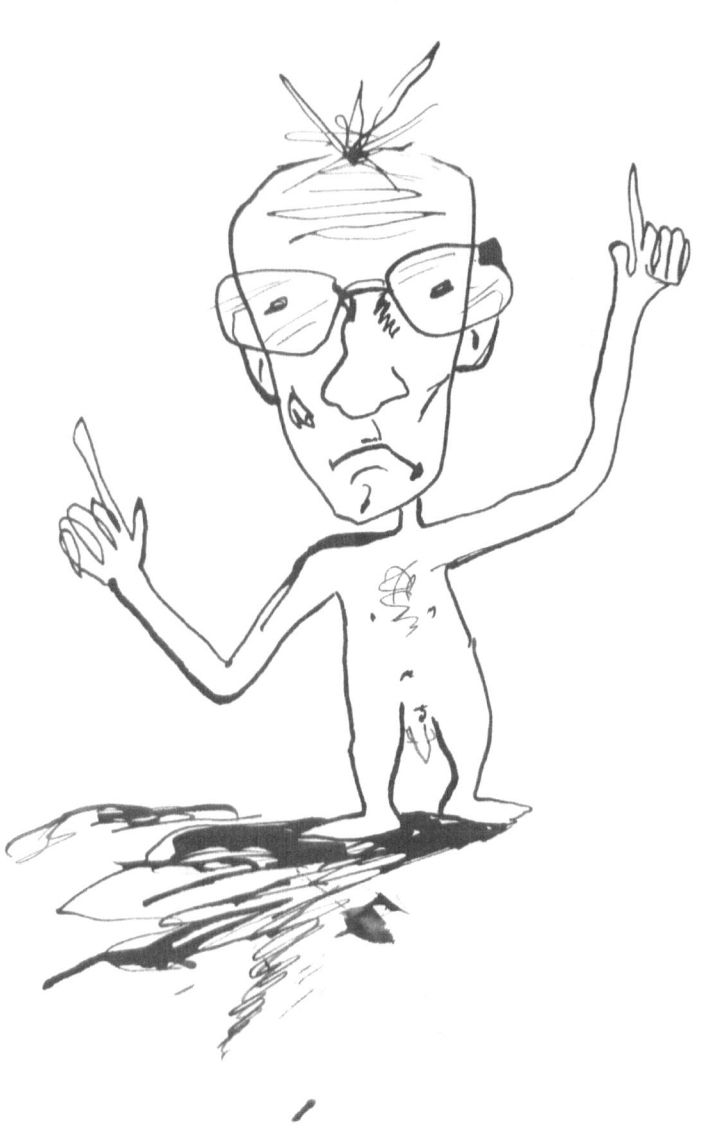

Power to the Migrants

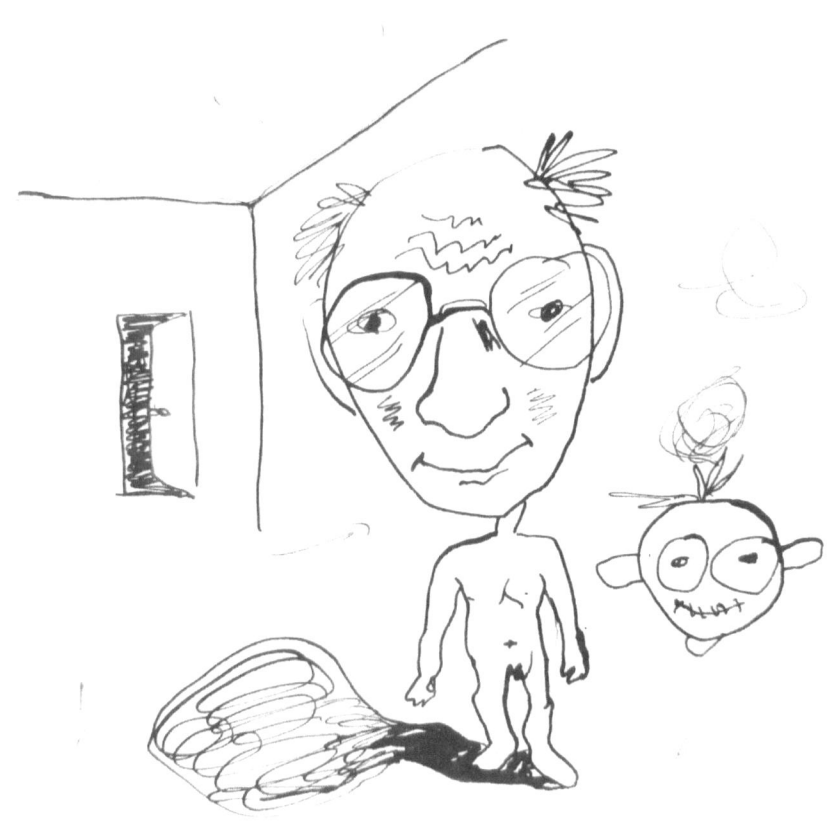

hospitality

hospitality

hospitality

hospitality

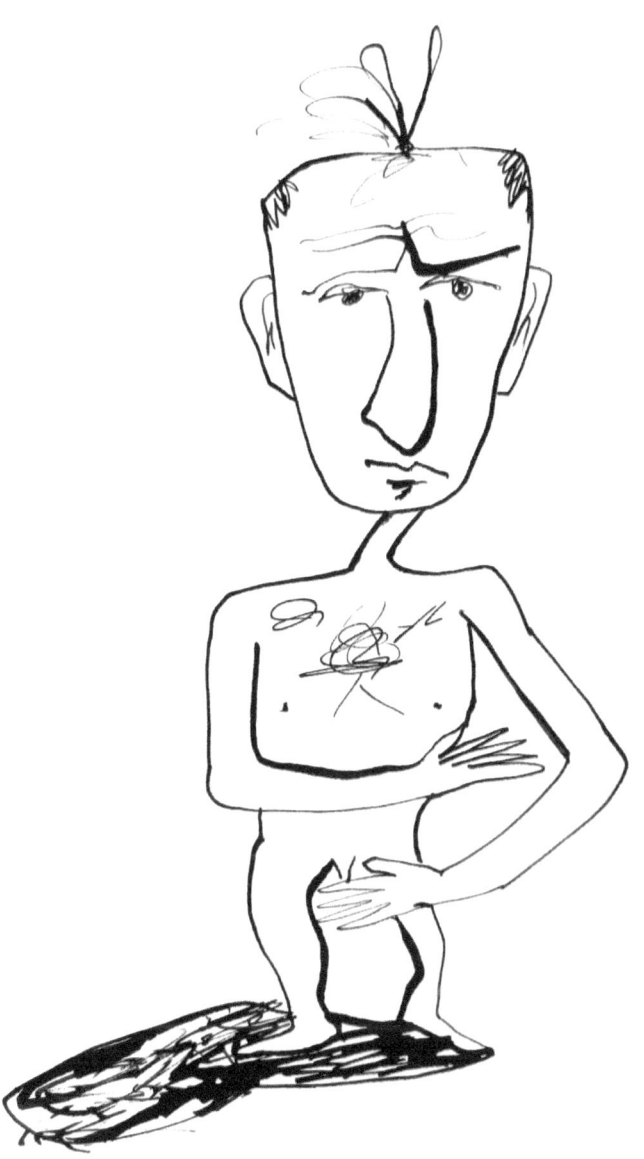

neither borders nor cages

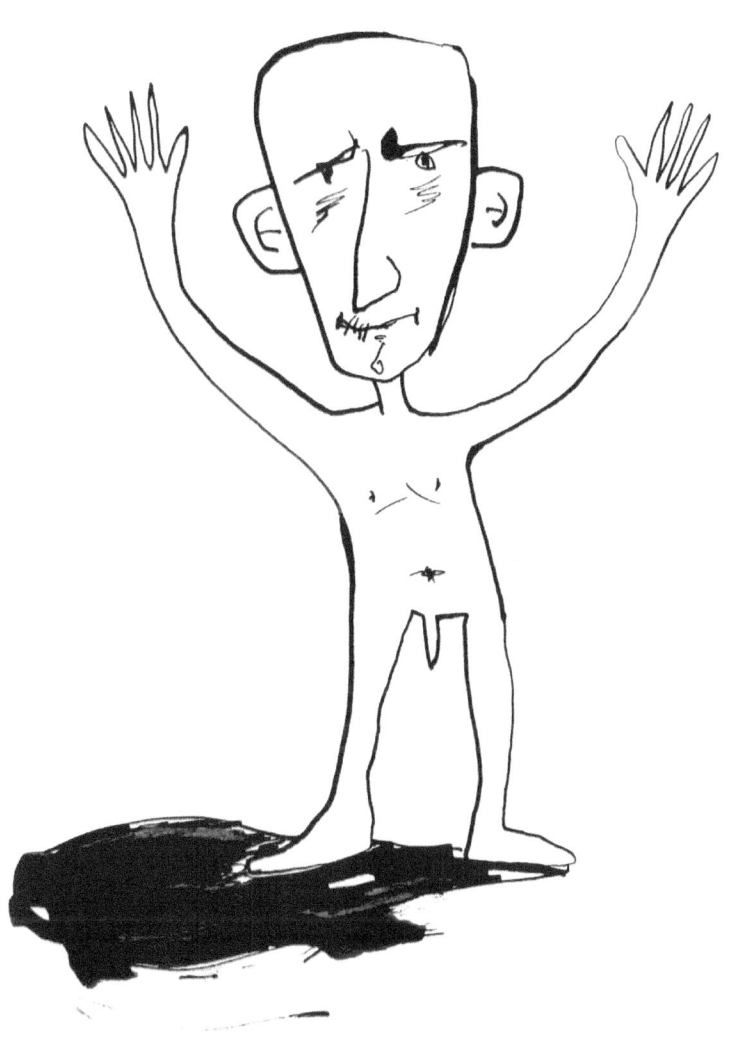

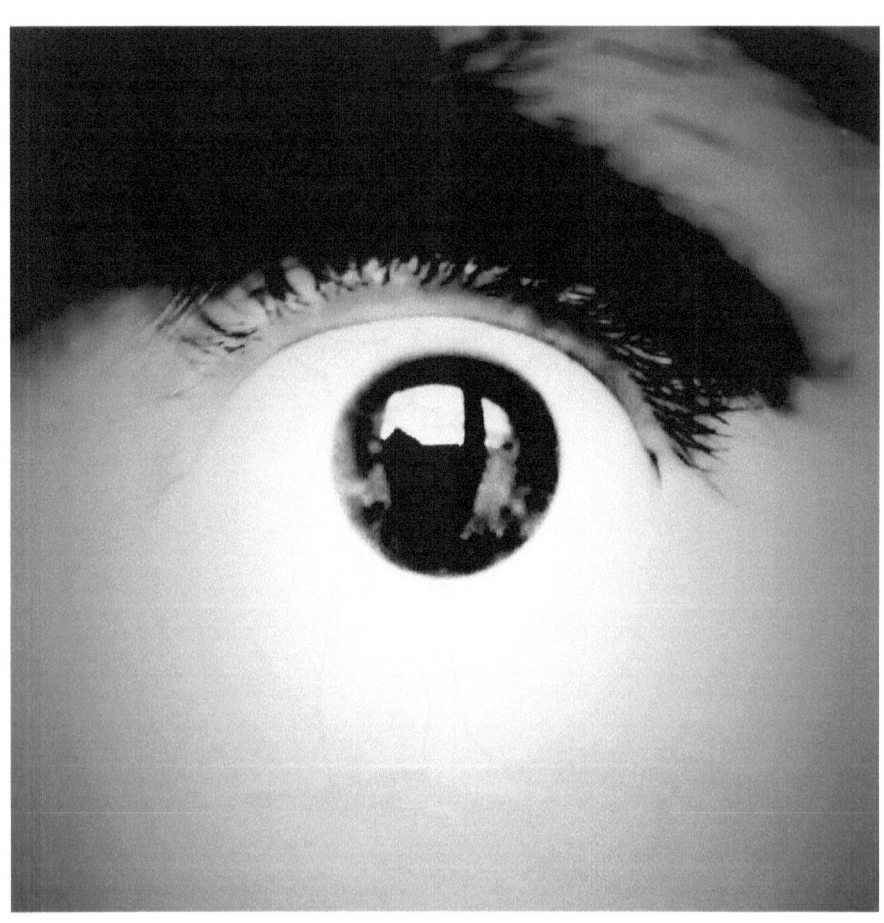

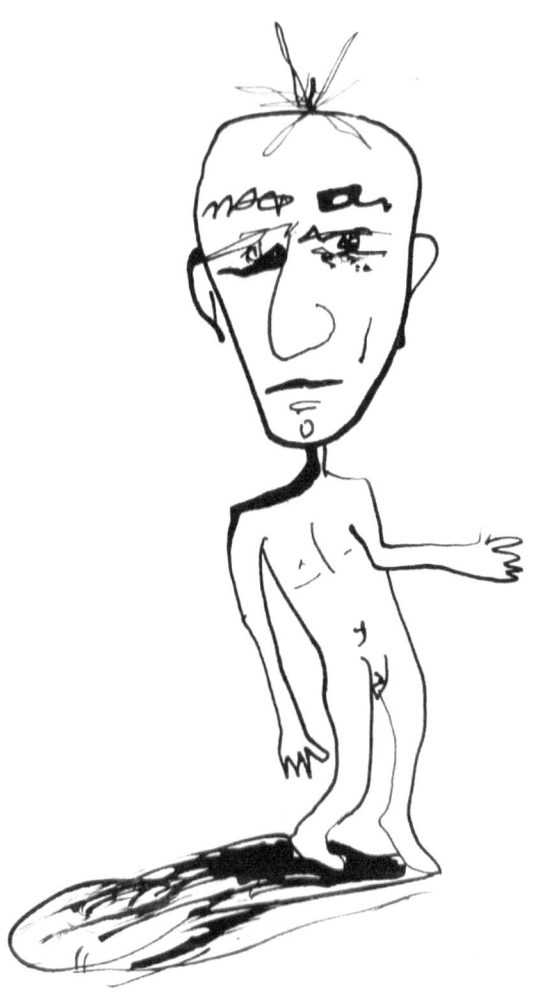

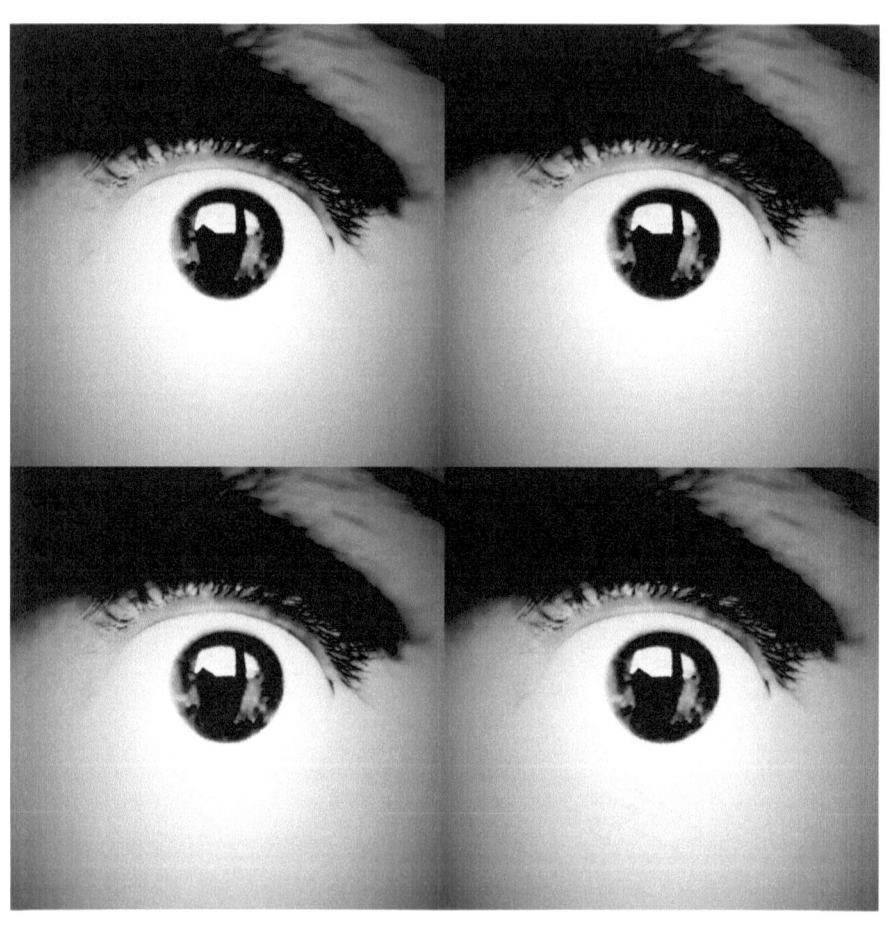

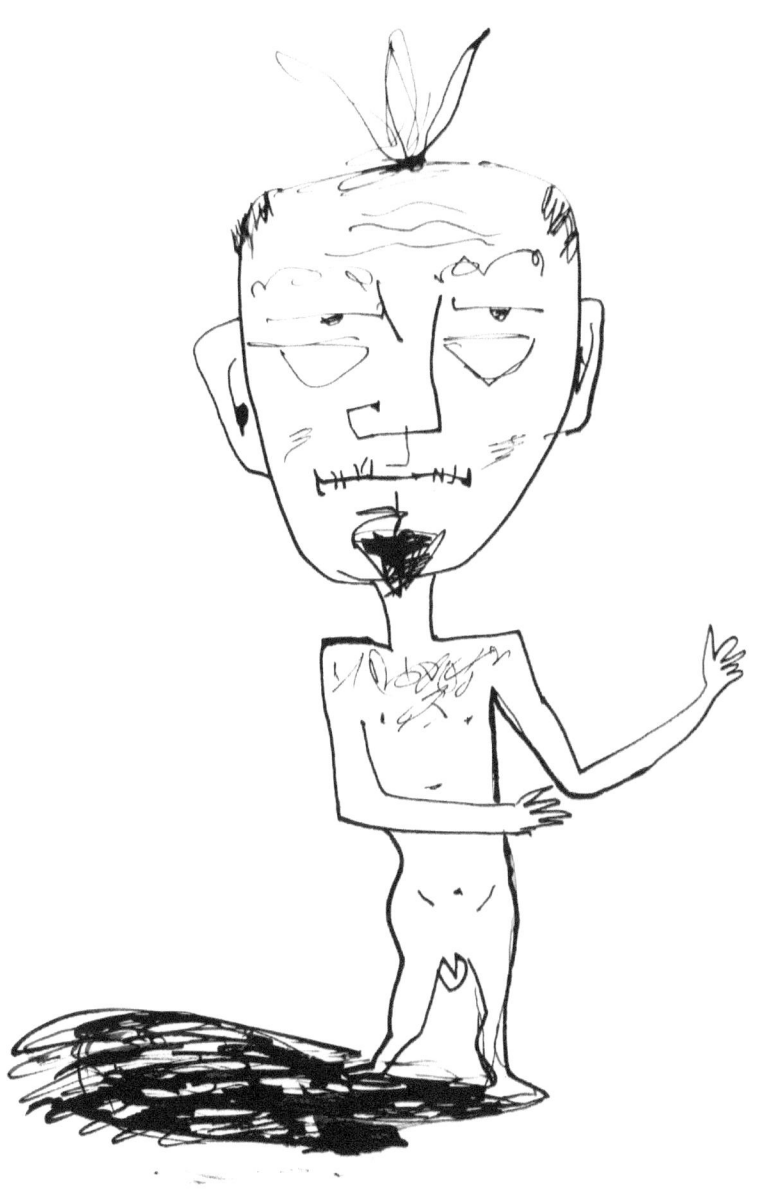

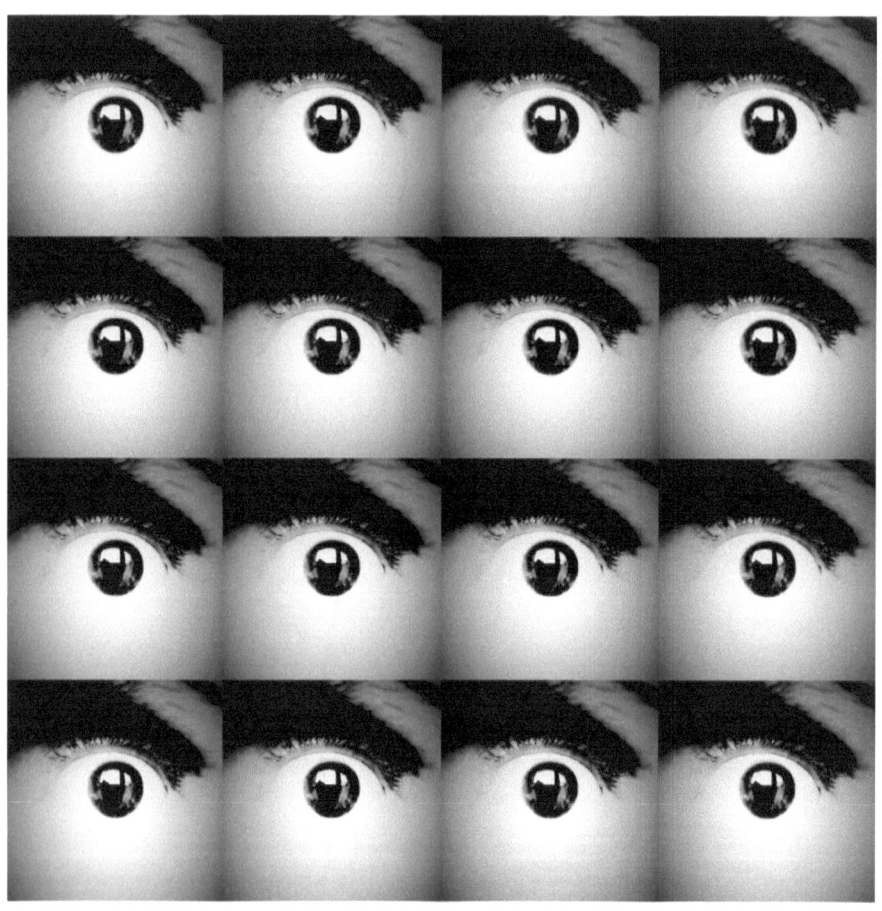

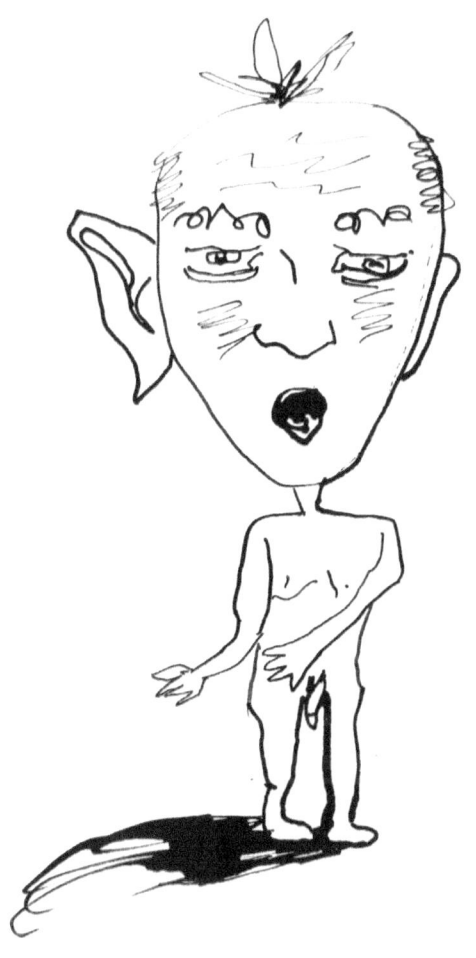

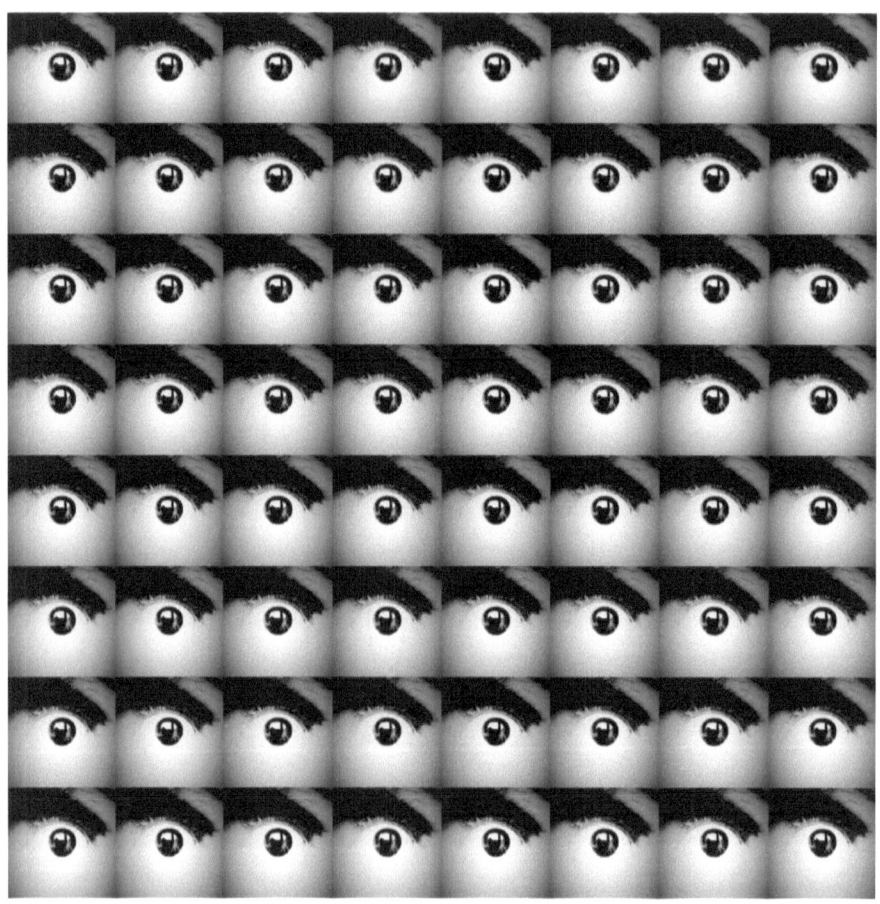

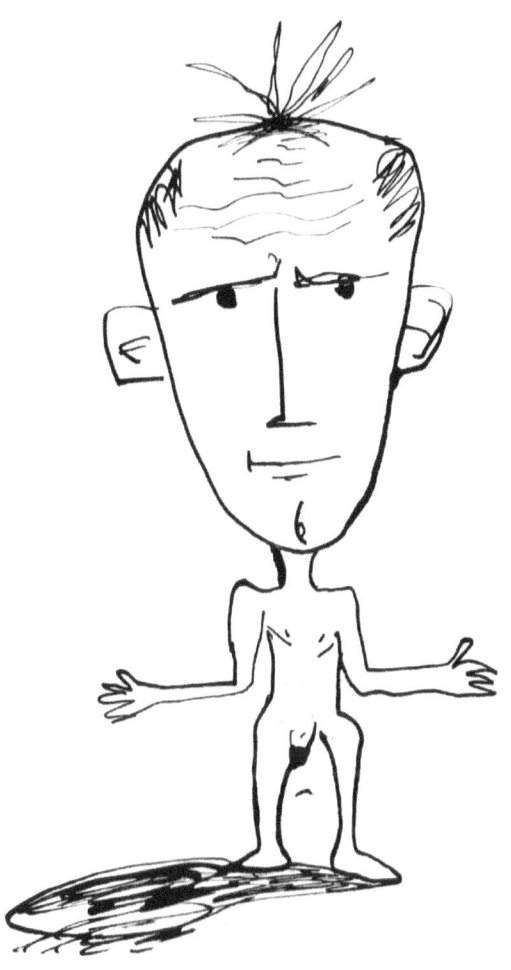

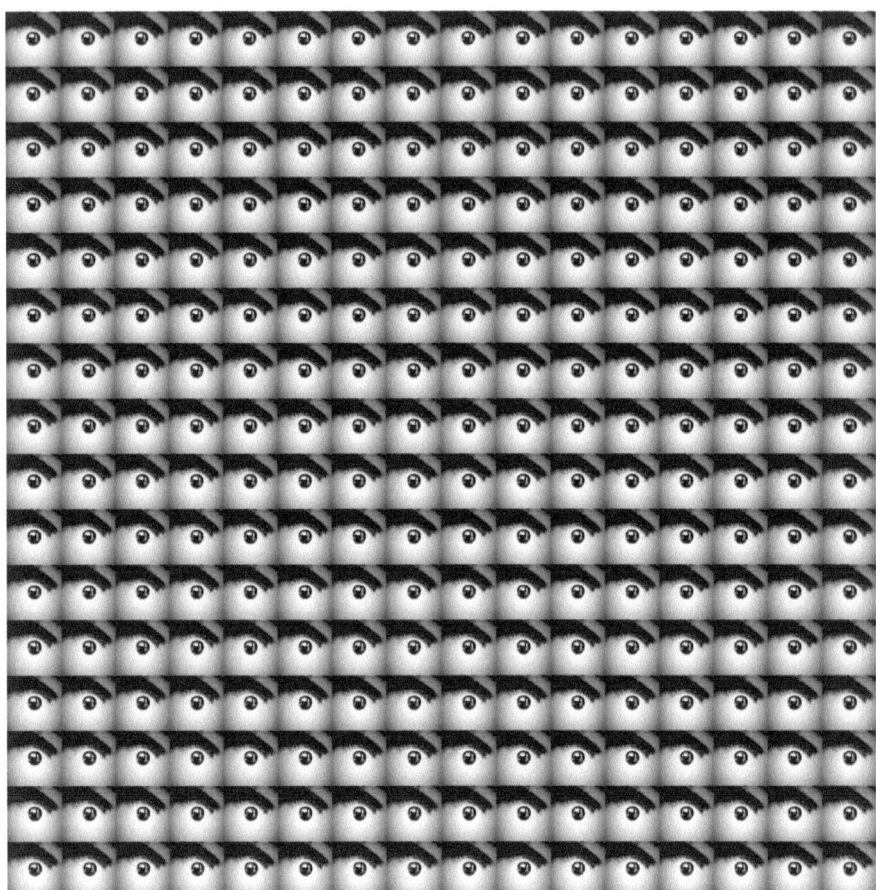

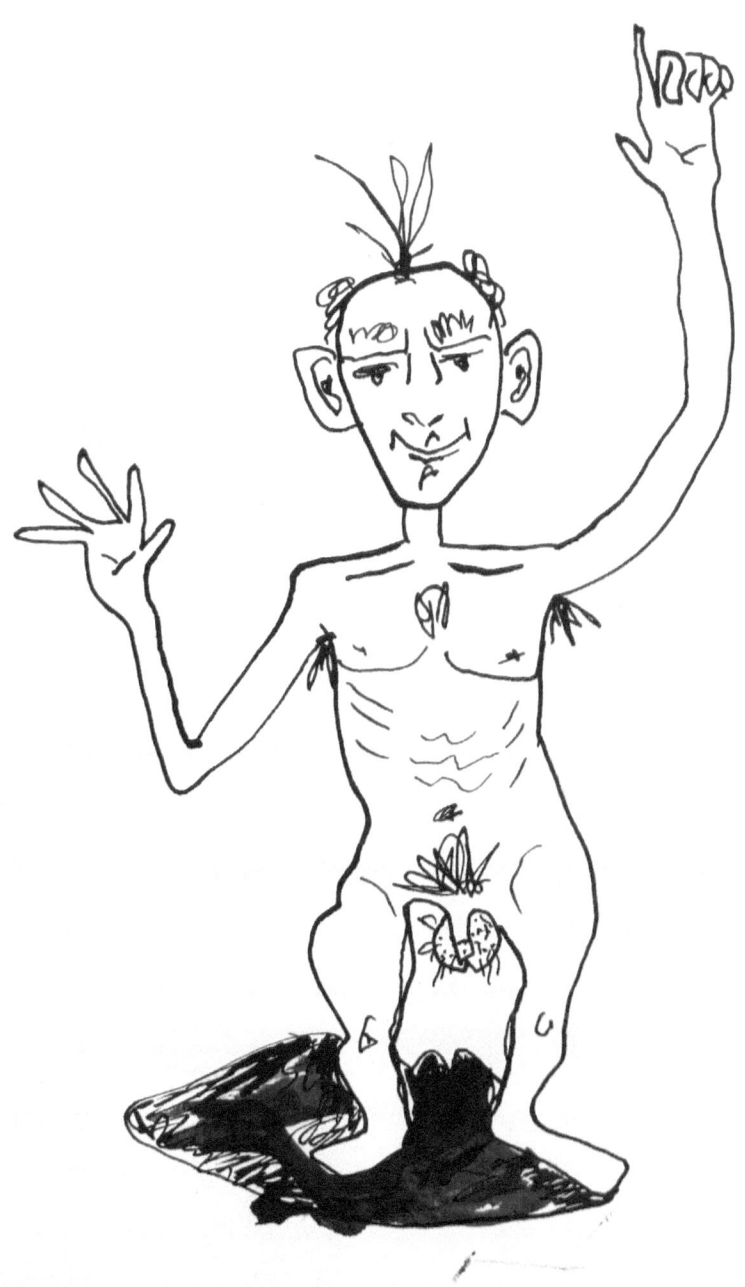

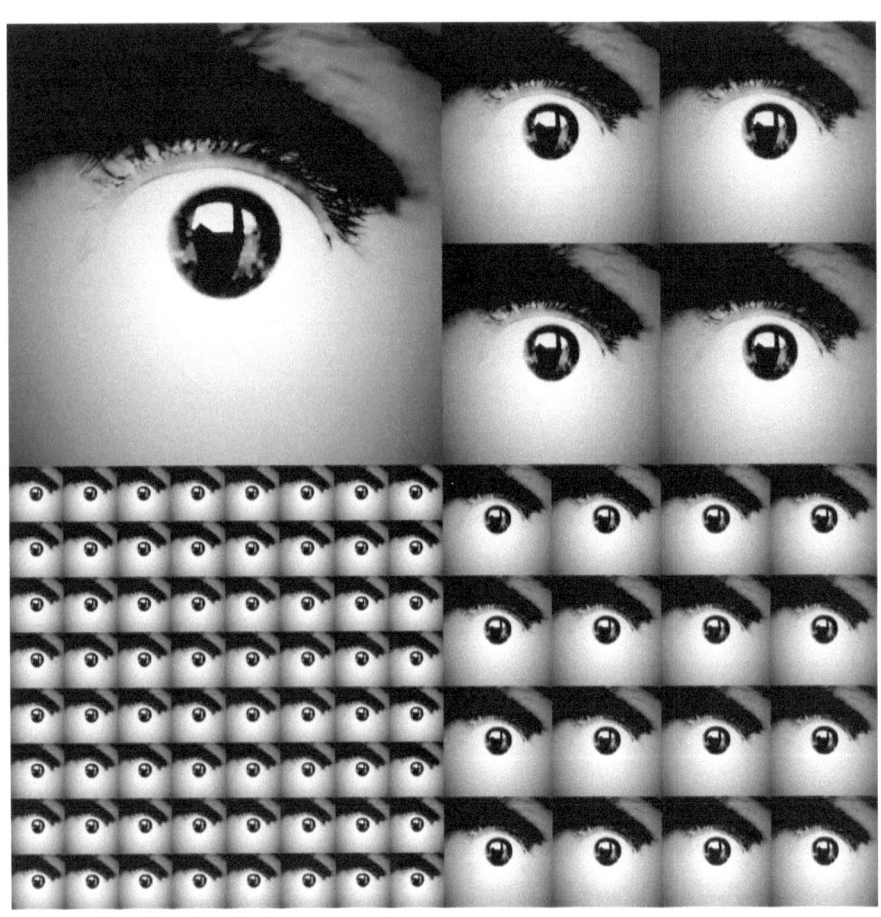

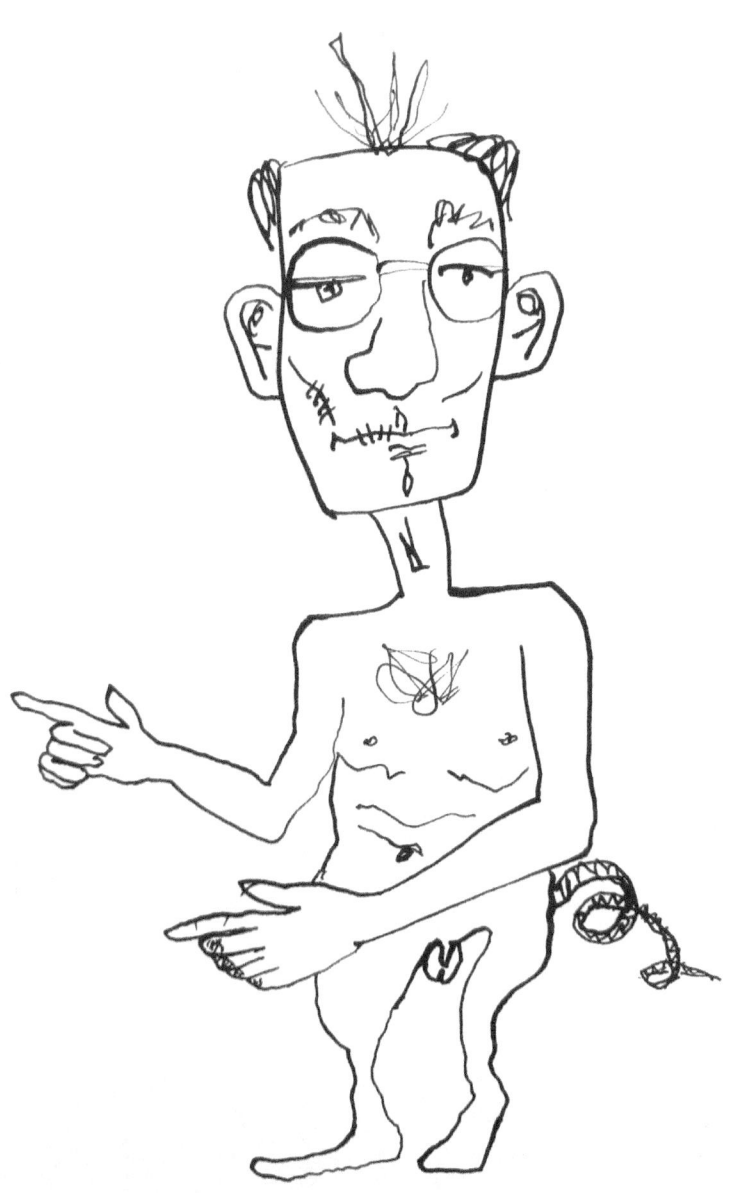

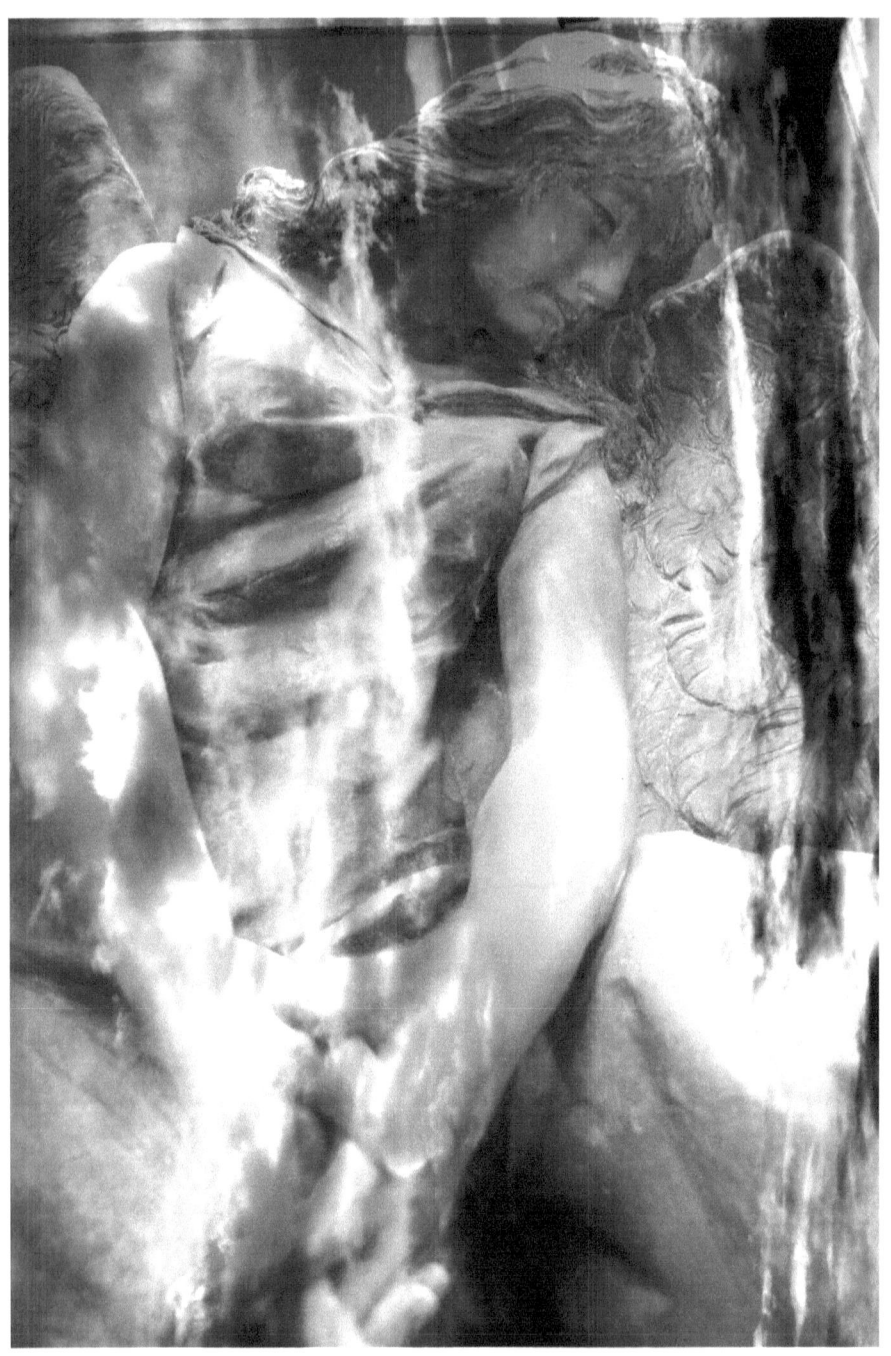

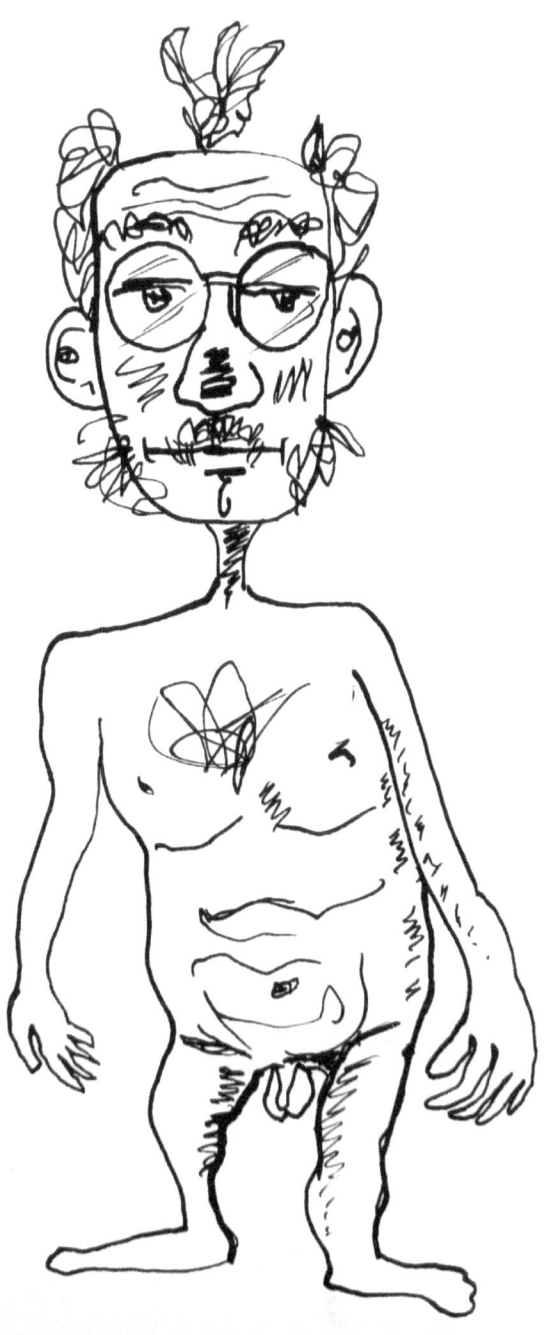

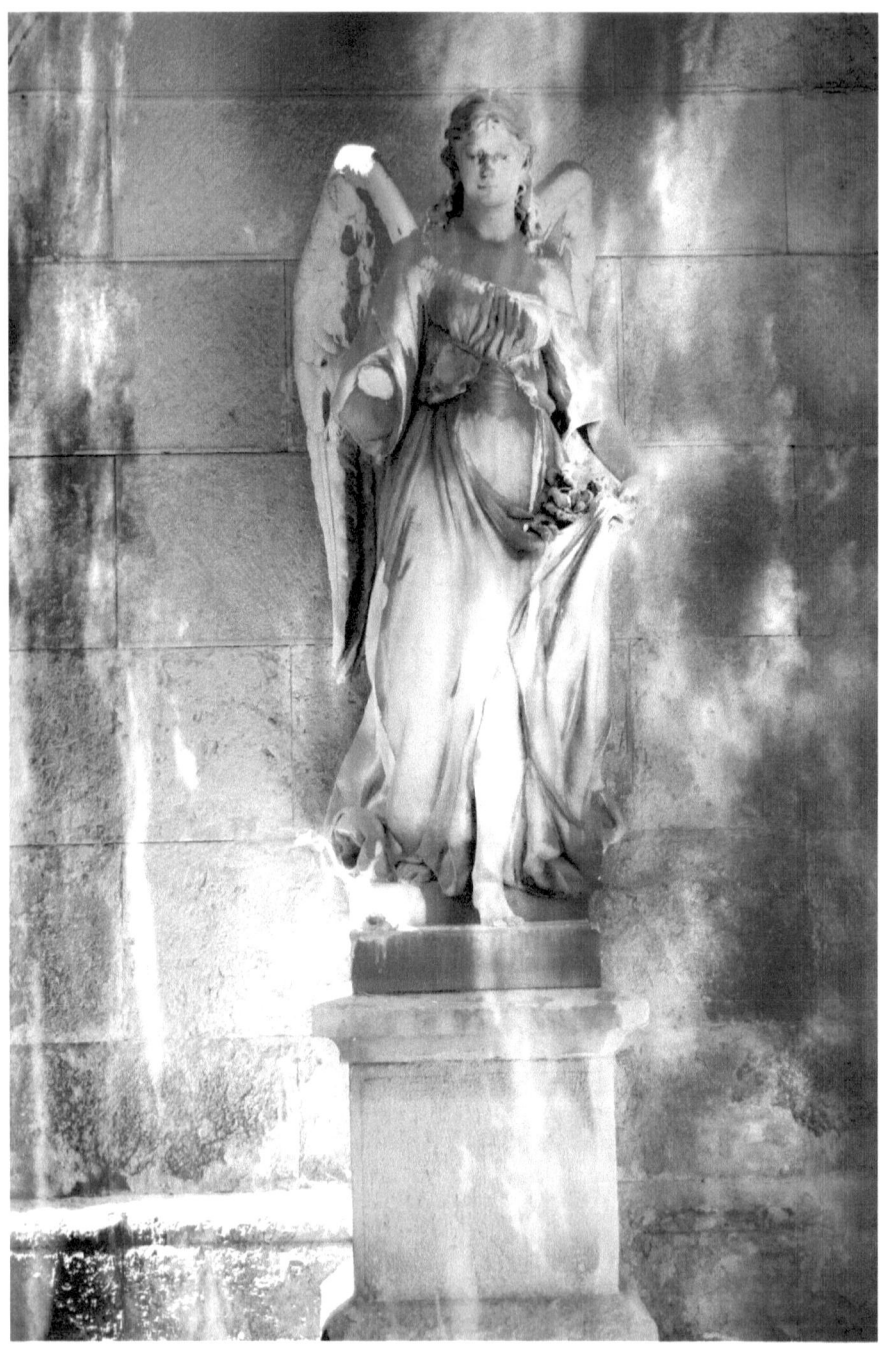

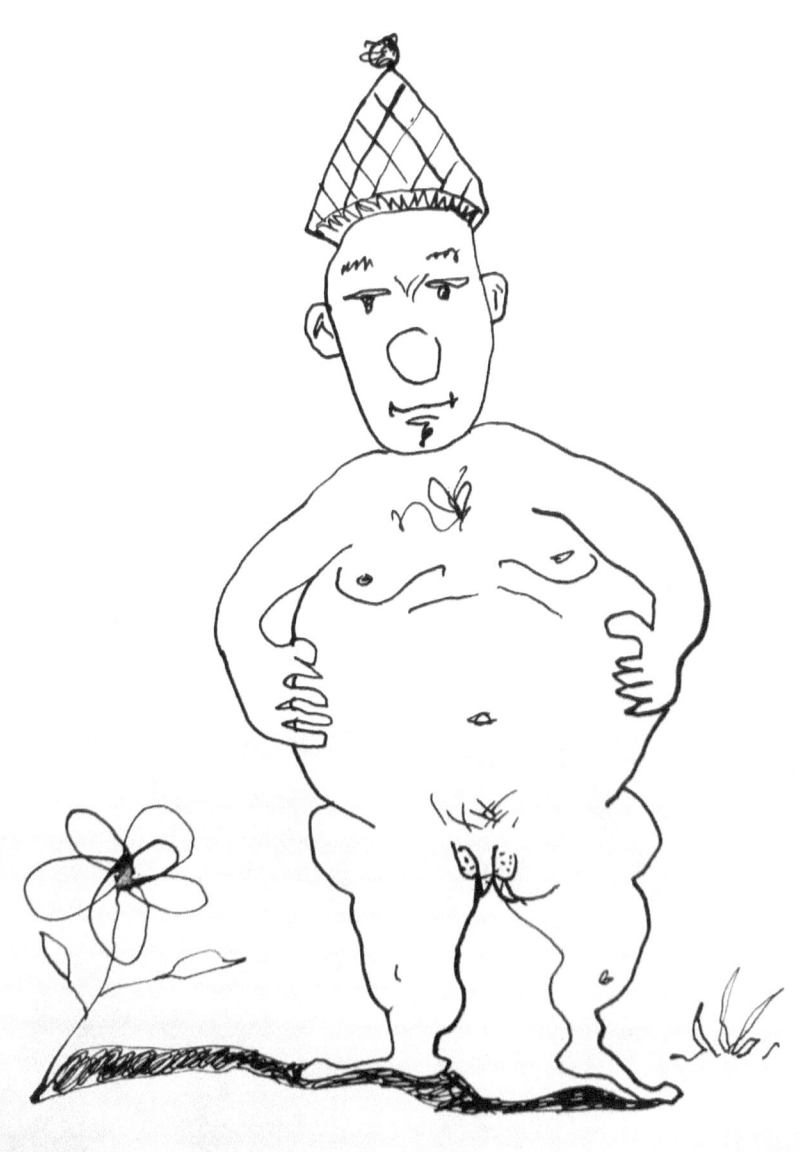

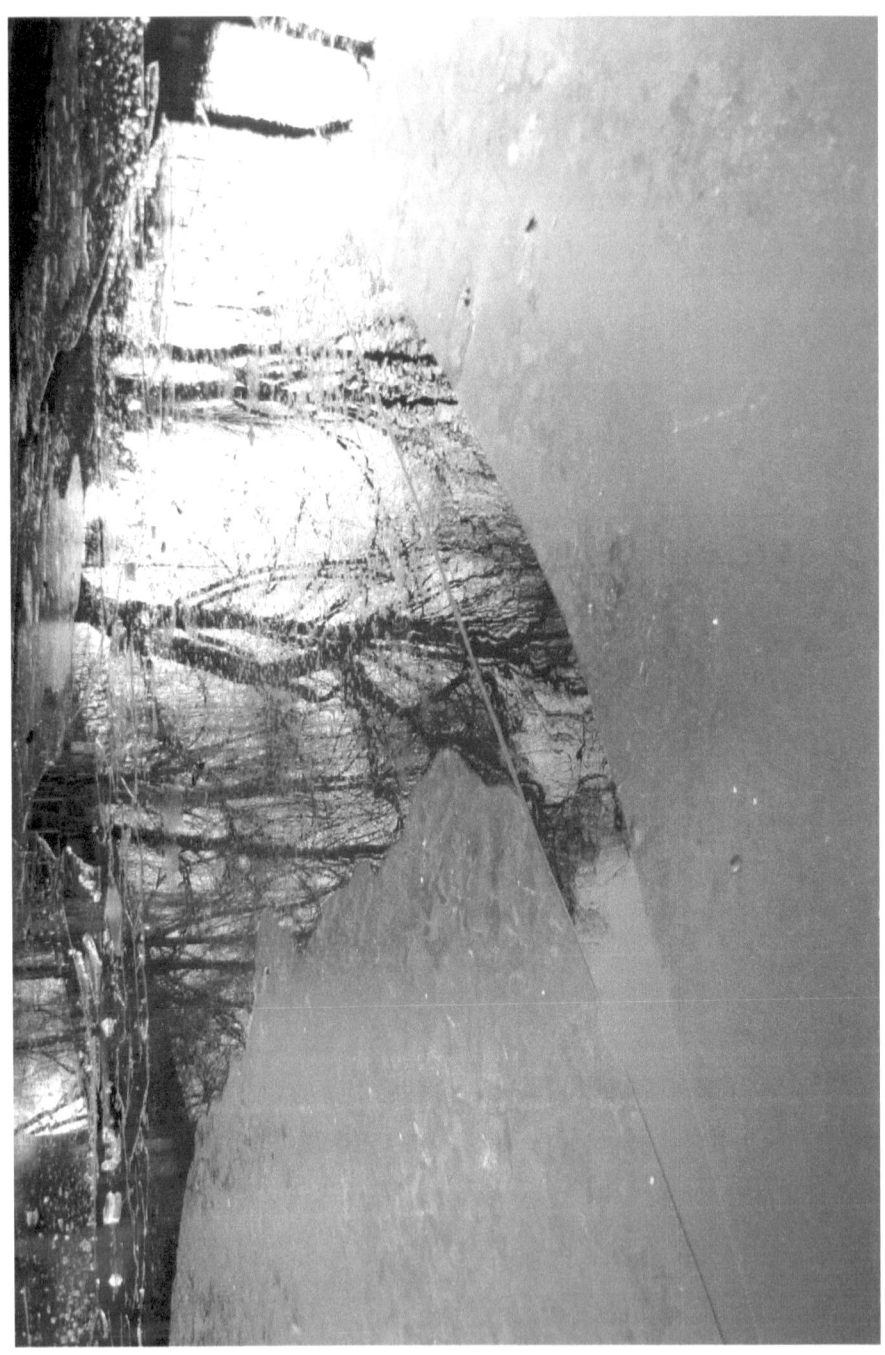

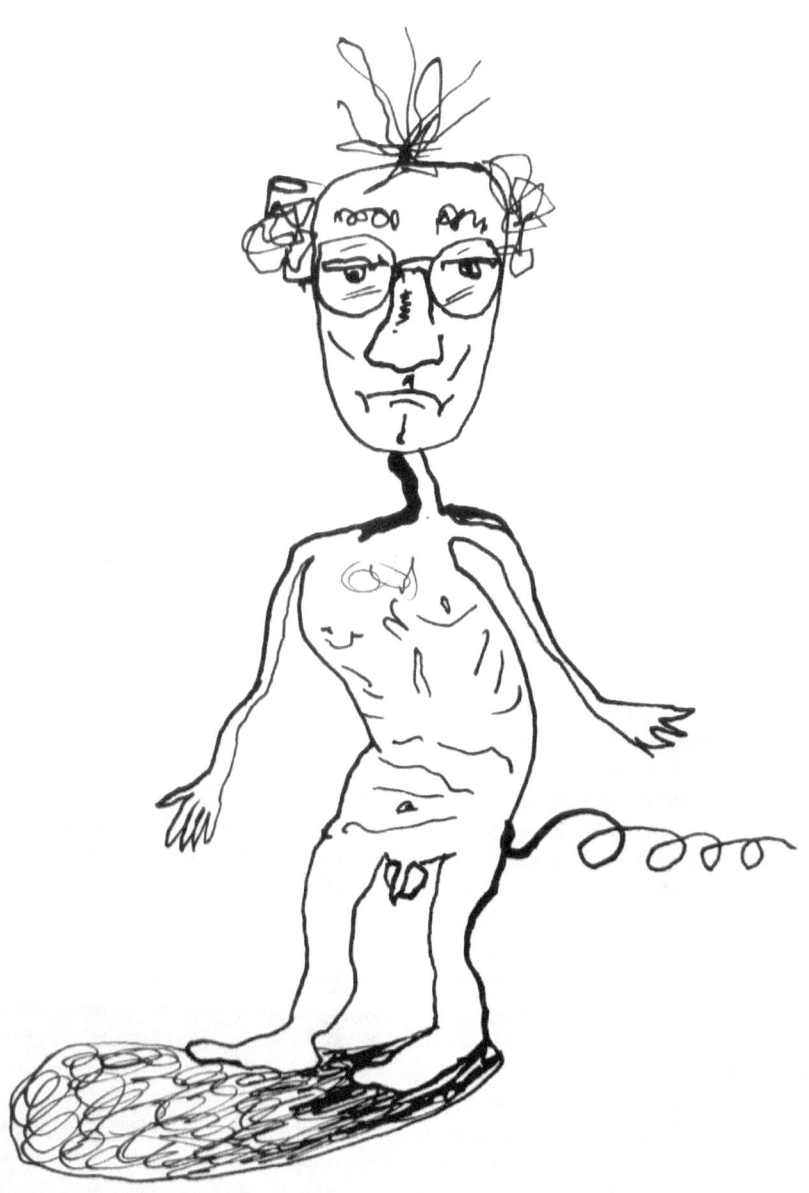

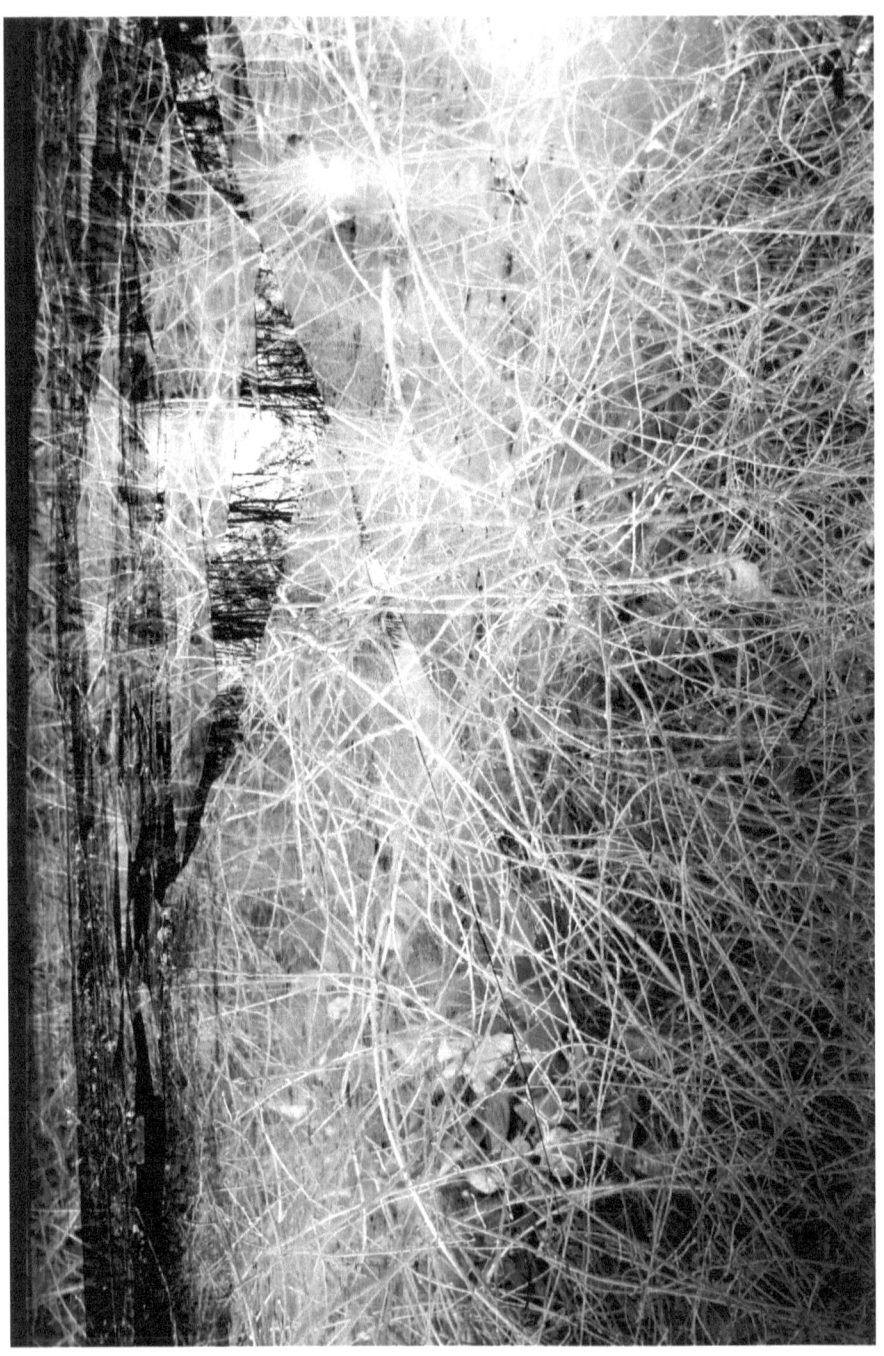

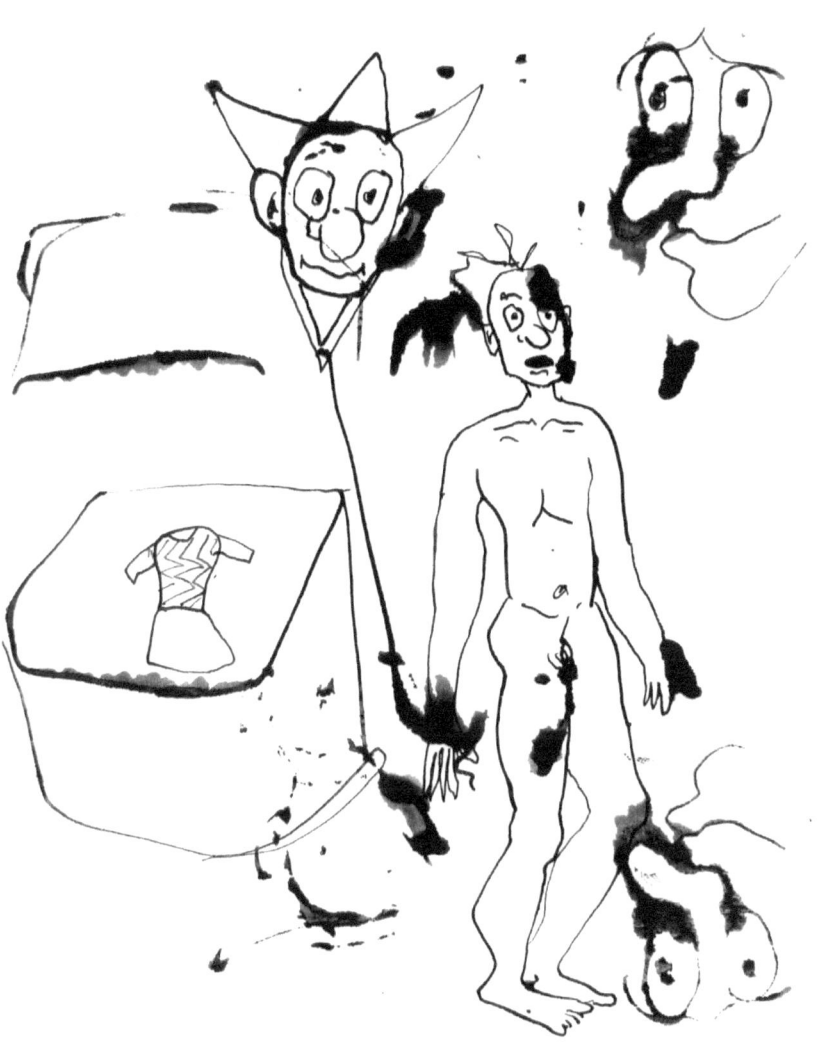

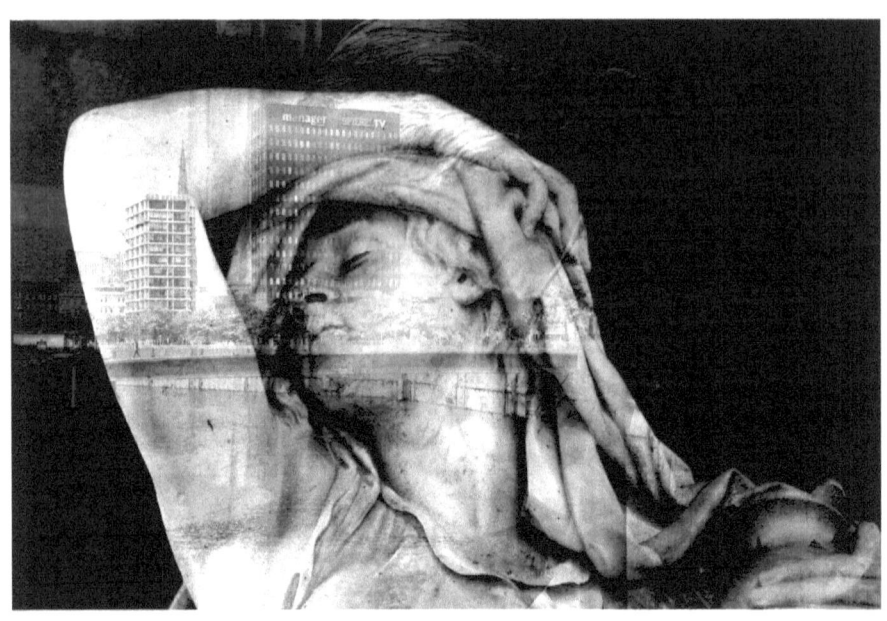

mistakes in history
(historical blunders)

mistakes

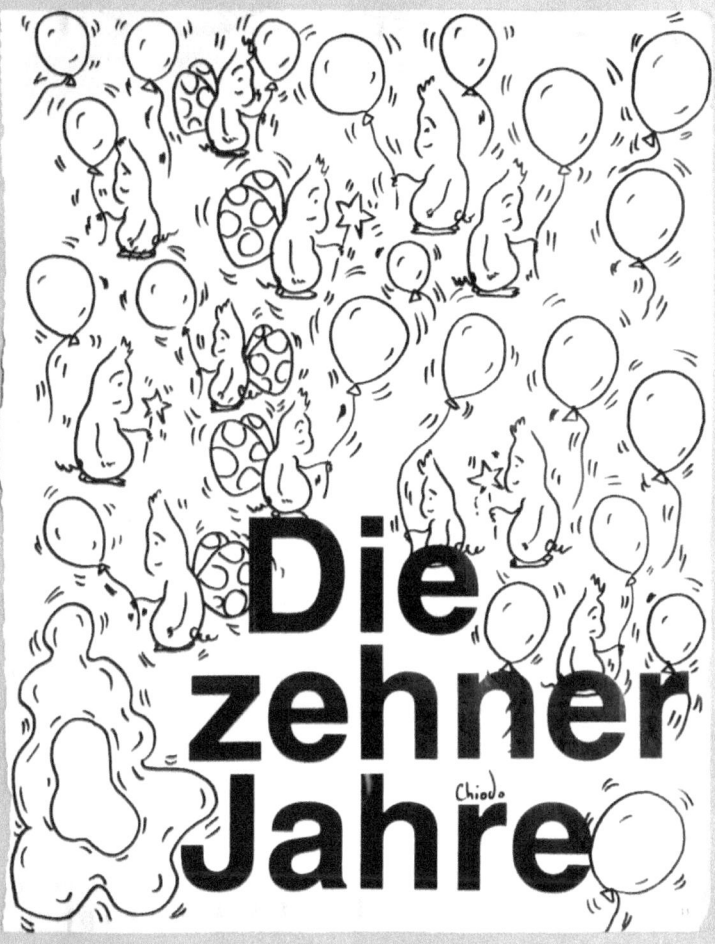

blunders

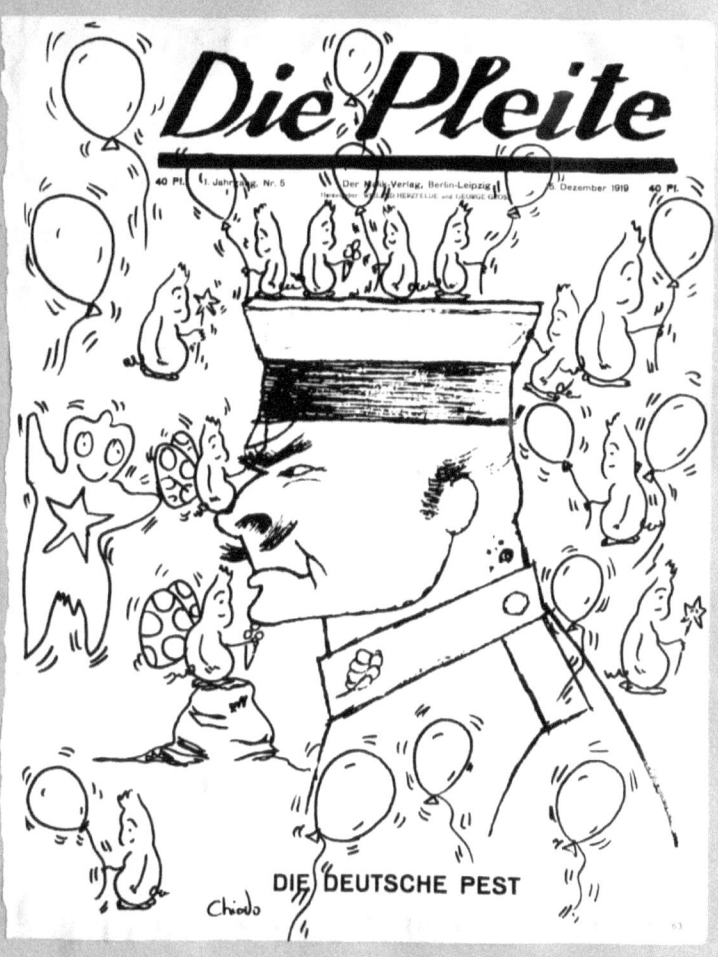

Die Pleite

40 Pf. 1. Jahrgang. Nr. 5 — Der Malik-Verlag, Berlin-Leipzig — 5. Dezember 1919 — 40 Pf.

Herausgeber: WIELAND HERZFELDE und GEORGE GROSZ

DIE DEUTSCHE PEST

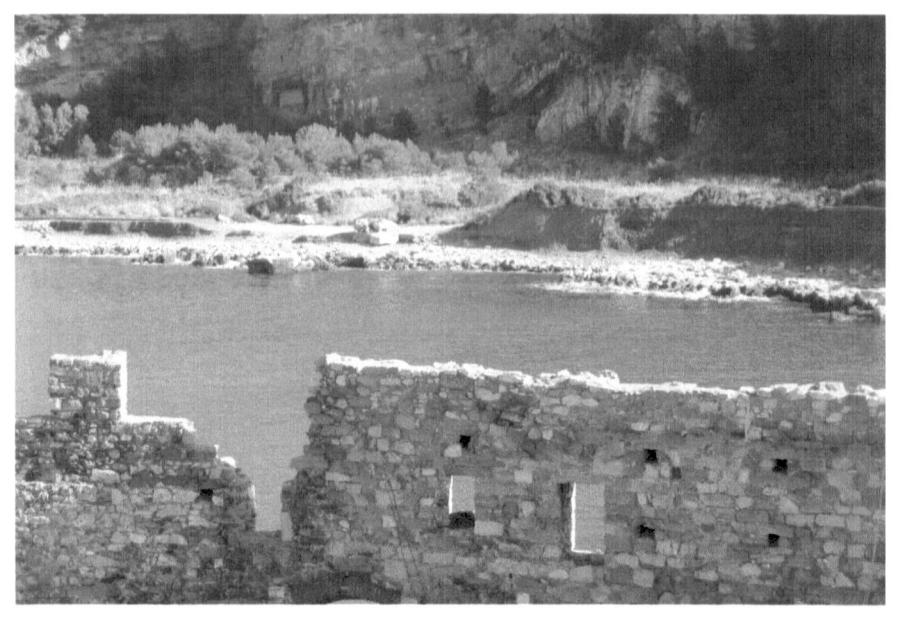

creativity matters

Creativity is the result of a cultural blend.

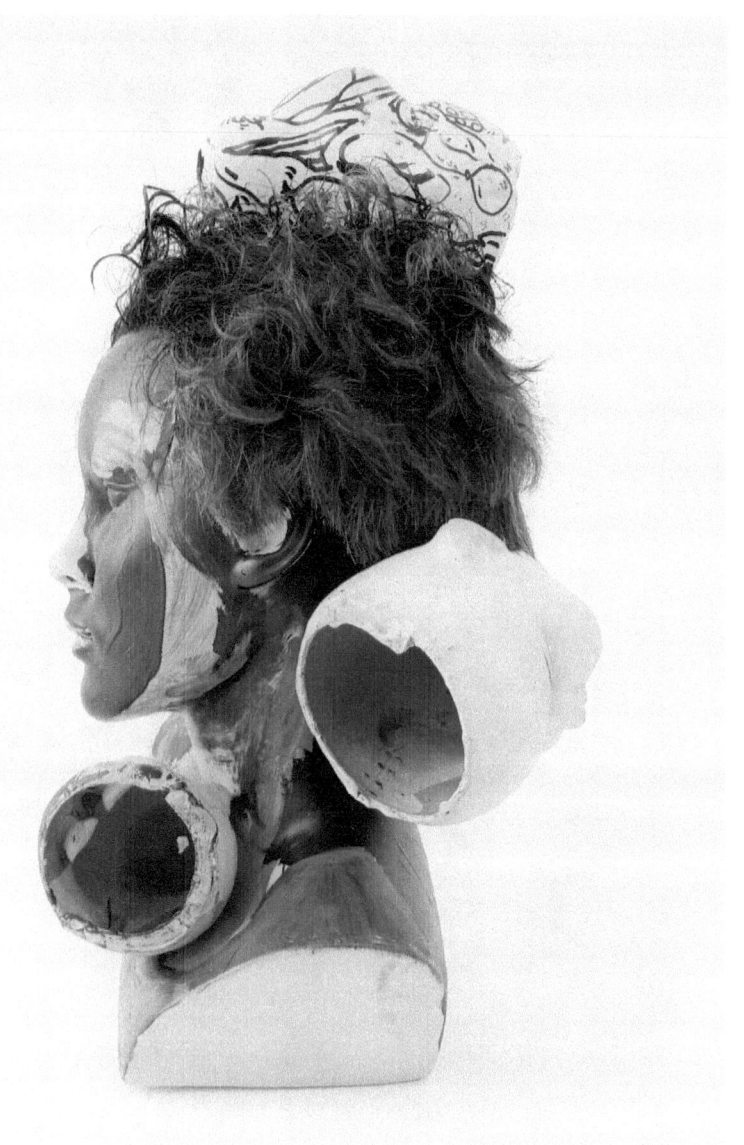

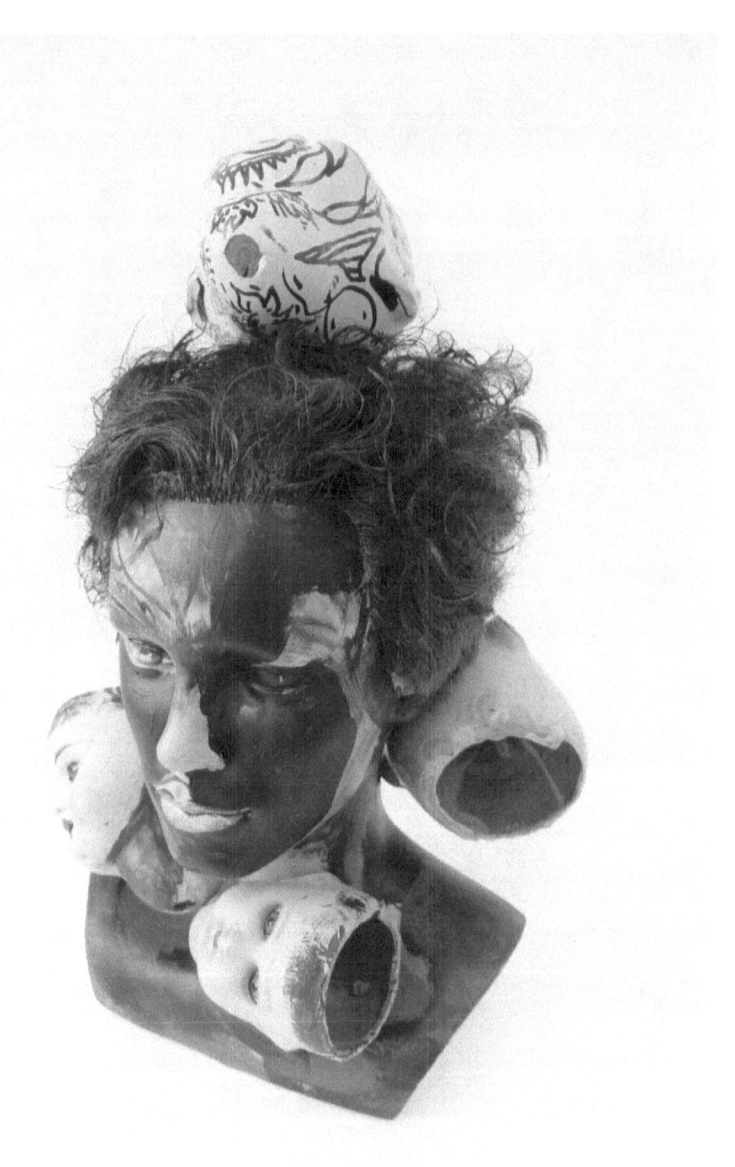

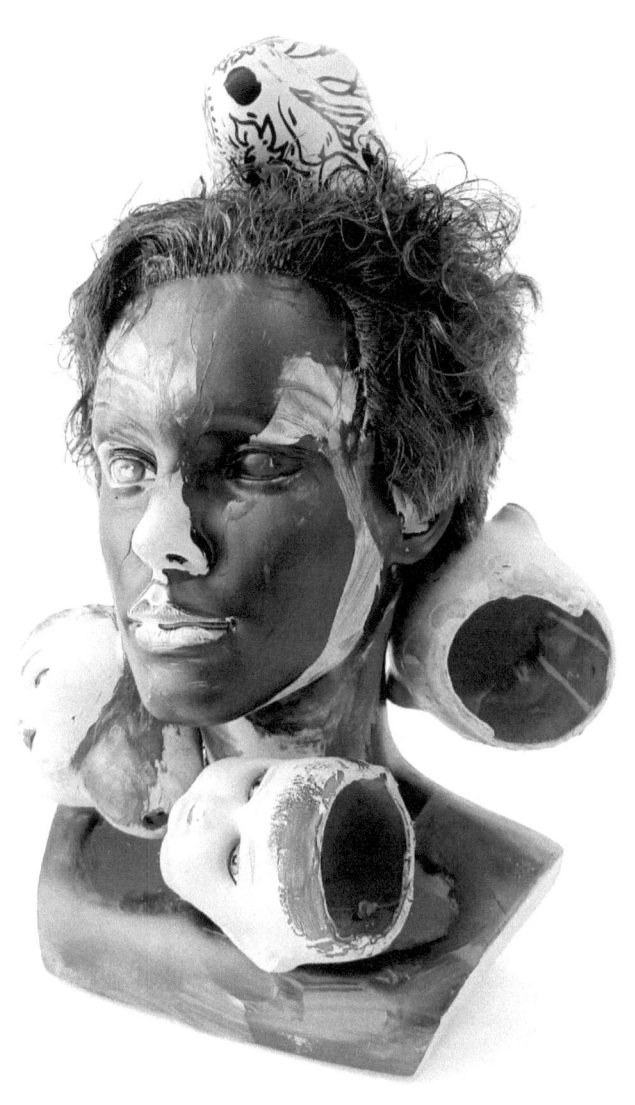

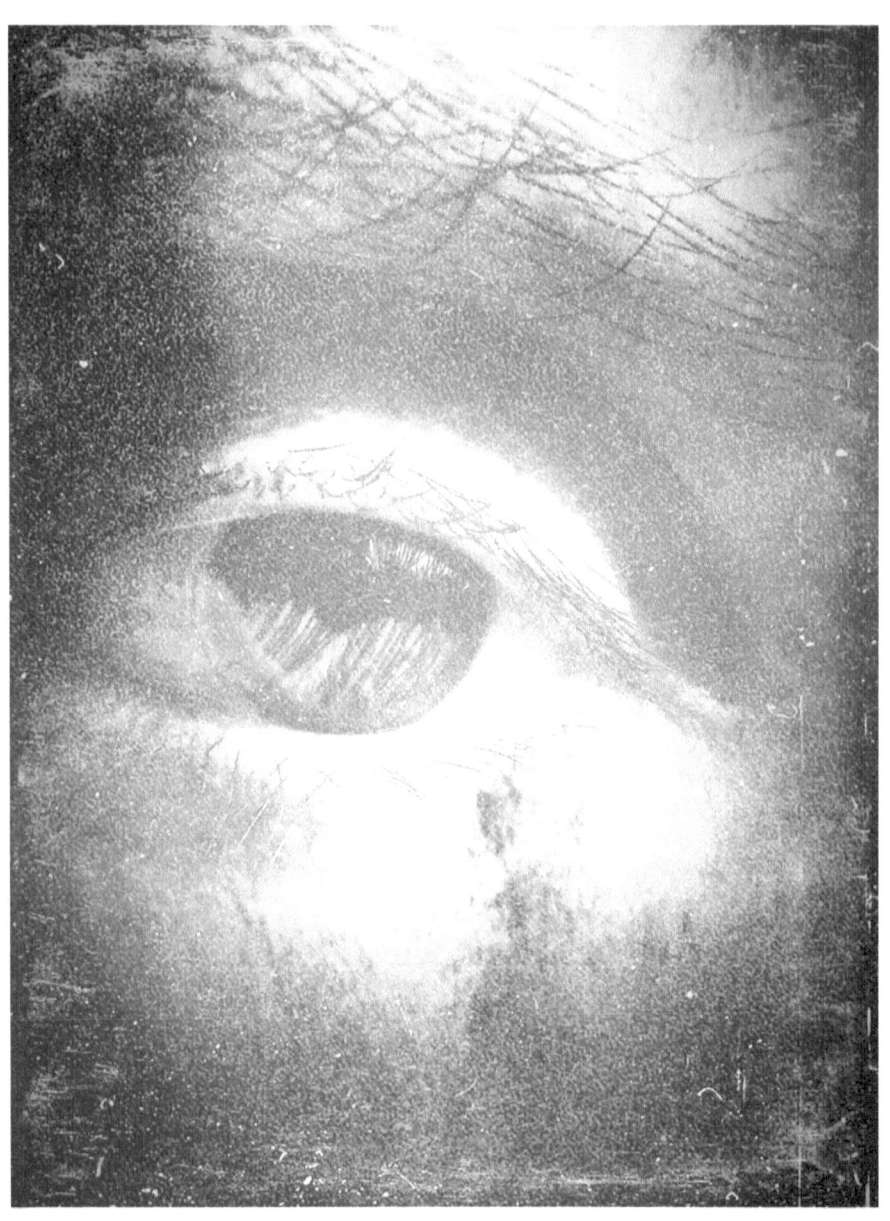

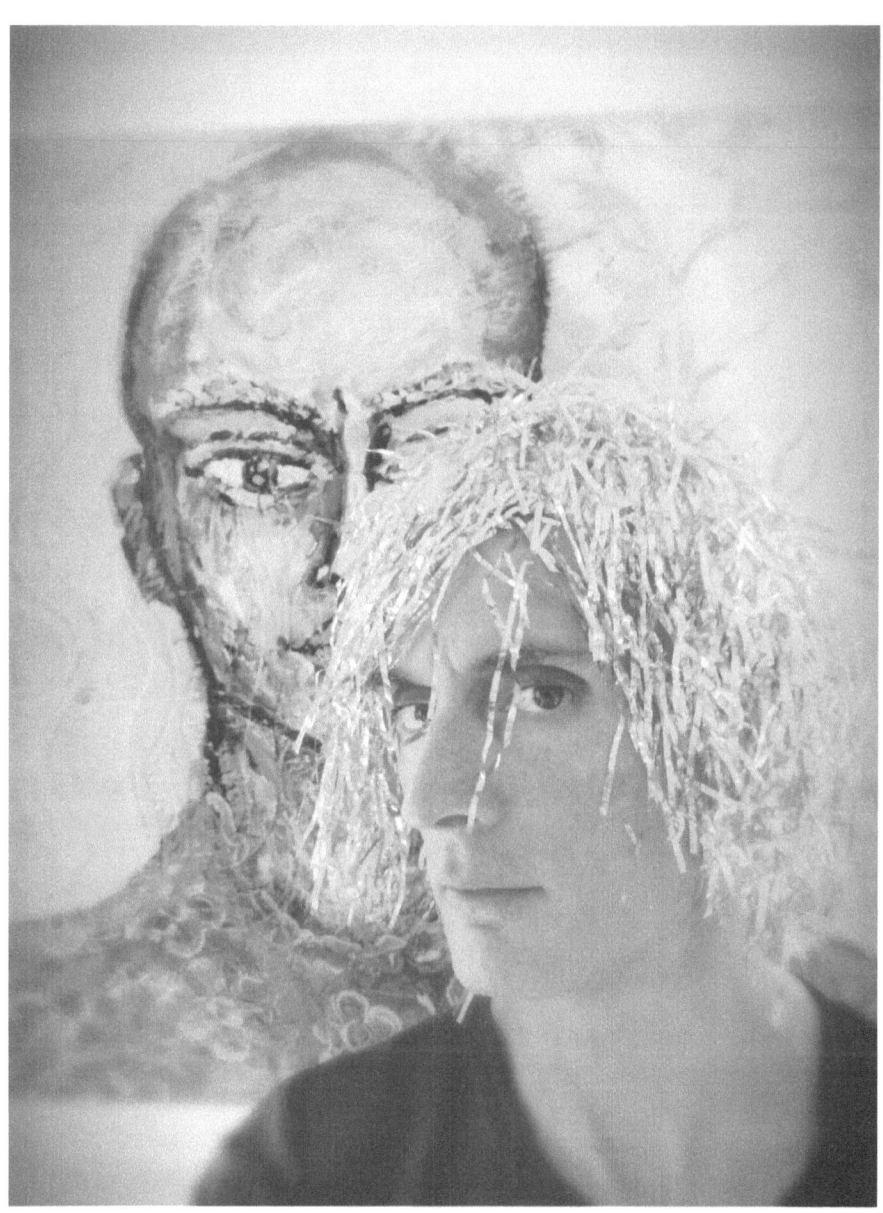

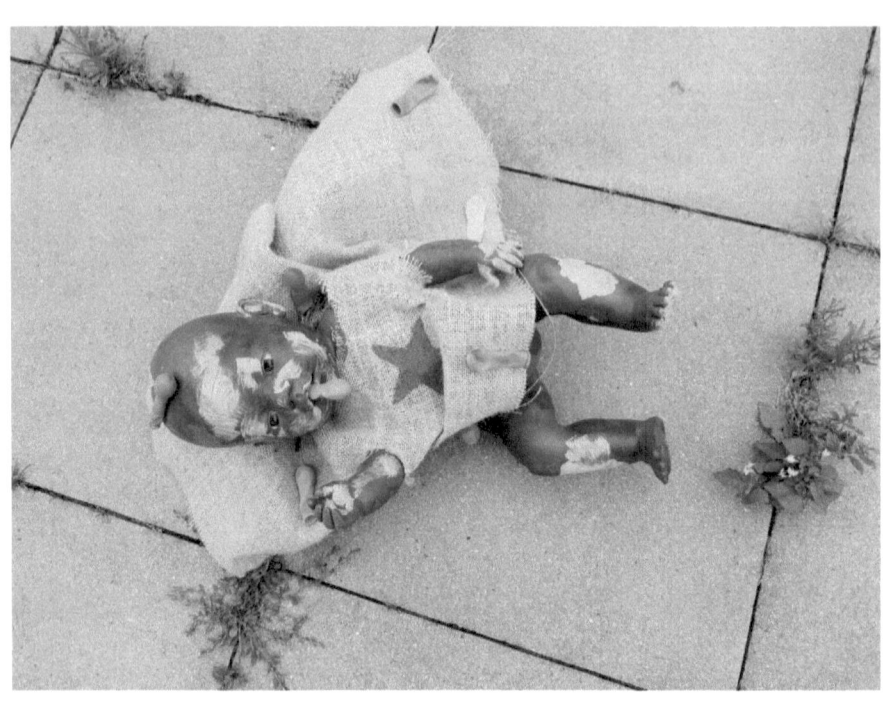

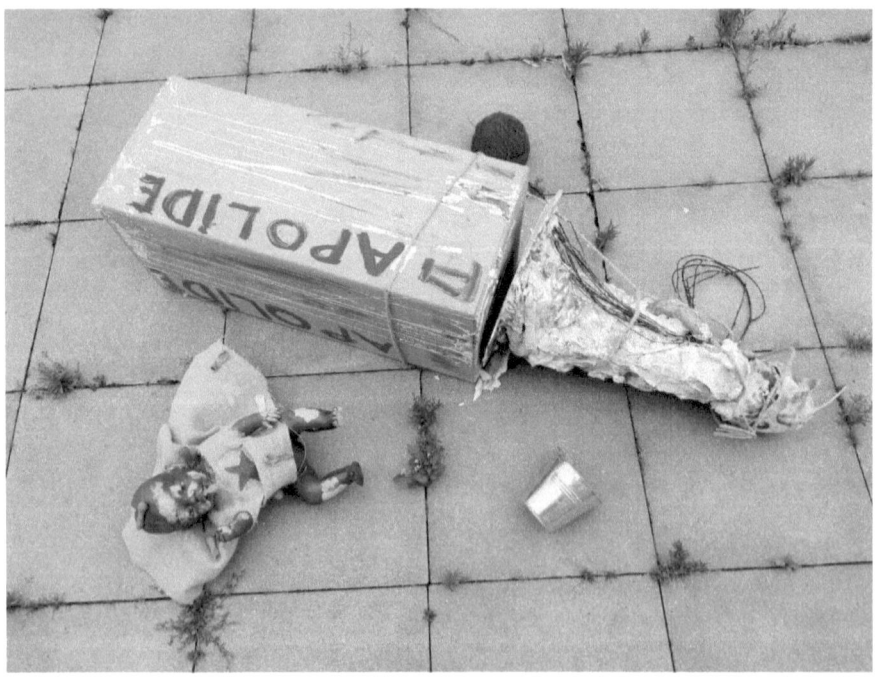

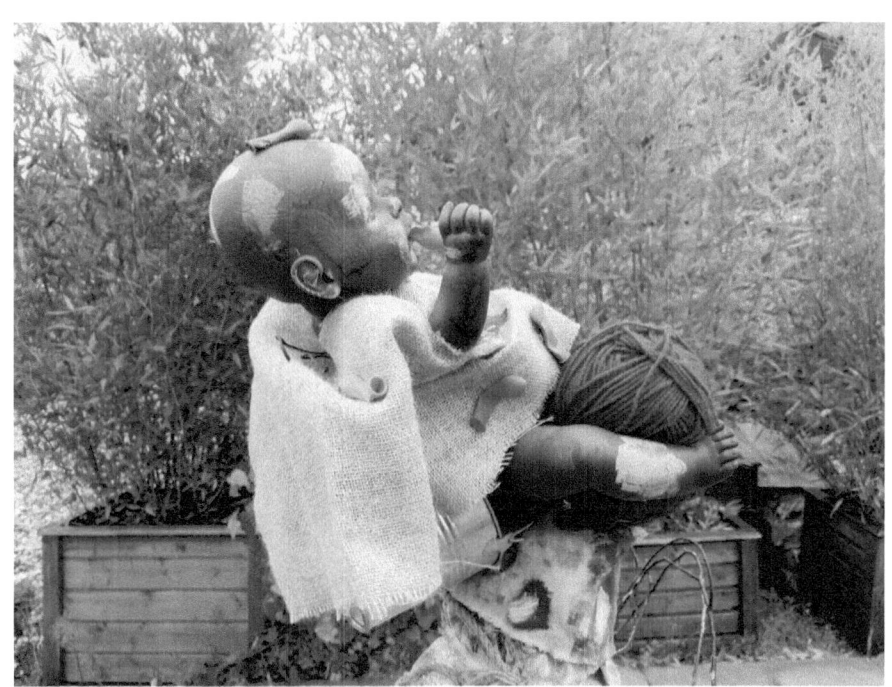

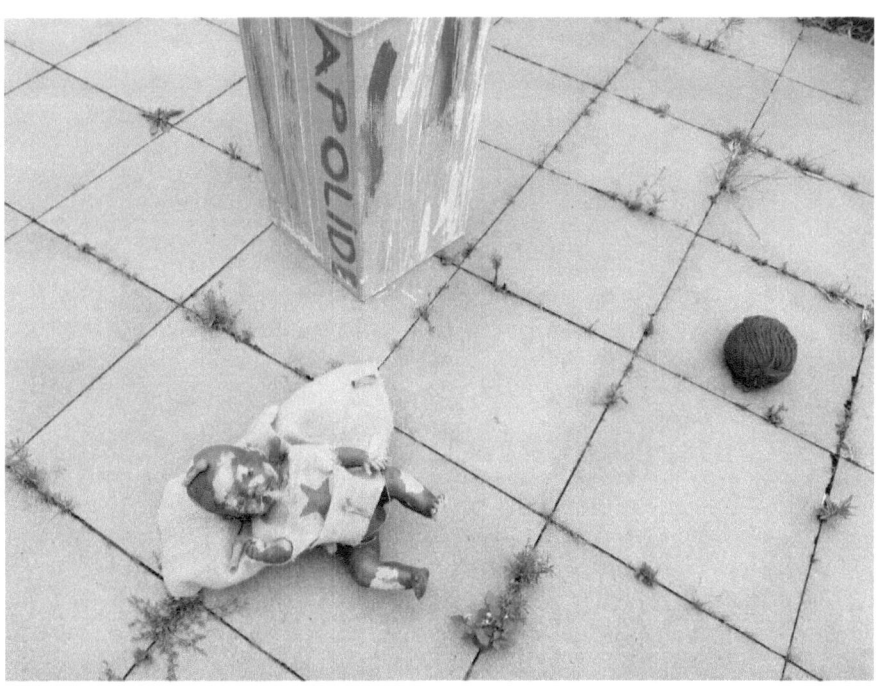

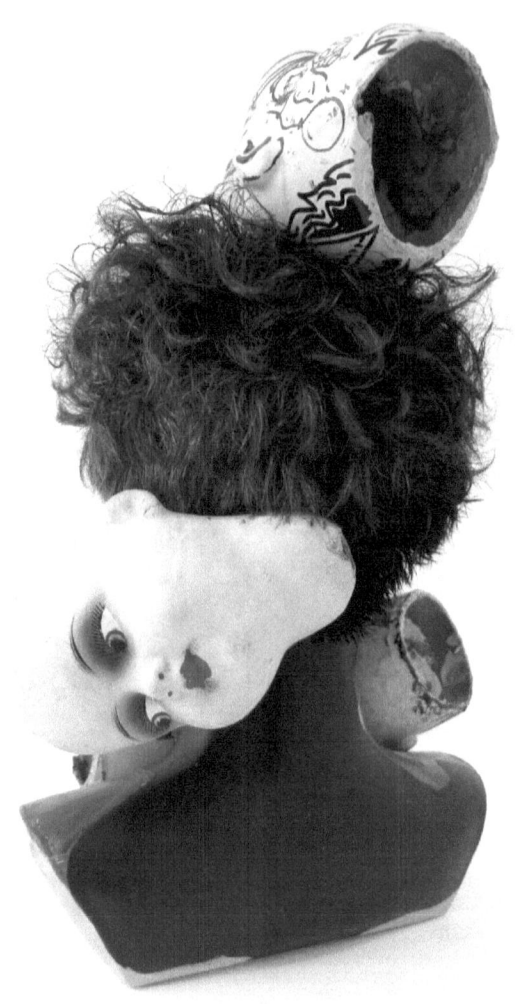

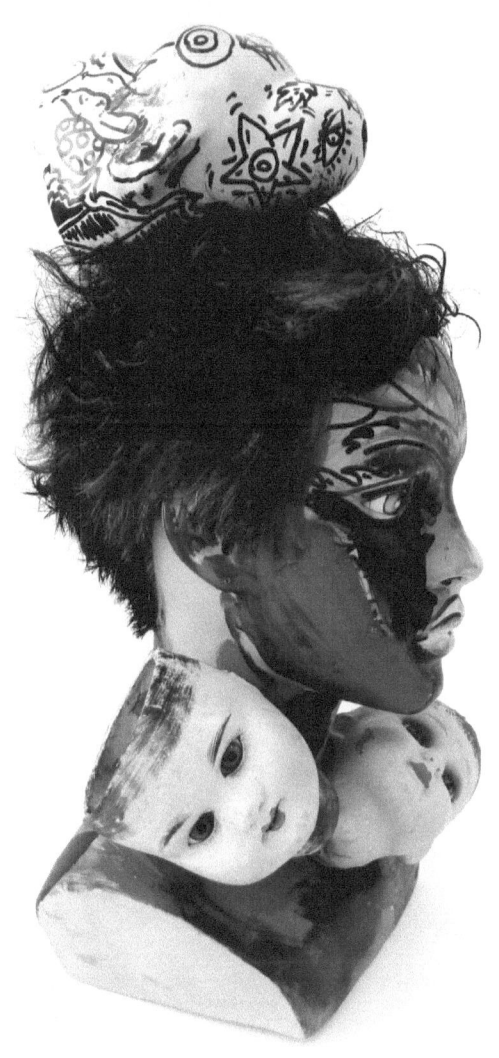

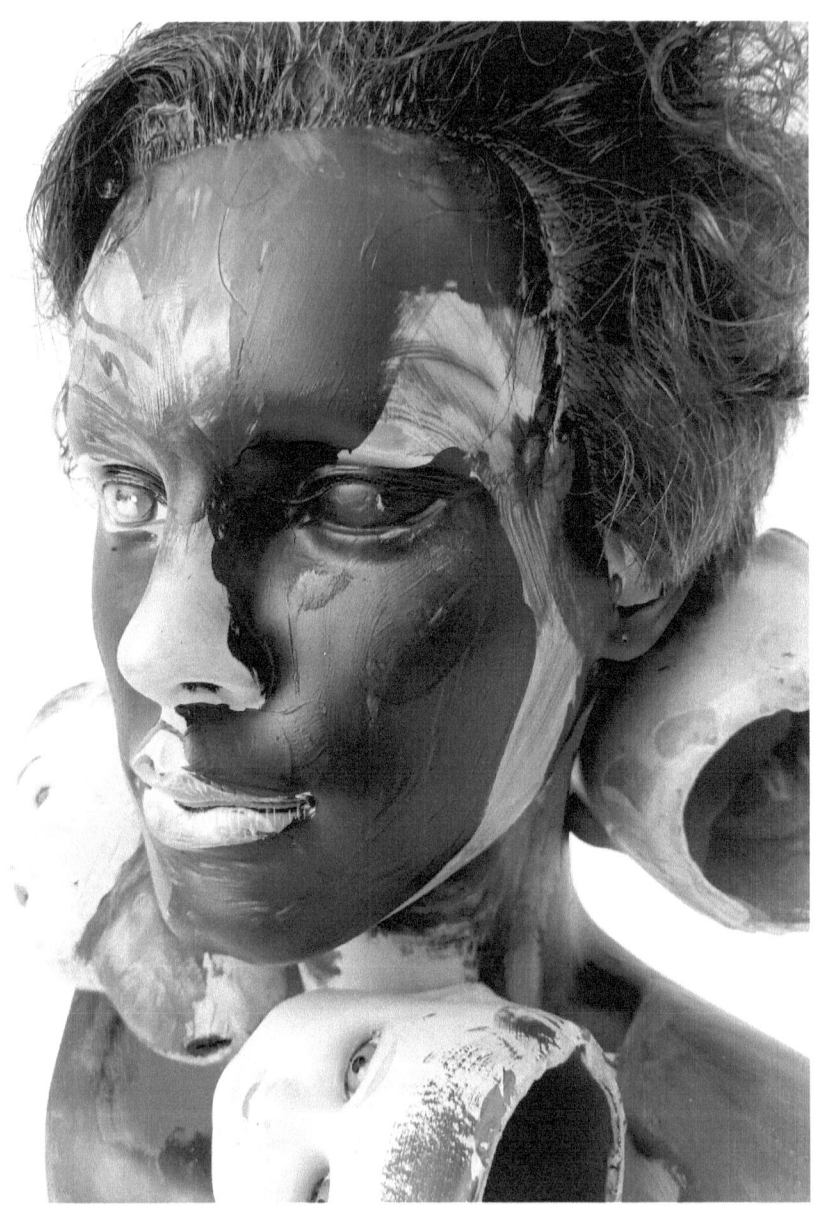

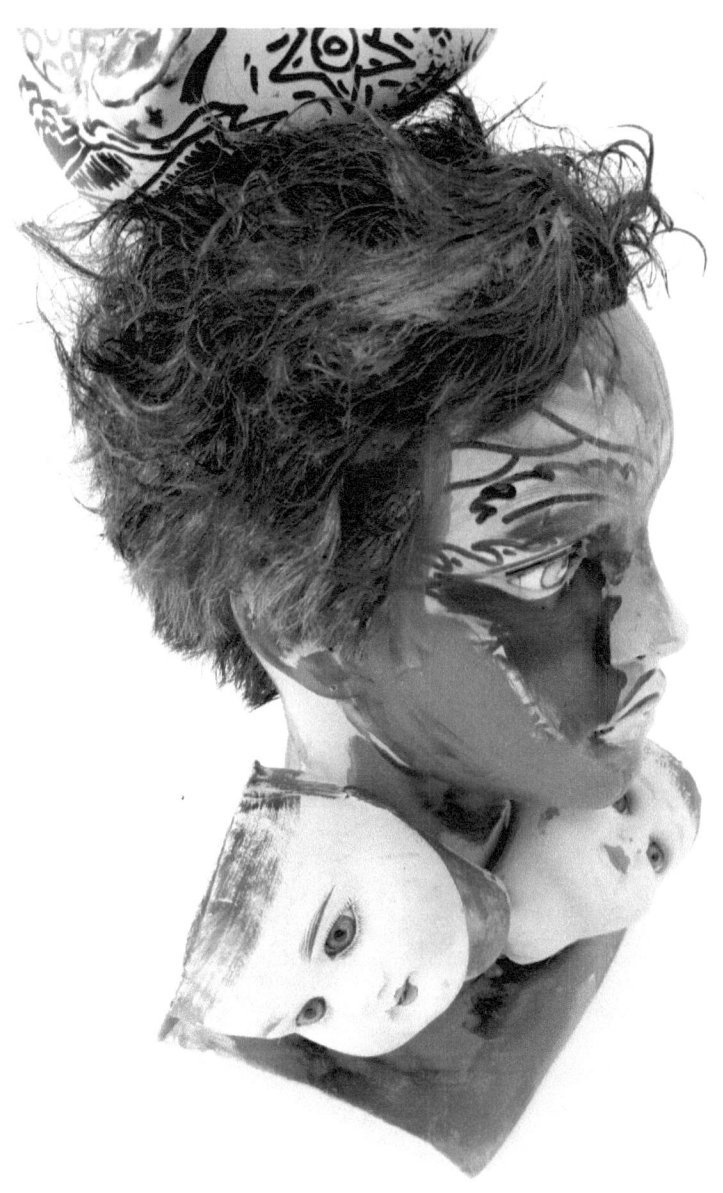

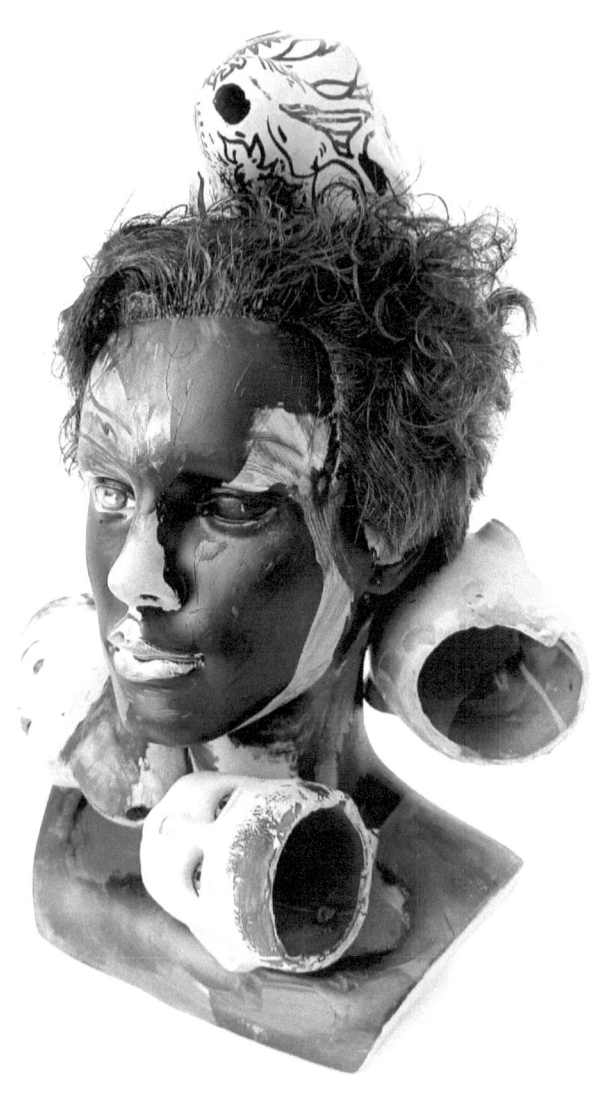

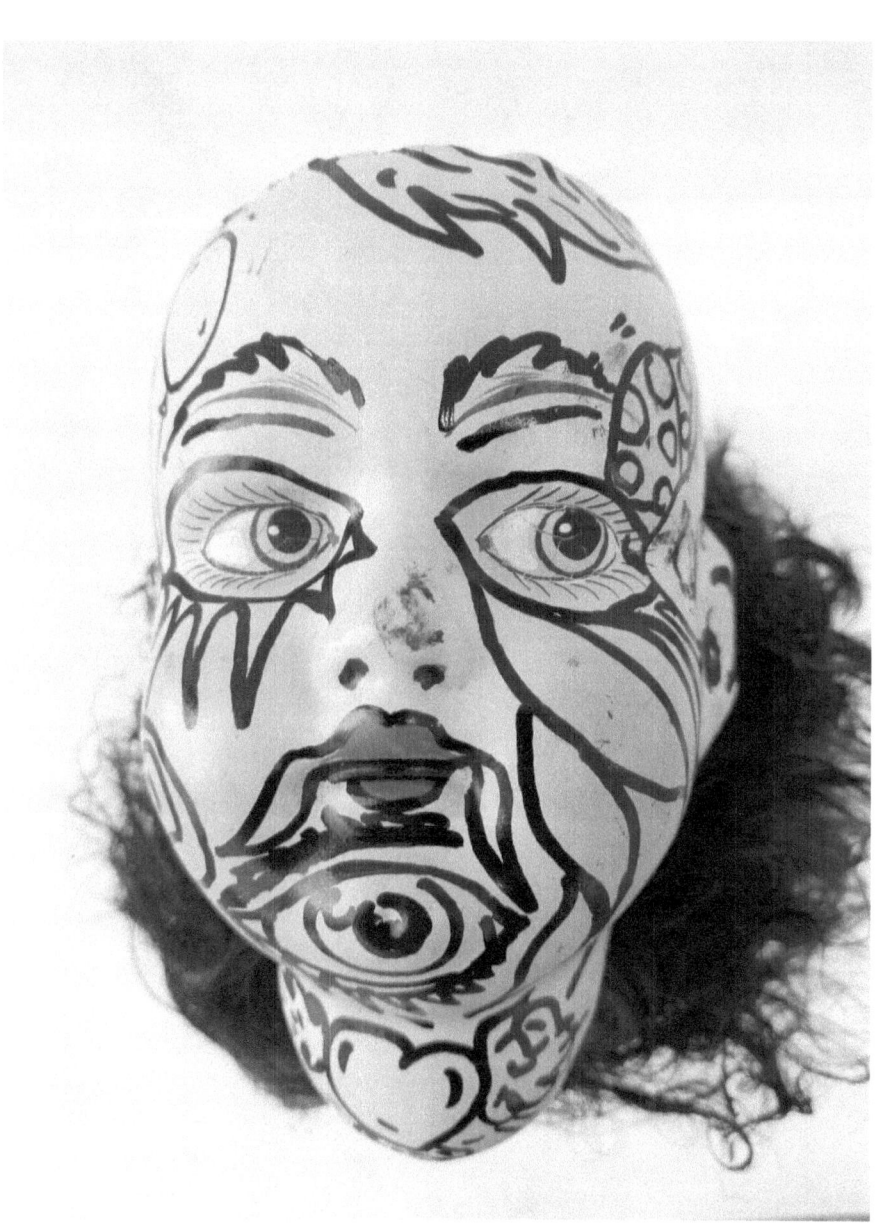

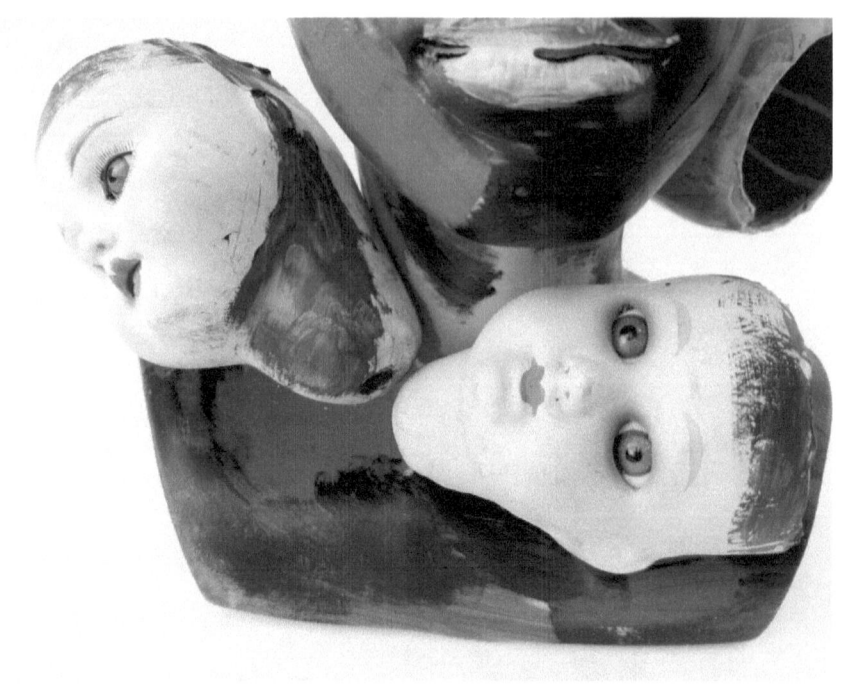

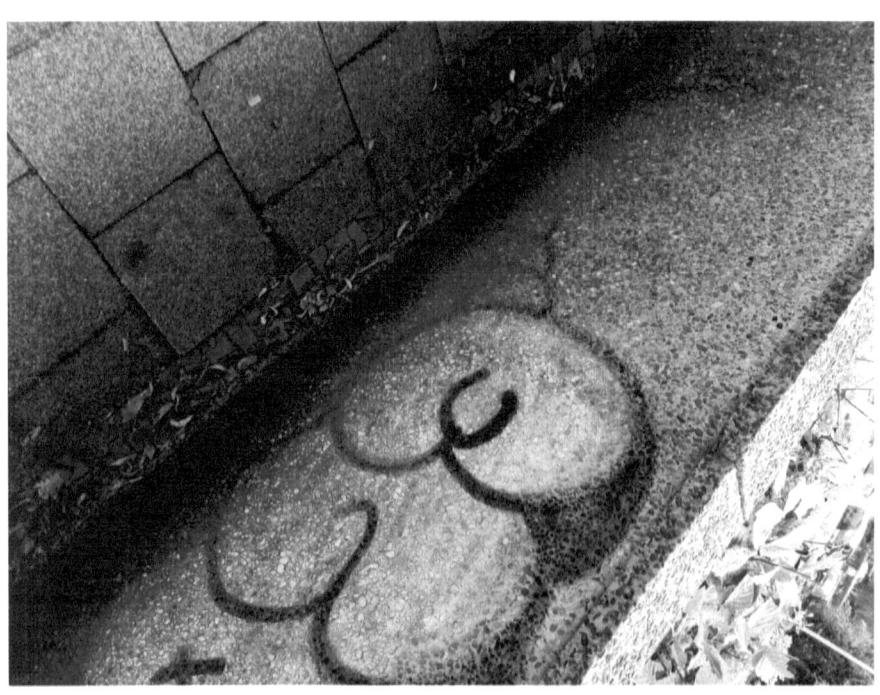

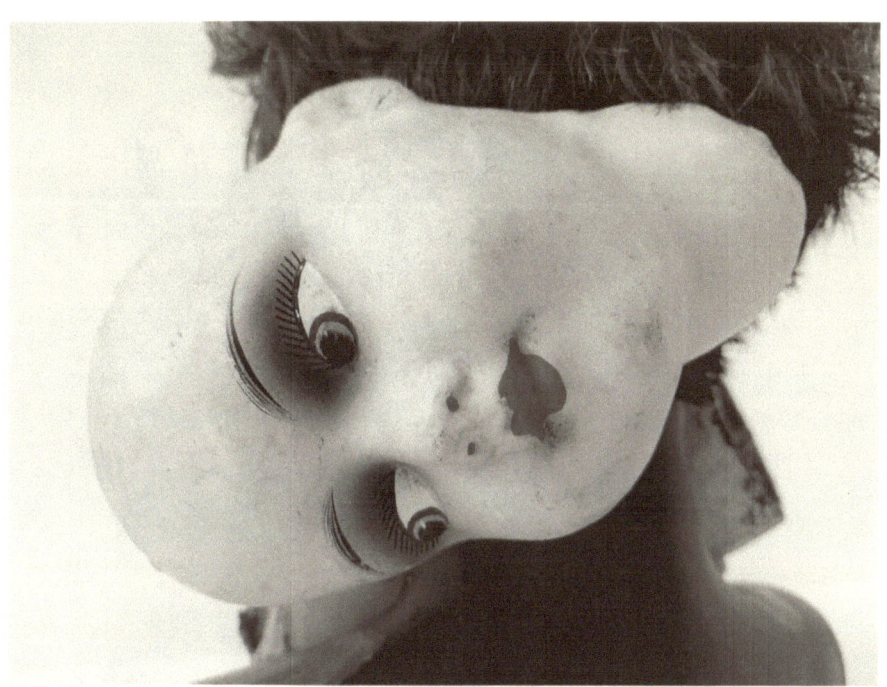

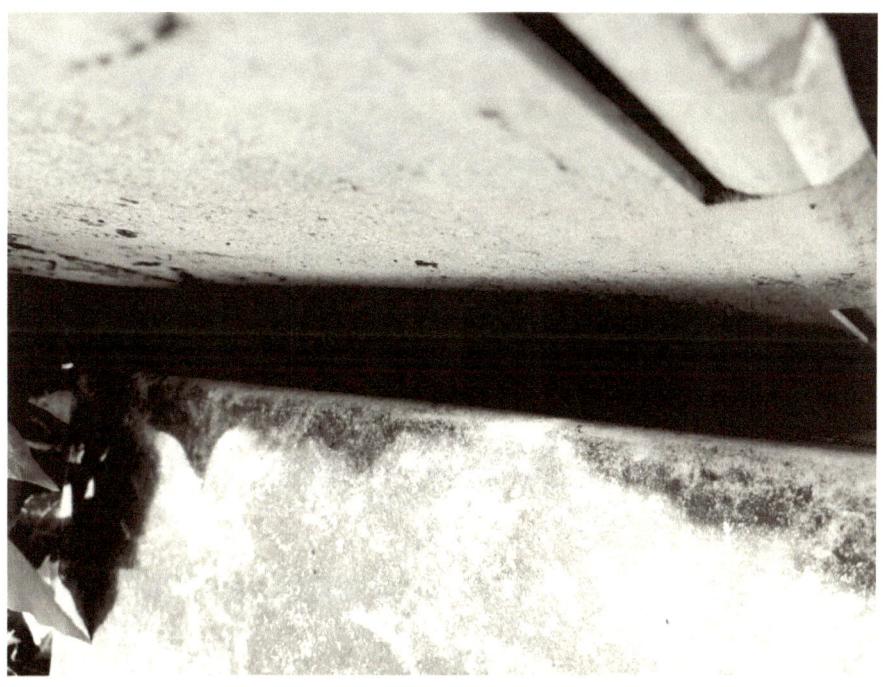

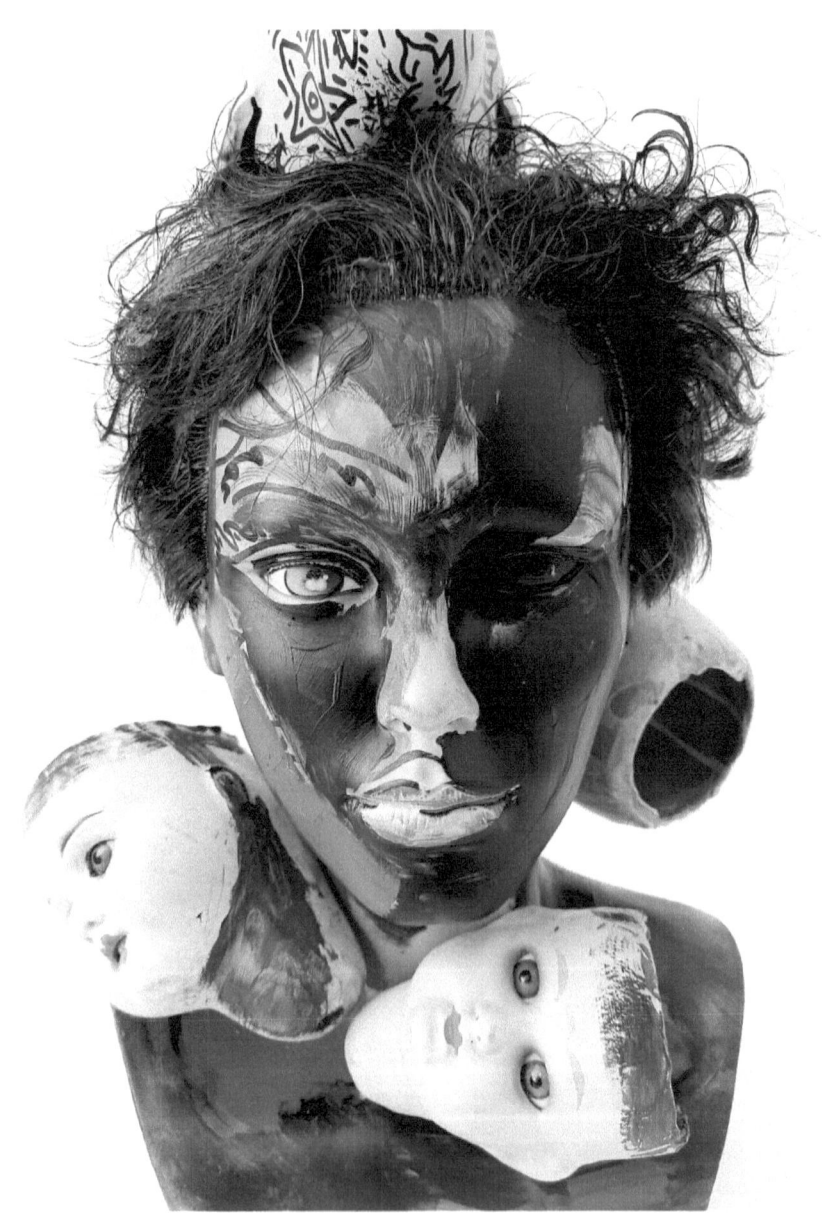

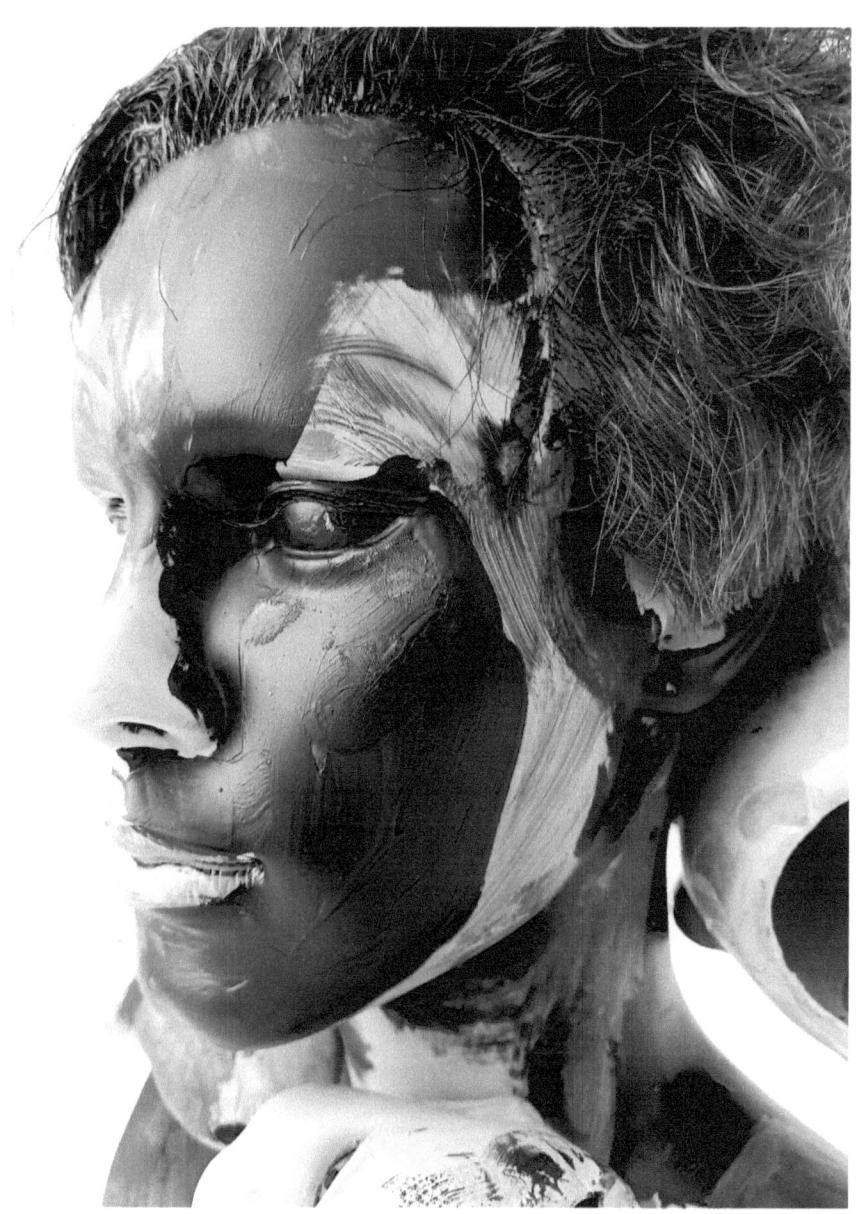

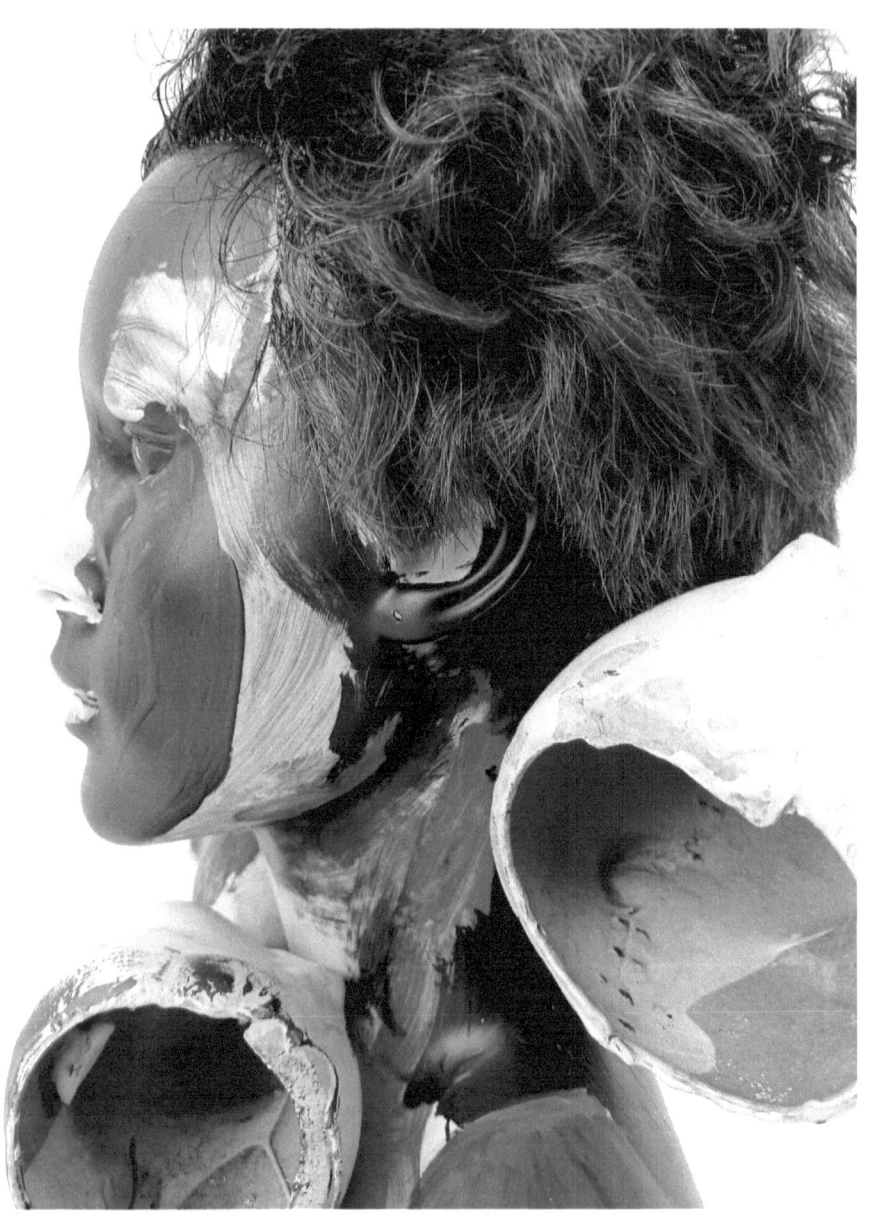

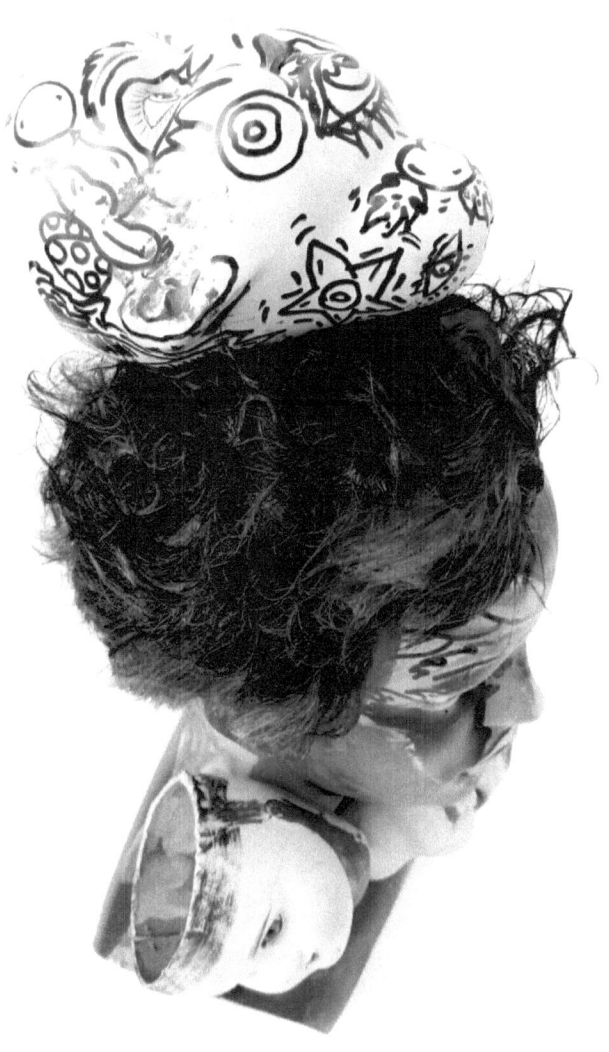

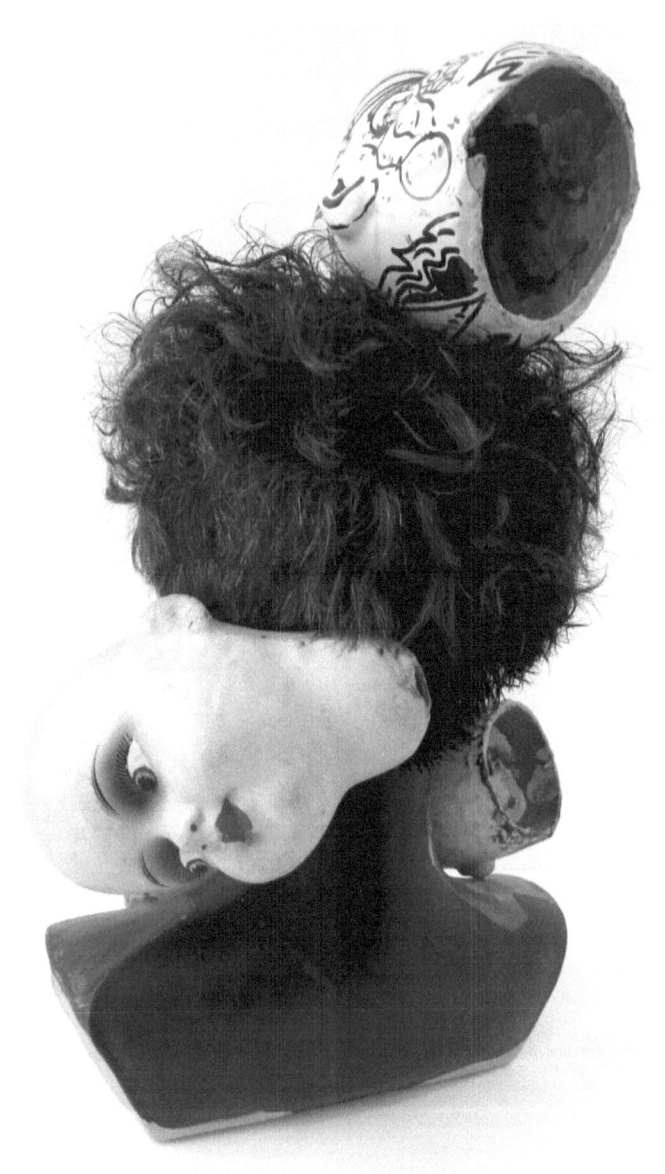

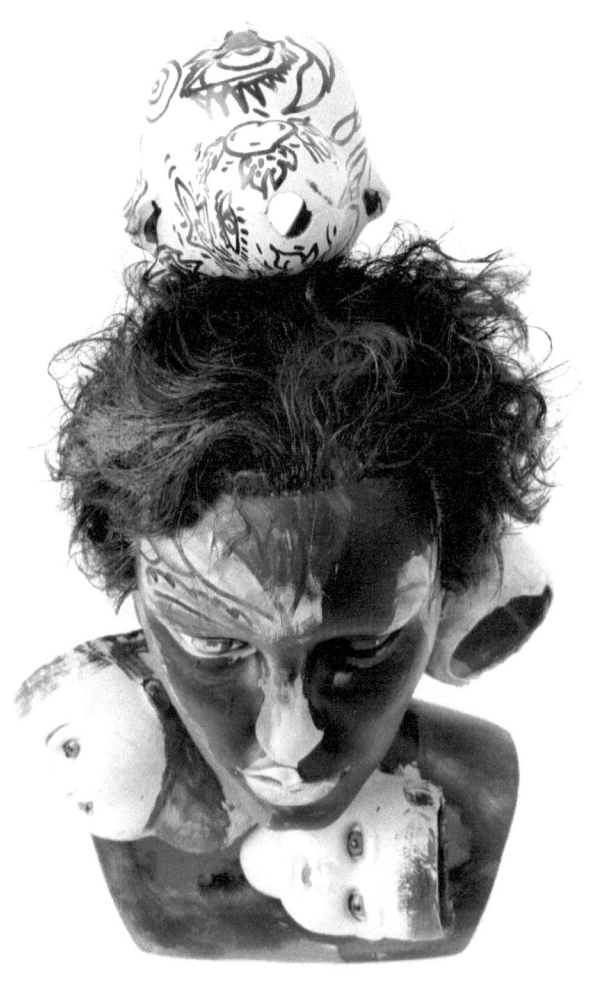

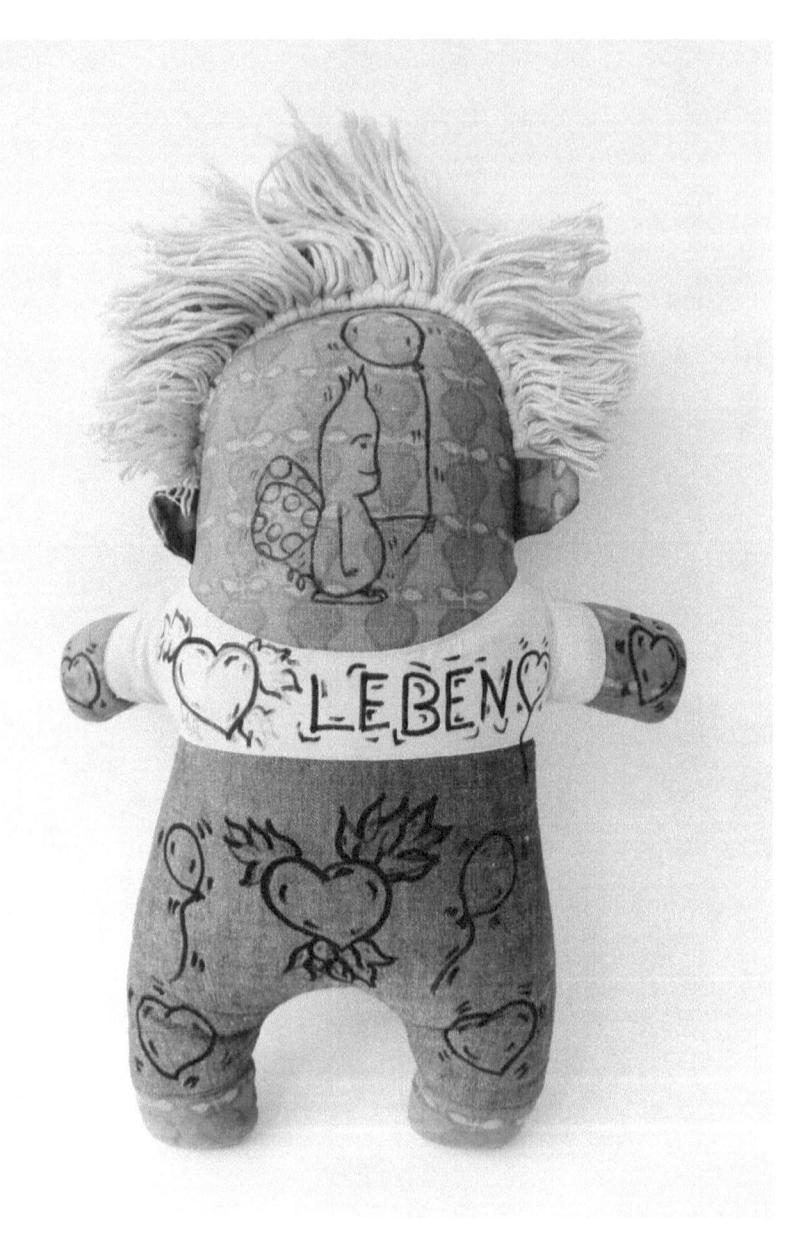

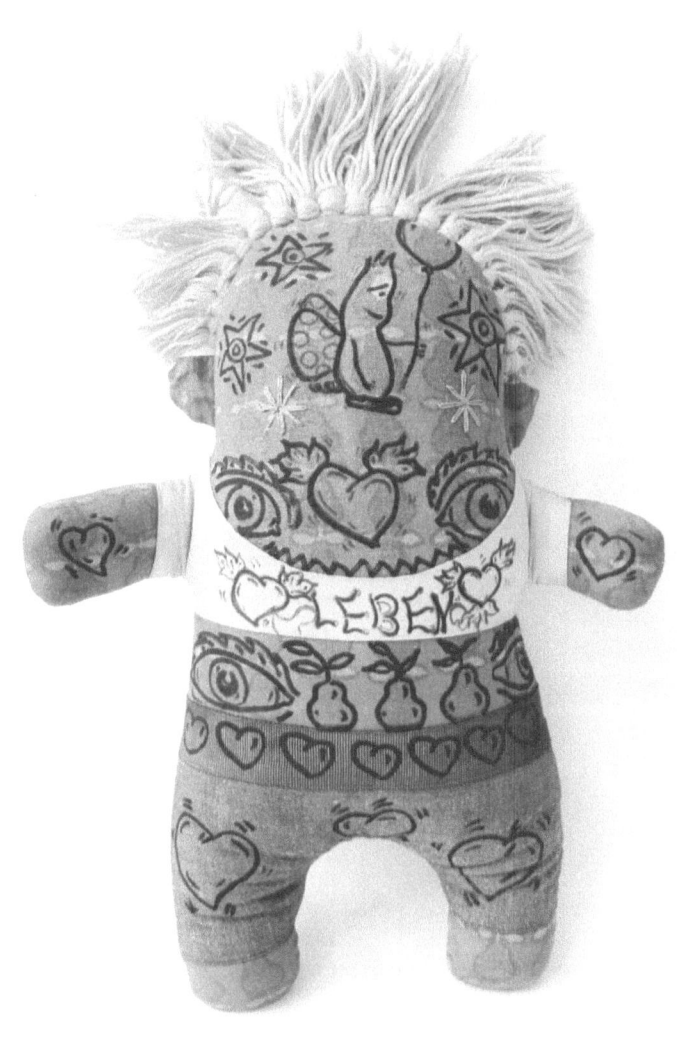

the
powers
that
be

Die Macht des Vorhandenen

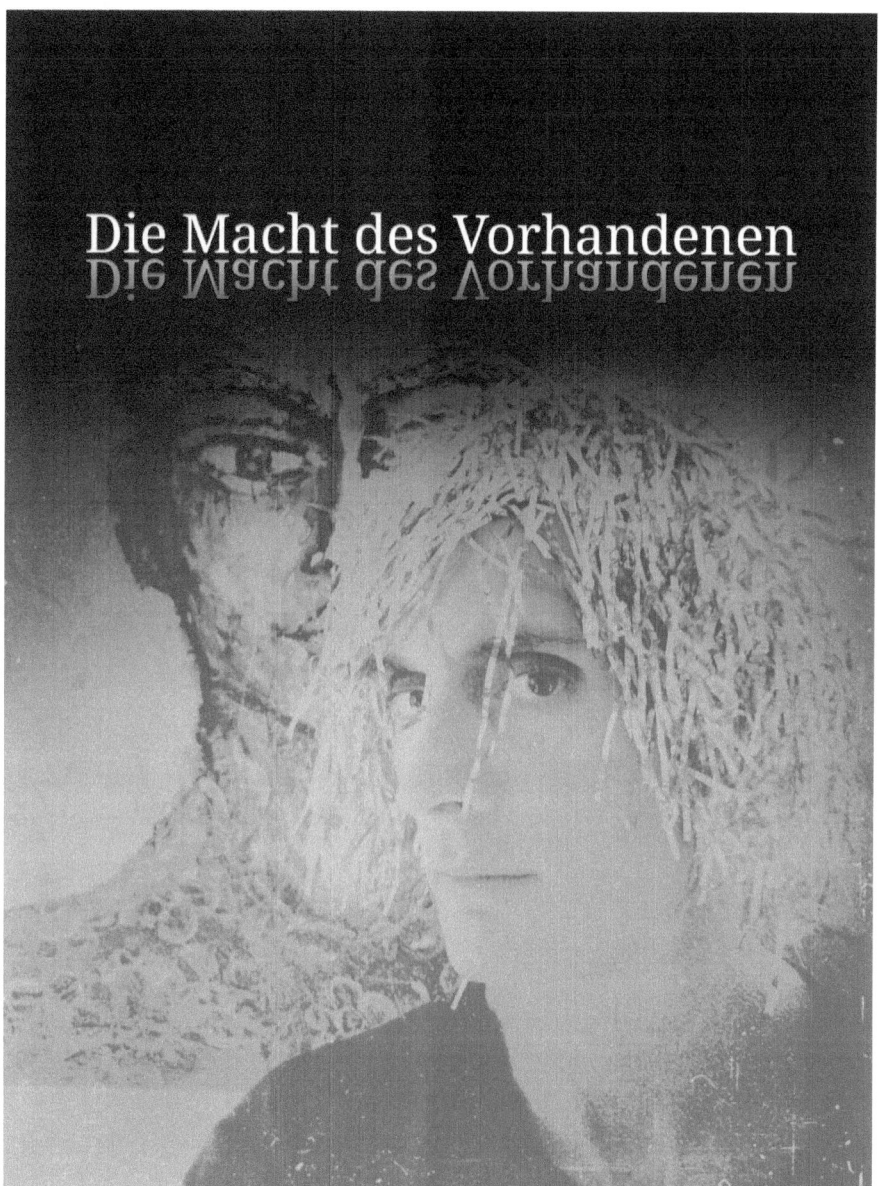

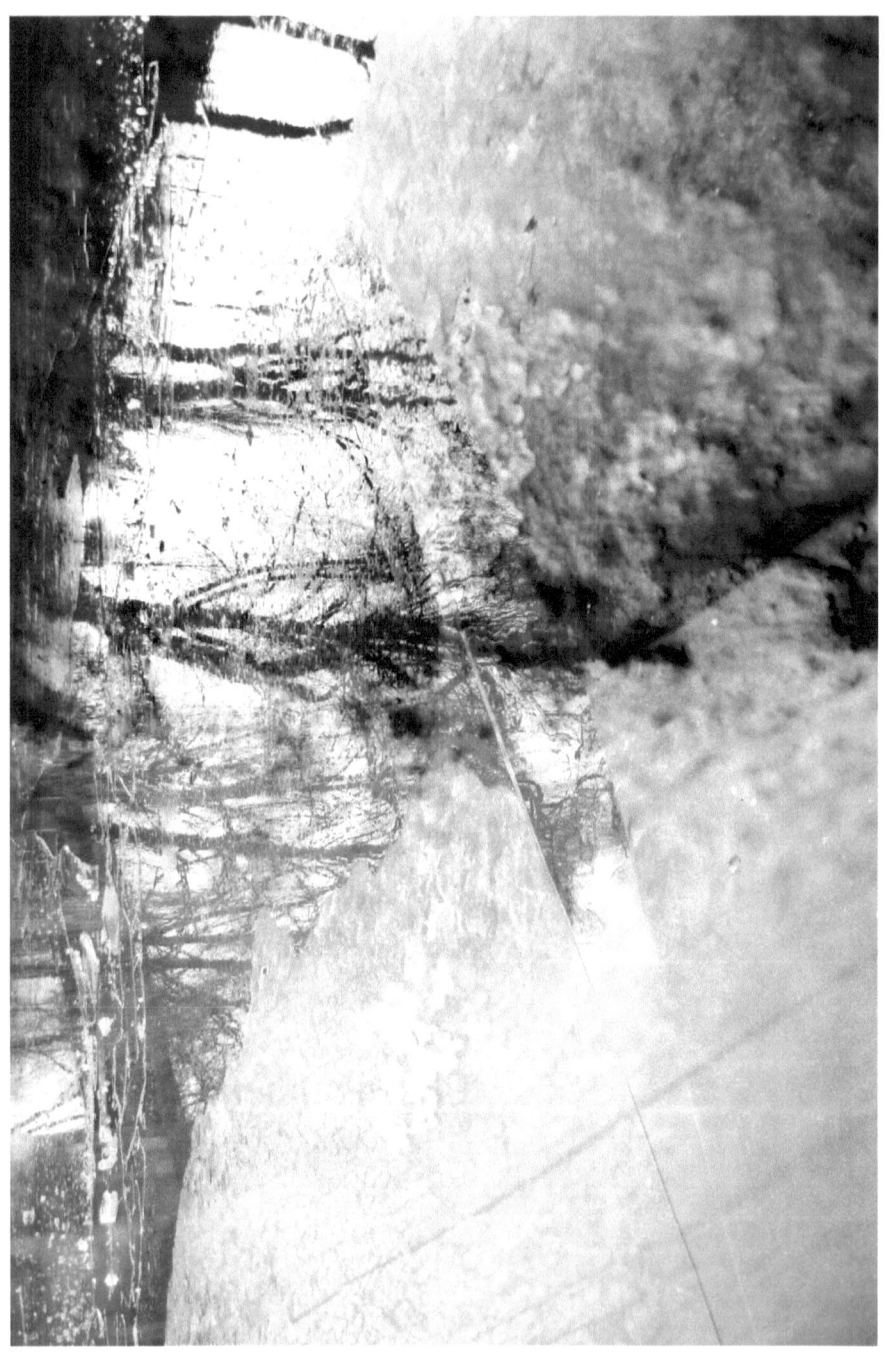

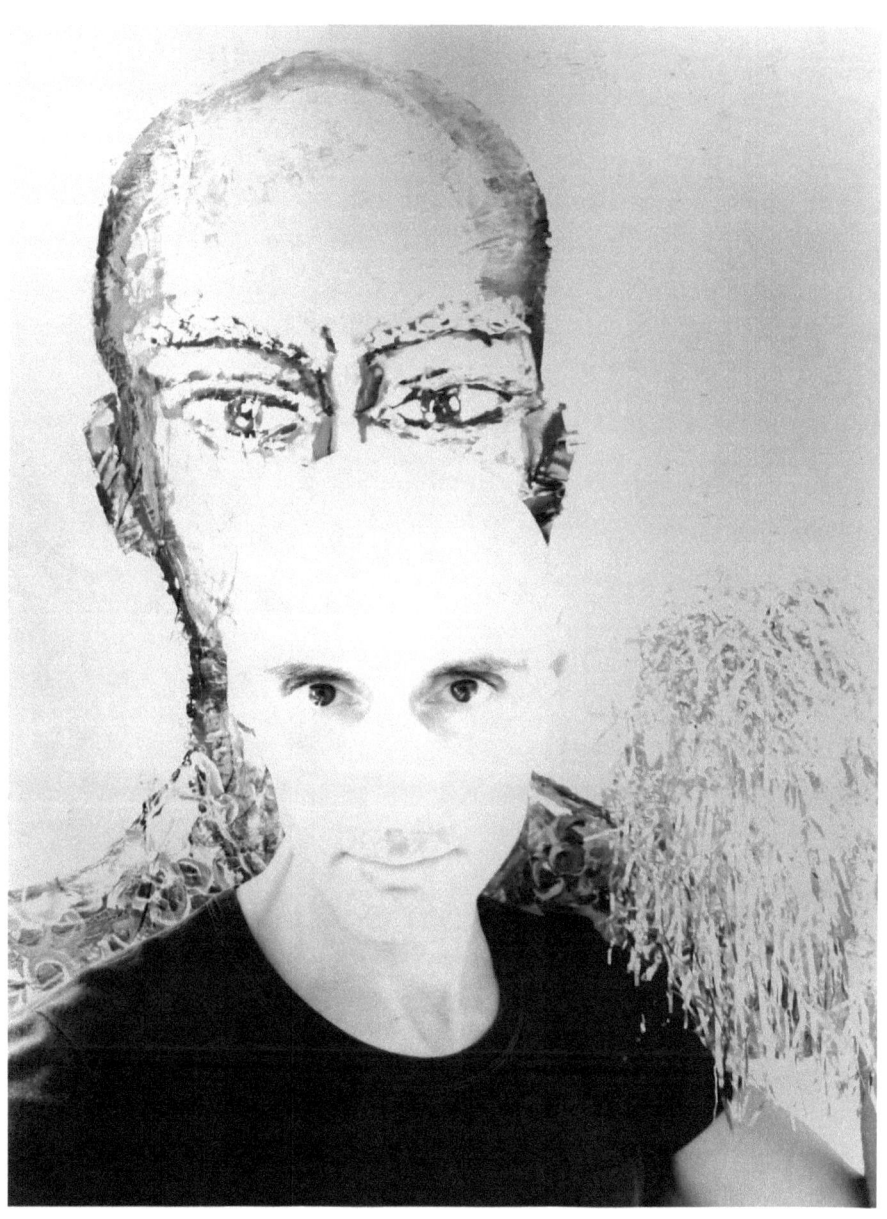

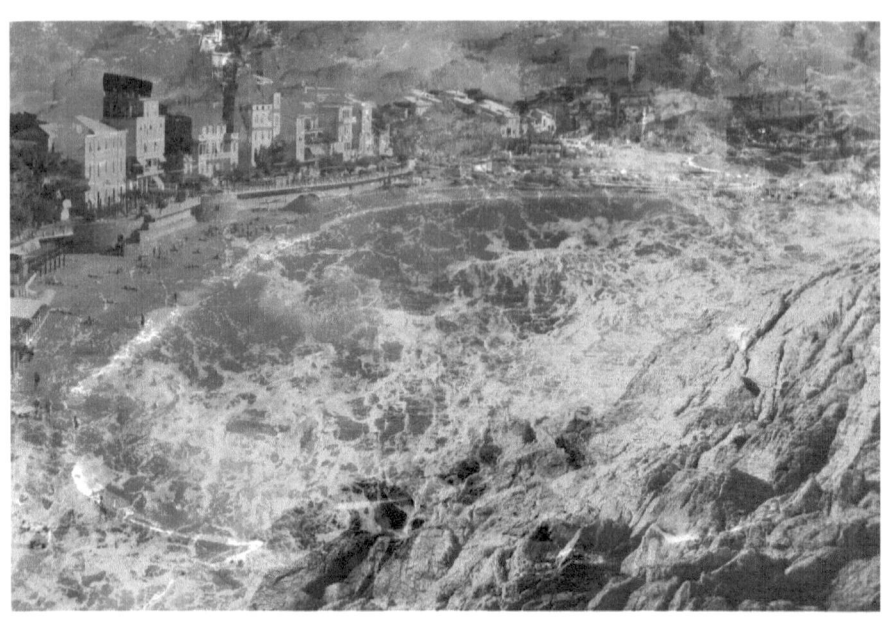

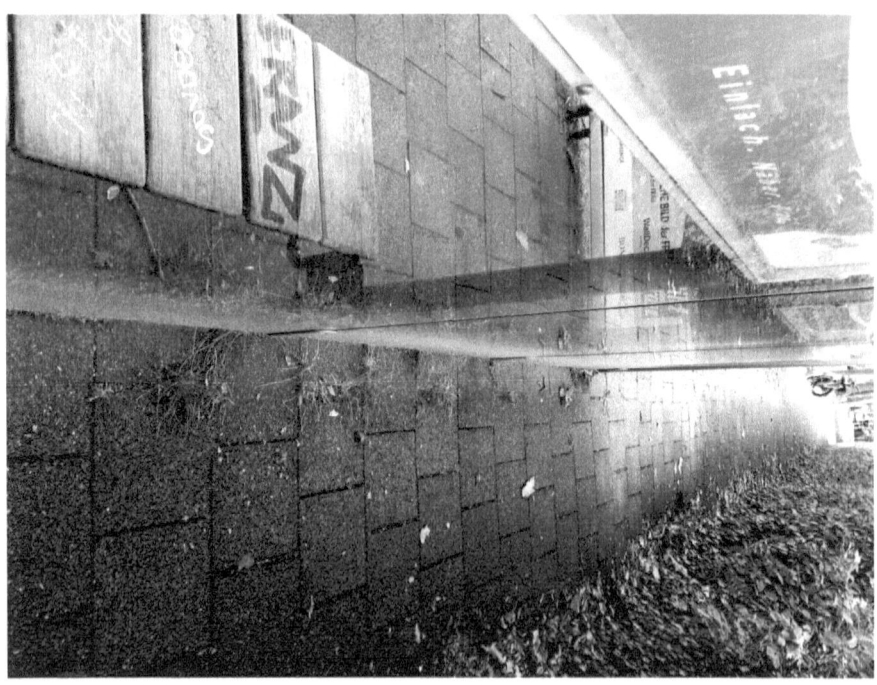

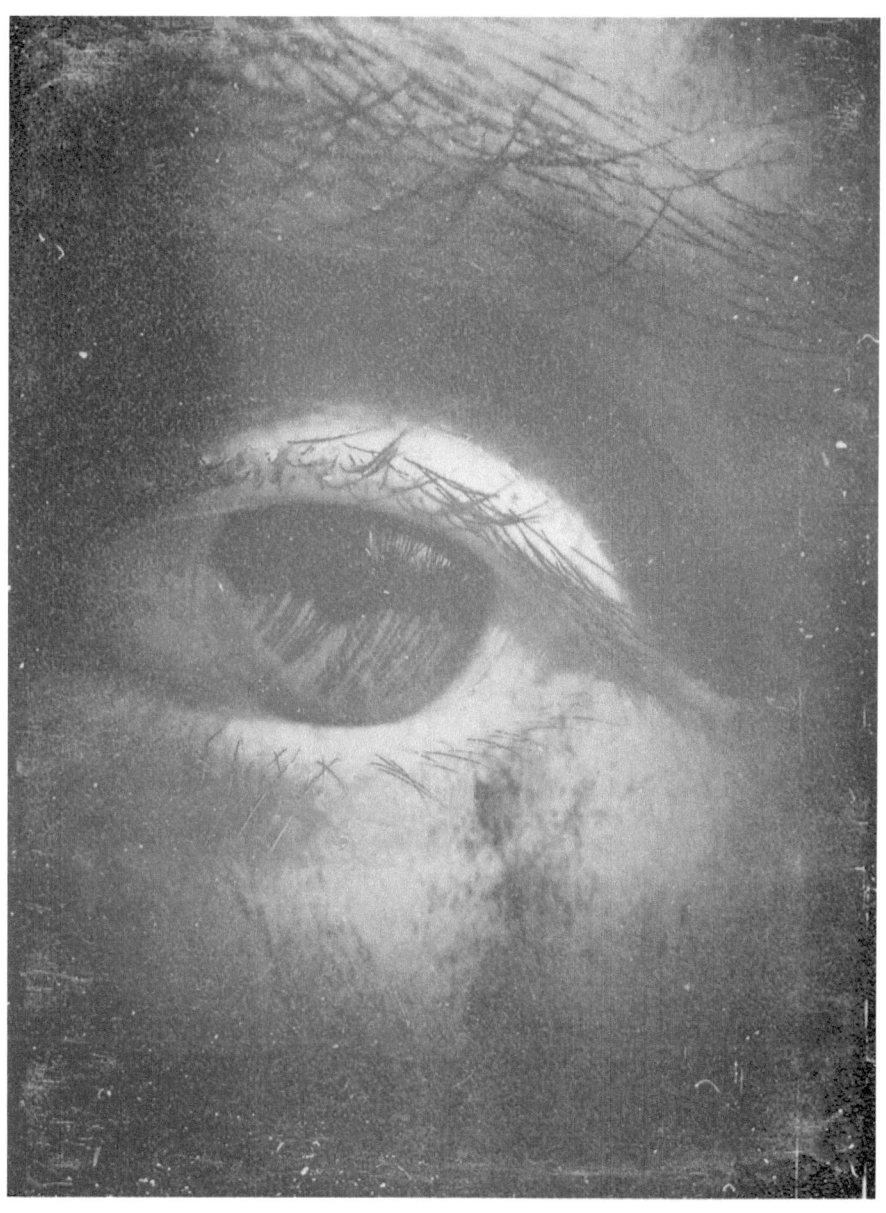

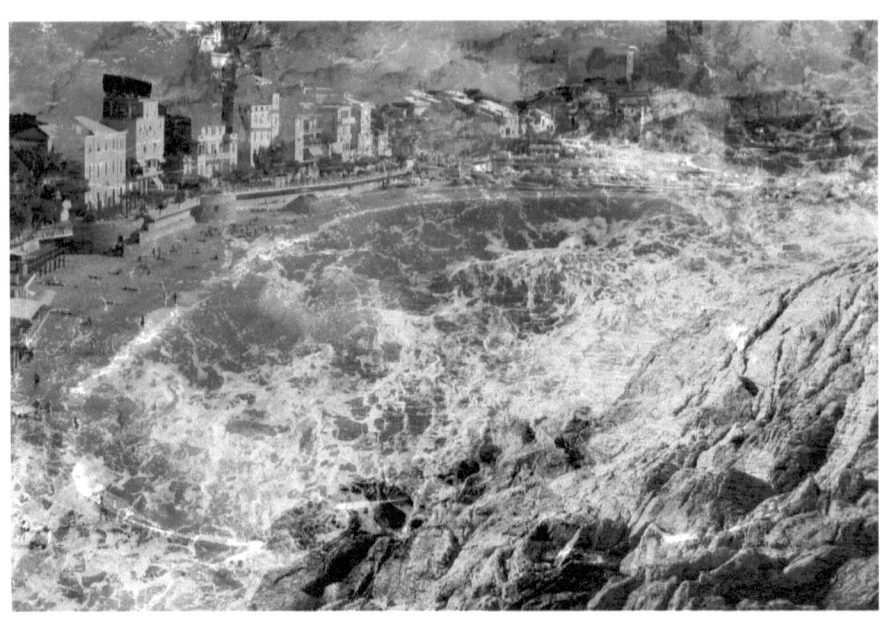

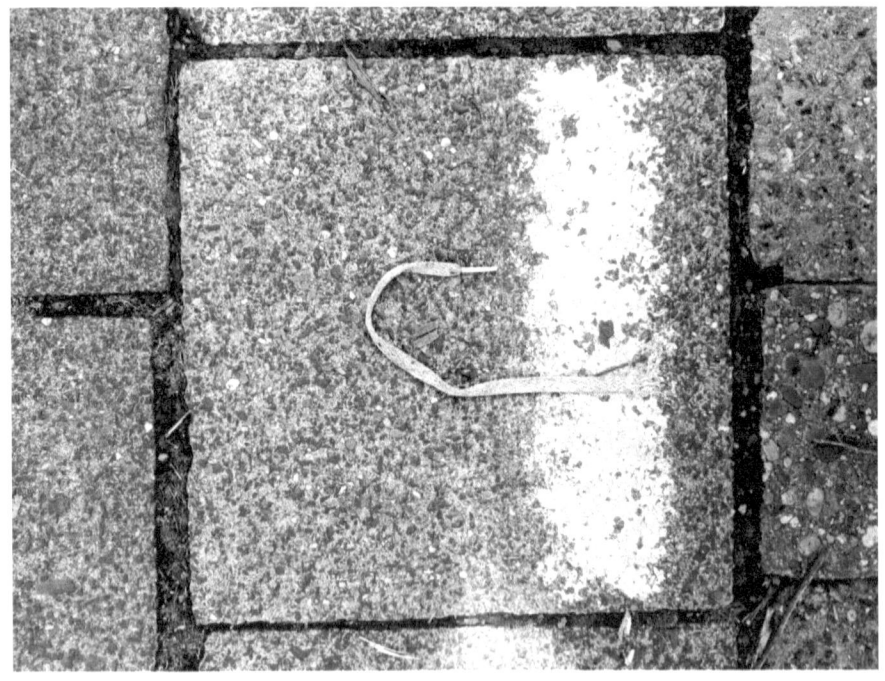

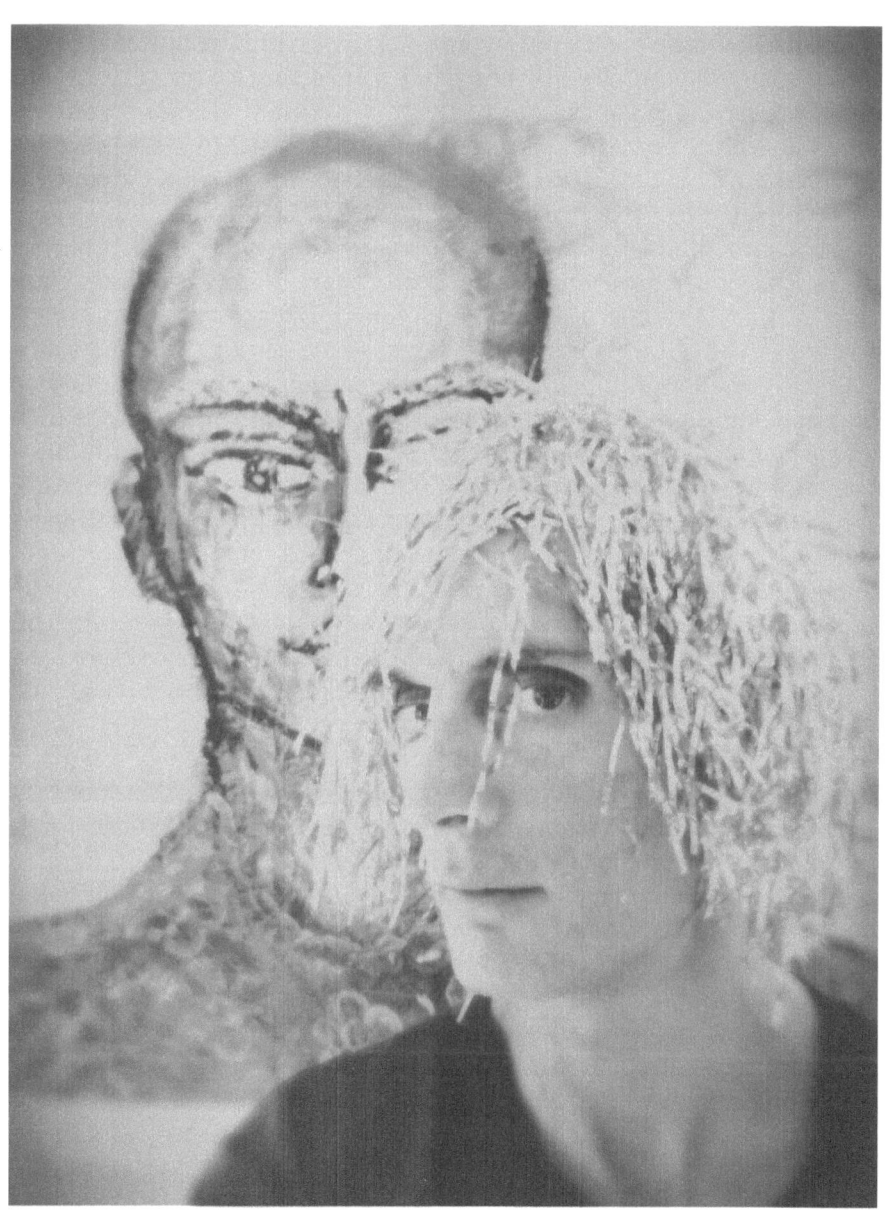

your.life.his.mine.theirs.ours.yours.hers.your.life.his.mine.theirs.o
urs.yours.hers.your.life.his.mine.theirs.ours.yours.hers.your.life.hi
s.mine.theirs.ours.yours.hers.your.life.his.mine.theirs.ours.yours.h
ers.your.life.his.mine.theirs.ours.yours.hers.your.life.his.mine.thei
rs.ours.yours.hers.your.life.his.mine.theirs.ours.yours.hers.your.lif
e.his.mine.theirs.ours.yours.hers.your.life.his.mine.theirs.ours.you
rs.hers.your.life.his.mine.theirs.ours.yours.hers.your.life.his.mine.t
heirs.ours.yours.hers.your.life.his.mine.theirs.ours.yours.hers.your
.life.his.mine.theirs.ours.yours.hers.your.life.his.mine.theirs.ours.y
ours.hers.your.life.his.mine.theirs.ours.yours.hers.your.life.his.min
e.theirs.ours.yours.hers.your.life.his.mine.theirs.ours.yours.hers.yo
ur.life.his.mine.theirs.ours.yours.hers.your.life.his.mine.theirs.our
s.yours.hers.your.life.his.mine.theirs.ours.yours.hers.your.life.his.
mine.theirs.ours.yours.hers.your.life.his.mine.theirs.ours.yours.her
s.your.life.his.mine.theirs.ours.yours.hers.your.life.his.mine.theirs.
ours.yours.hers.your.life.his.mine.theirs.ours.yours.hers.your.life.h
is.mine.theirs.ours.yours.hers.your.life.his.mine.theirs.ours.yours.
hers.your.life.his.mine.theirs.ours.yours.hers.your.life.his.mine.the
irs.ours.yours.hers.your.life.his.mine.theirs.ours.yours.hers.your.lif
e.his.mine.theirs.ours.yours.hers.your.life.his.mine.theirs.ours.you
rs.hers.your.life.his.mine.theirs.ours.yours.hers.your.life.his.mine.t
heirs.ours.yours.hers.your.life.his.mine.theirs.ours.yours.hers.your
.life.his.mine.theirs.ours.yours.hers.your.life.his.mine.theirs.ours.y
ours.hers.your.life.his.mine.theirs.ours.yours.hers.your.life.his.min
e.theirs.ours.yours.hers.your.life.his.mine.theirs.ours.yours.hers.yo
ur.life.his.mine.theirs.ours.yours.hers.your.life.his.mine.theirs.our
s.yours.hers.your.life.his.mine.theirs.ours.yours.hers.your.life.his.
mine.theirs.ours.yours.hers.your.life.his.mine.theirs.ours.yours.her
s.your.life.his.mine.theirs.ours.yours.hers.your.life.his.mine.theirs.
ours.yours.hers.your.life.his.mine.theirs.ours.yours.hers.your.life.h
is.mine.theirs.ours.yours.hers.your.life.his.mine.theirs.ours.yours.
hers.your.life.his.mine.theirs.ours.yours.hers.your.life.his.mine.the
irs.ours.yours.hers.your.life.his.mine.theirs.ours.yours.hers.your.lif
e.his.mine.theirs.ours.yours.hers.your.life.his.mine.theirs.ours.you
rs.hers.your.life.his.mine.theirs.ours.yours.hers.your.life.his.mine.t
heirs.ours.yours.hers.your.life.his.mine.theirs.ours.yours.hers.your
.life.his.mine.theirs.ours.yours.hers.your.life.his.mine.theirs.ours.y
ours.hers.your.life.his.mine.theirs.ours.yours.hers.your.life.his.min
e.theirs.ours.yours.hers.your.life.his.mine.theirs.ours.yours.hers.yo
ur.life.his.mine.theirs.ours.yours.hers.your.life.his.mine.theirs.our
s.yours.hers.your.life.his.mine.theirs.ours.yours.hers.your.life.his.

your.life.his.mine.theirs.ours.yours.hers.your.life.his.mine.theirs.o
urs.yours.hers.your.life.his.mine.theirs.ours.yours.hers.your.life.hi
s.mine.theirs.ours.yours.hers.your.life.his.mine.theirs.ours.yours.h
ers.your.life.his.mine.theirs.ours.yours.hers.your.life.his.mine.thei
rs.ours.yours.hers.your.life.his.mine.theirs.ours.yours.hers.your.lif
e.his.mine.theirs.ours.yours.hers.your.life.his.mine.theirs.ours.you
rs.hers.your.life.his.mine.theirs.ours.yours.hers.your.life.his.mine.t
heirs.ours.yours.hers.your.life.his.mine.theirs.ours.yours.hers.your
.life.his.mine.theirs.ours.yours.hers.your.life.his.mine.theirs.ours.y
ours.hers.your.life.his.mine.theirs.ours.yours.hers.your.life.his.min
e.theirs.ours.yours.hers.your.life.his.mine.theirs.ours.yours.hers.yo
ur.life.his.mine.theirs.ours.yours.hers.your.life.his.mine.theirs.our
s.yours.hers.your.life.his.mine.theirs.ours.yours.hers.your.life.his.
mine.theirs.ours.yours.hers.your.life.his.mine.theirs.ours.yours.her
s.your.life.his.mine.theirs.ours.yours.hers.your.life.his.mine.theirs.
ours.yours.hers.your.life.his.mine.theirs.ours.yours.hers.your.life.h
is.mine.theirs.ours.yours.hers.your.life.his.mine.theirs.ours.yours.
hers.your.life.his.mine.theirs.ours.yours.hers.your.life.his.mine.the
irs.ours.yours.hers.your.life.his.mine.theirs.ours.yours.hers.your.lif
e.his.mine.theirs.ours.yours.hers.your.life.his.mine.theirs.ours.you
rs.hers.your.life.his.mine.theirs.ours.yours.hers.your.life.his.mine.t
heirs.ours.yours.hers.your.life.his.mine.theirs.ours.yours.hers.your
.life.his.mine.theirs.ours.yours.hers.your.life.his.mine.theirs.ours.y
ours.hers.your.life.his.mine.theirs.ours.yours.hers.your.life.his.min
e.theirs.ours.yours.hers.your.life.his.mine.theirs.ours.yours.hers.yo
ur.life.his.mine.theirs.ours.yours.hers.your.life.his.mine.theirs.our
s.yours.hers.your.life.his.mine.theirs.ours.yours.hers.your.life.his.
mine.theirs.ours.yours.hers.your.life.his.mine.theirs.ours.yours.her
s.your.life.his.mine.theirs.ours.yours.hers.your.life.his.mine.theirs.
ours.yours.hers.your.life.his.mine.theirs.ours.yours.hers.your.life.h
is.mine.theirs.ours.yours.hers.your.life.his.mine.theirs.ours.yours.
hers.your.life.his.mine.theirs.ours.yours.hers.your.life.his.mine.the
irs.ours.yours.hers.your.life.his.mine.theirs.ours.yours.hers.your.lif
e.his.mine.theirs.ours.yours.hers.your.life.his.mine.theirs.ours.you
rs.hers.your.life.his.mine.theirs.ours.yours.hers.your.life.his.mine.t
heirs.ours.yours.hers.your.life.his.mine.theirs.ours.yours.hers.your
.life.his.mine.theirs.ours.yours.hers.your.life.his.mine.theirs.ours.y
ours.hers.your.life.his.mine.theirs.ours.yours.hers.your.life.his.min
e.theirs.ours.yours.hers.your.life.his.mine.theirs.ours.yours.hers.yo
ur.life.his.mine.theirs.ours.yours.hers.your.life.his.mine.theirs.our
s.yours.hers.your.life.his.mine.theirs.ours.yours.hers.your.life.his.

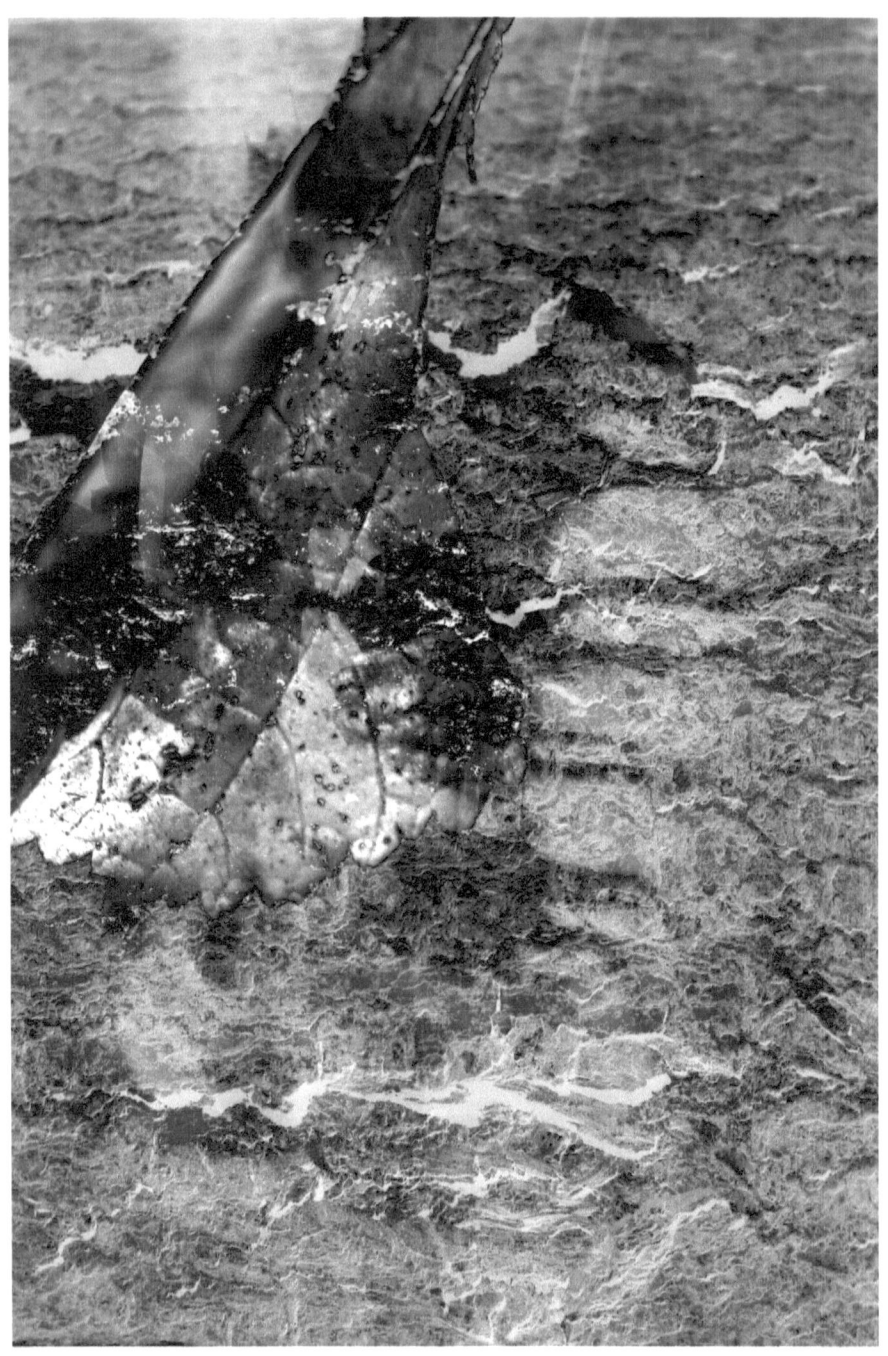

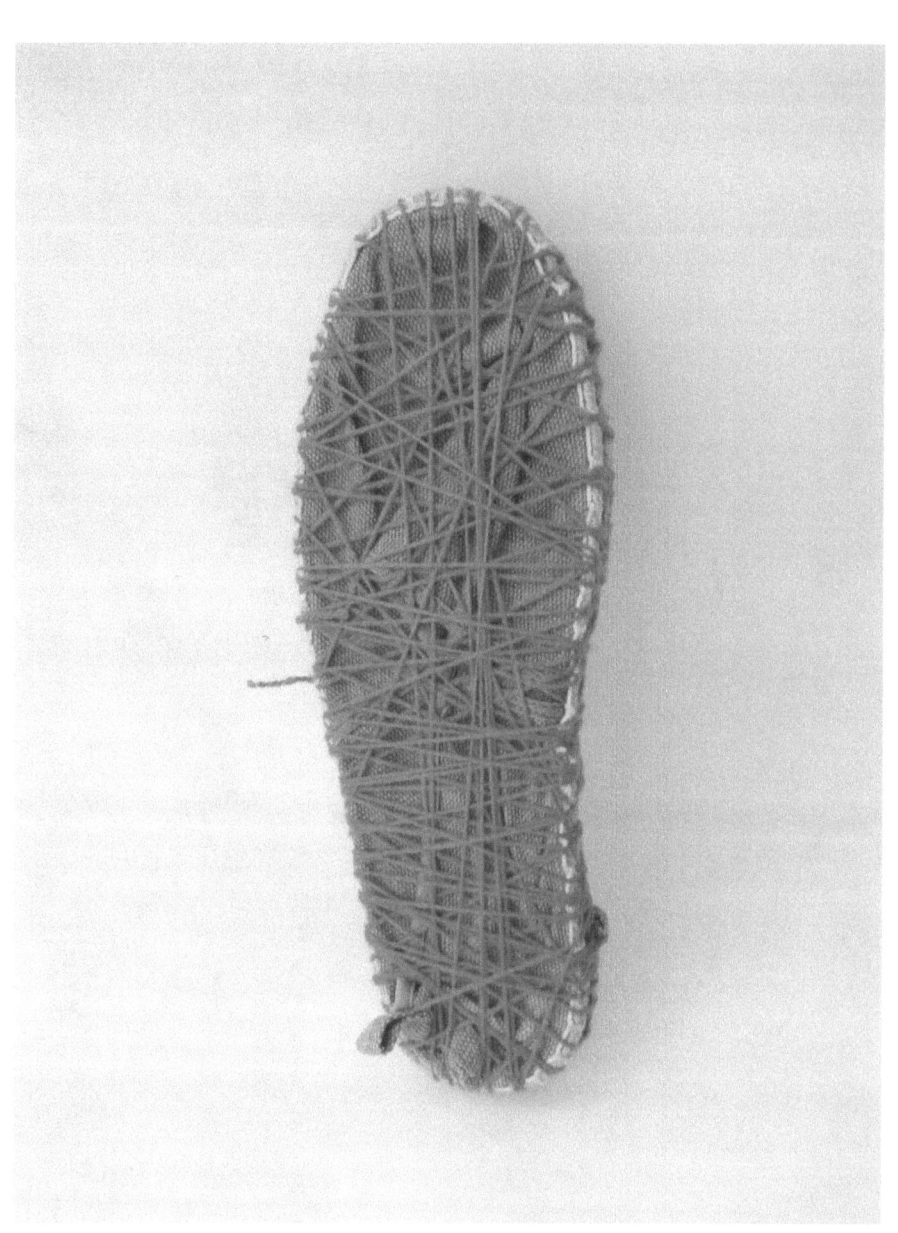

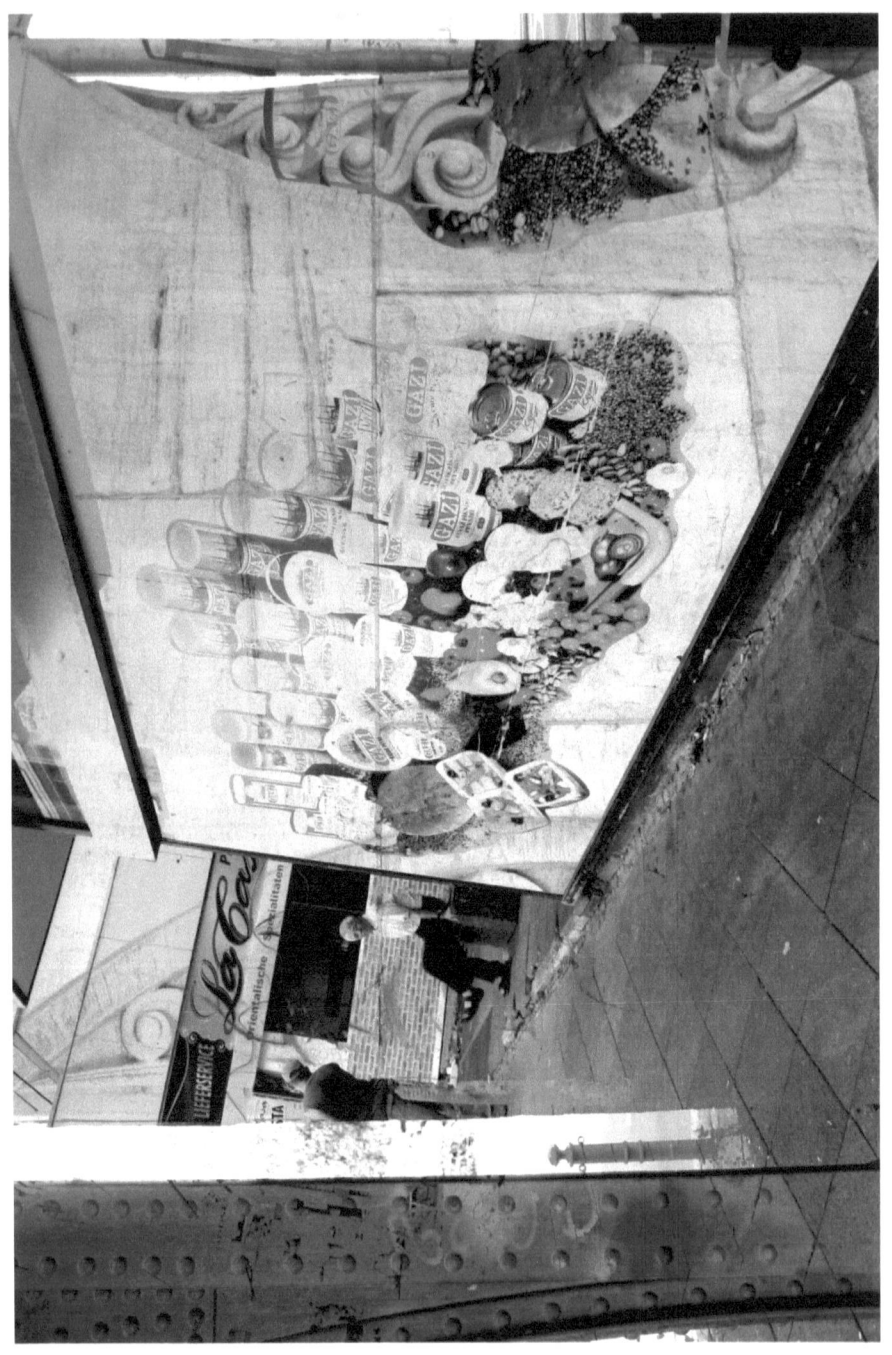

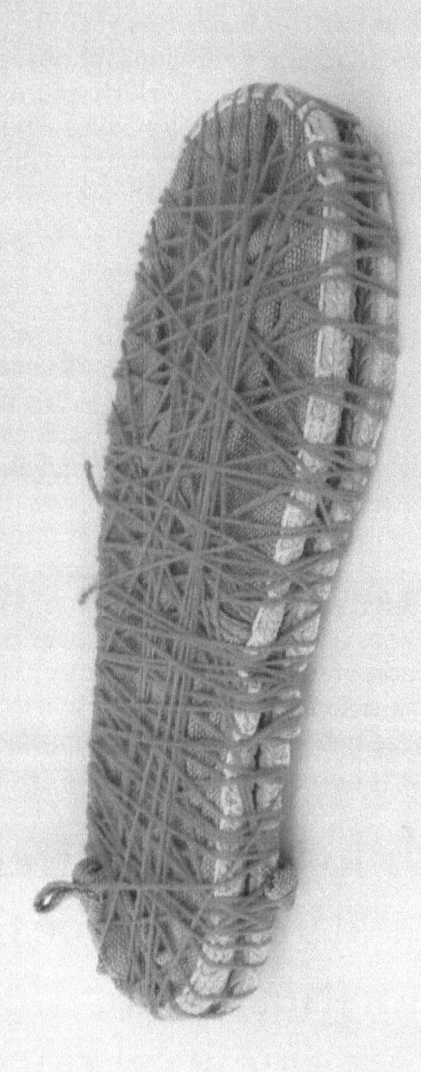

religions. philosophies. differences. humanism. natural sciences. interiority.minorities.minorities.majorities.small.large.neutral.pure.spurious.democracy.acceptance.religions. philosophies. differences. humanism. natural sciences. interiority.minorities.minorities.majorities.small.large.neutral.pure.spurious.democracy.acceptance.religions. philosophies. differences. humanism. natural sciences. interiority.minorities.minorities.majorities.small.large.eutral.pure.spurious.democracy.acceptance.religions. philosophies. differences. humanism. natural sciences. interiority.minorities.minorities.majorities.small.large.neutral.pure.spurious.democracy.acceptance.religions. philosophies. differences. humanism. natural sciences. interiority.minorities.minorities.majorities.small.large.neutral.pure.spurious.democracy.acceptance.religions. philosophies. differences. humanism. natural sciences. interiority.inorities.minorities.majorities.small.large.neutral.pure.spurious.emocracy.acceptance.religions. philosophies. differences. humanism. natural sciences. interiority.minorities.minorities.majorities.small.large.neutral.pure.spurious.democracy.acceptance.religions. philosophies. differences. humanism. natural sciences. interiority.minorities.minorities.majorities.small.large.neutral.pure.spurious.democracy.acceptance.religions. philosophies. differences. humanism. natural sciences. interiority.minorities.minorities.ajorities.small.large.neutral.pure.spurious.democracy.acceptance.religions. philosophies. differences. humanism. natural sciences.

religions.philosophies.differences. humanism.natural sciences.interiority.minorities.minorities.ajorities.small.large.neutral.pure.spurious.**democracy**.acceptance. democracy.small. democracy.large. democracy.neutral.

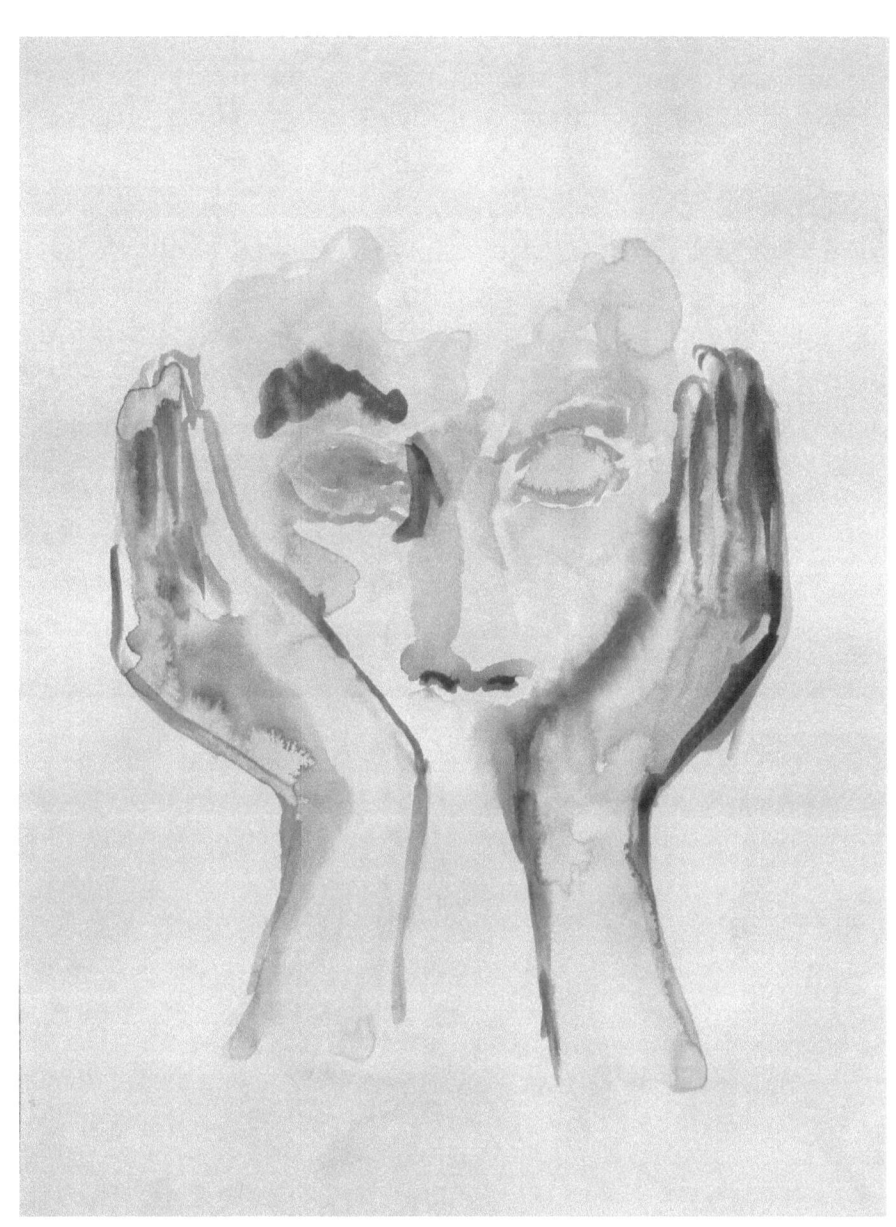

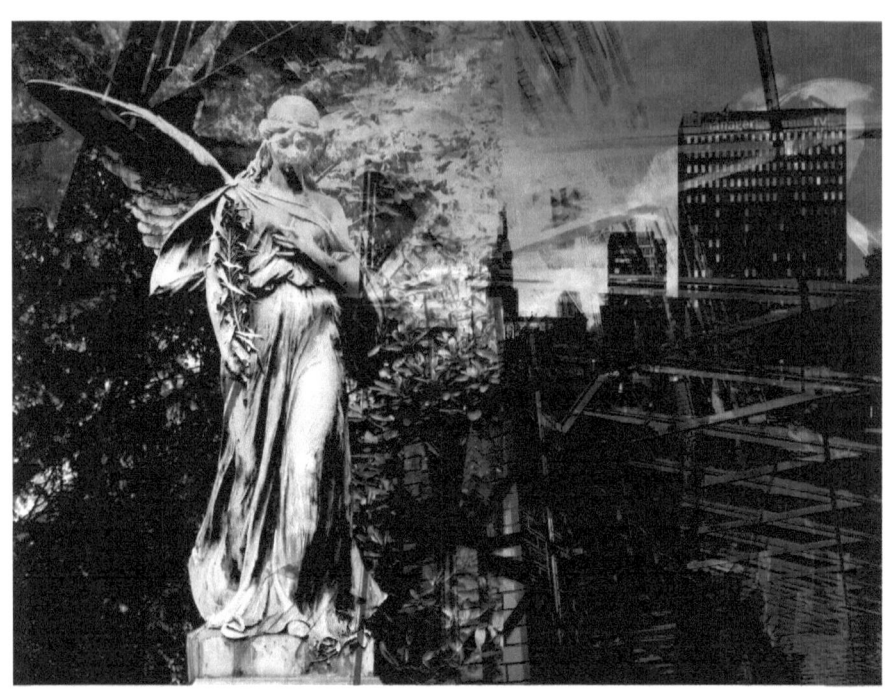

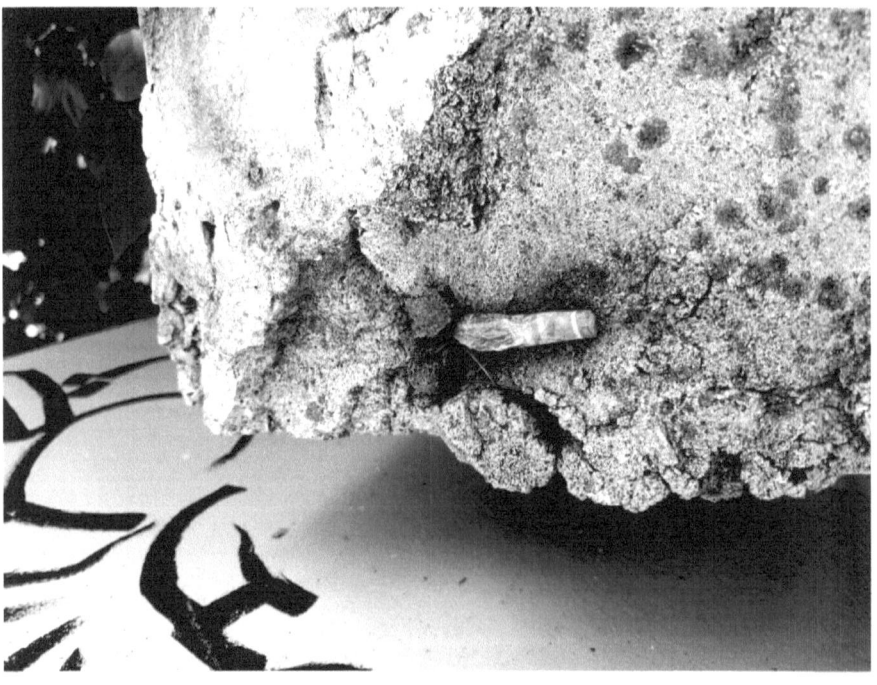

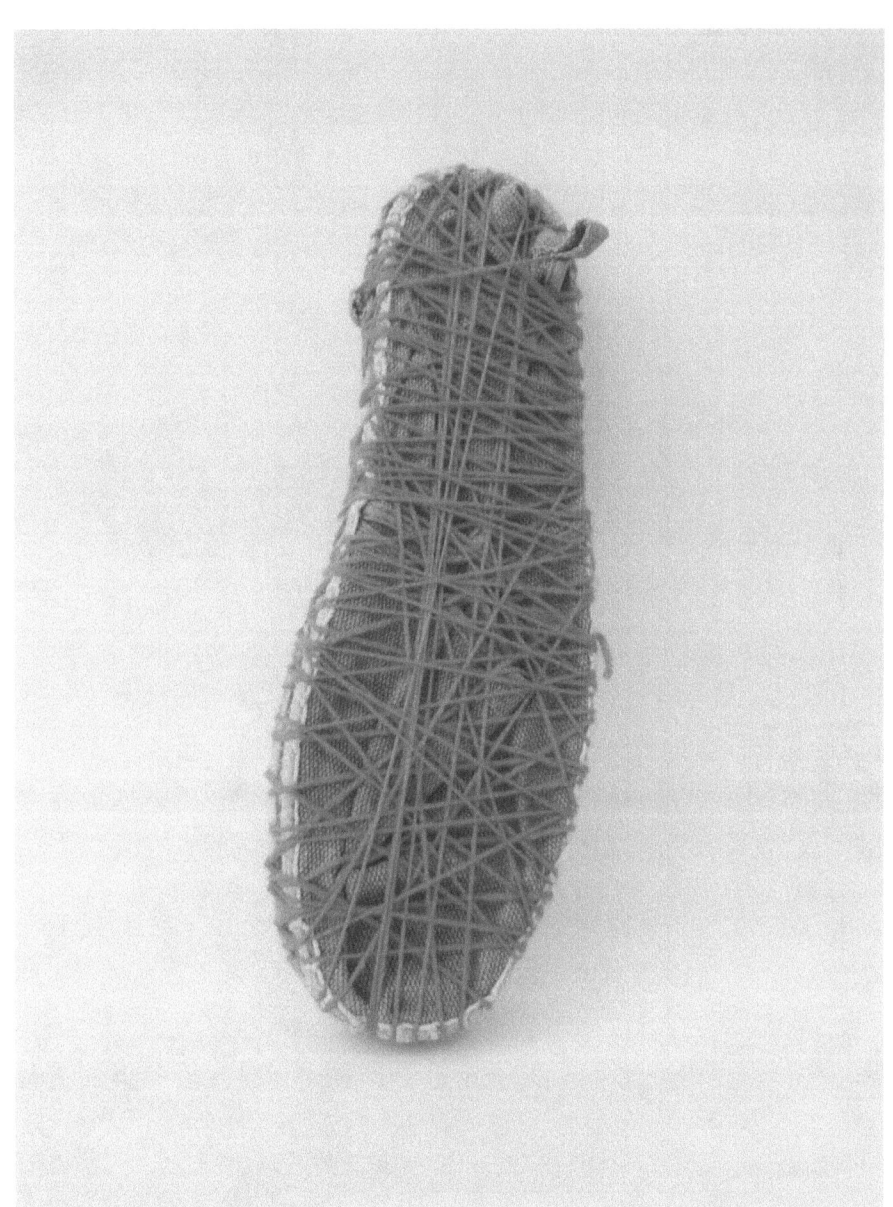

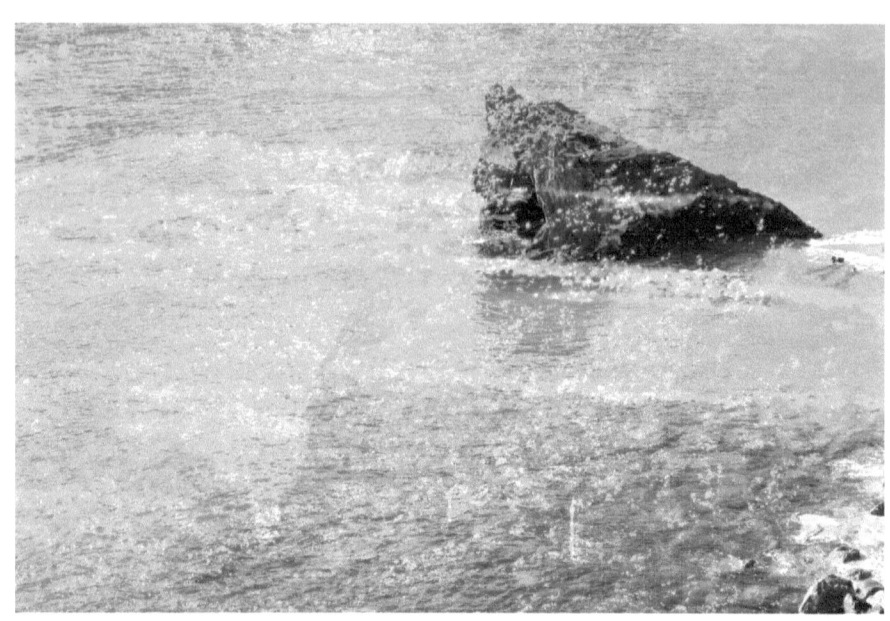

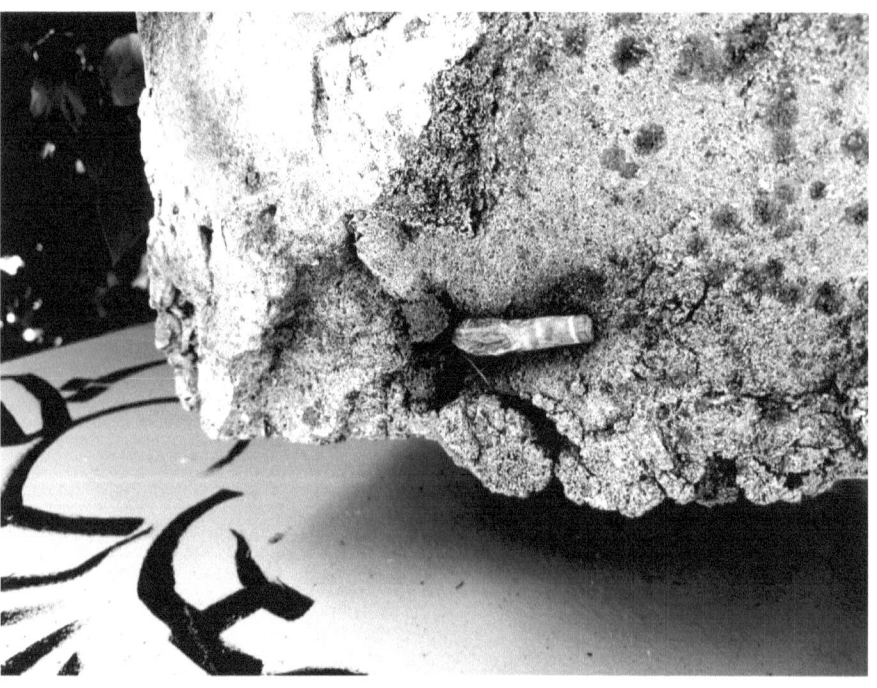

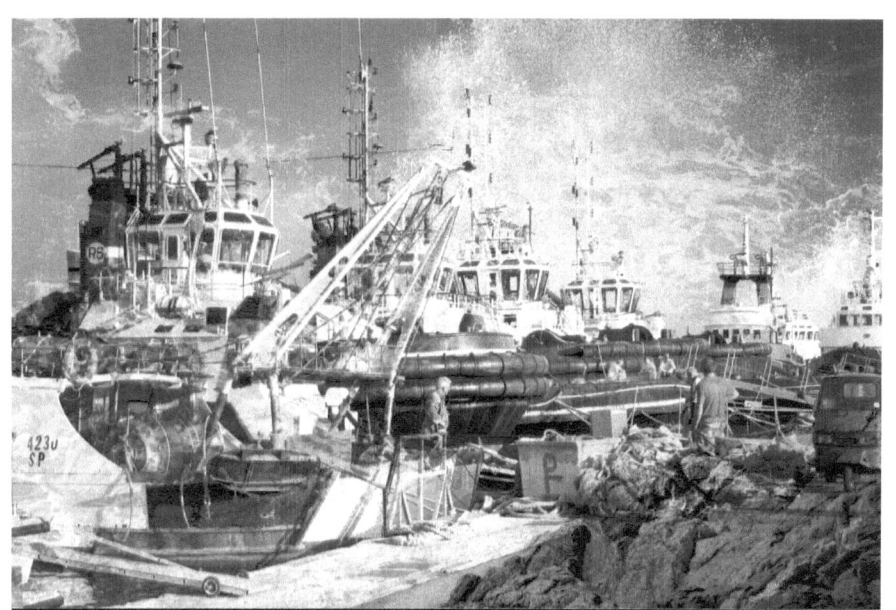

democracy.democracy.democra-
cy.democracy.democracy.demo-
cracy.democracy.democracy.de-
mocracy.democracy.democracy.-
democracy.democracy.democra-
cy.democracy.democracy.demo-
cracy.democracy.democracy.de-
mocracy.democracy.democracy.-
democracy.democracy.democra-
cy.democracy.democracy.demo-
cracy.democracy.democracy.de-

mocracy.democracy.democracy.-
democracy.democracy.democra-
cy.democracy.democracy.demo-
cracy.democracy.democracy.de-
mocracy.democracy.democracy.-
democracy.democracy.democra-
cy.democracy.democracy.demo-
cracy.democracy.democracy.de-
mocracy.democracy.democracy.-
democracy.democracy.democra-
cy.democracy.democracy.demo-
cracy.democracy.democracy.de-
mocracy.democracy.democracy.-
democracy.democracy.democra-
cy.democracy.democracy.demo-
cracy.democracy.democracy.de-
mocracy.democracy.democracy.-
democracy.democracy.democra-
cy.democracy.democracy.demo-
cracy.democracy.democracy.

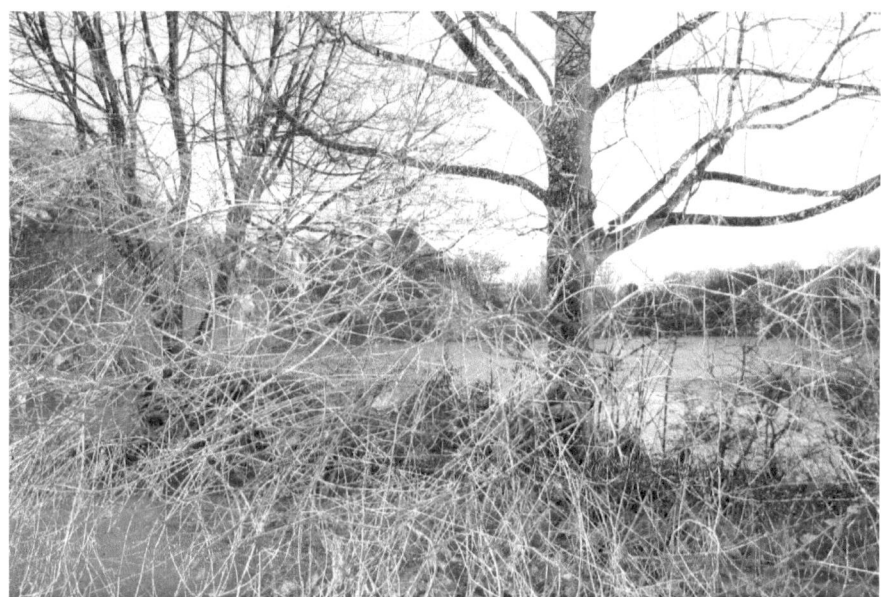

small.large.neutral.small.large.neutral.small.large.neutral.small.lar
ge.neutral.small.large.neutral.small.large.neutral.small.large.neutr
al.small.large.neutral.small.large.neutral.small.large.neutral.small.l
arge.neutral.small.large.neutral.small.large.neutral.small.large.neu
tral.small.large.neutral.small.large.neutral.small.large.neutral.smal
l.large.neutral.small.large.neutral.small.large.neutral.small.large.n
eutral.small.large.neutral.small.large.neutral.small.large.neutral.s
mall.large.neutral.small.large.neutral.small.large.neutral.small.larg
e.neutral.small.large.neutral.small.large.neutral.small.large.neutral
.small.large.neutral.small.large.neutral.small.large.neutral.small.la
rge.neutral.small.large.neutral.small.large.neutral.small.large.neut
ral.small.large.neutral.small.large.neutral.small.large.neutral.small
.large.neutral.small.large.neutral.small.large.neutral.small.large.ne
utral.small.large.neutral.small.large.neutral.small.large.neutral.sm
all.large.neutral.small.large.neutral.small.large.neutral.small.large.
neutral.small.large.neutral.small.large.neutral.small.large.neutral.s
mall.large.neutral.small.large.neutral.small.large.neutral.small.larg
e.neutral.small.large.neutral.small.large.neutral.small.large.neutral
.small.large.neutral.small.large.neutral.small.large.neutral.small.la
rge.neutral.small.large.neutral.small.large.neutral.small.large.neut
ral.small.large.neutral.small.large.neutral.small.large.neutral.small
.large.neutral.small.large.neutral.small.large.neutral.small.large.ne
utral.small.large.neutral.small.large.neutral.small.large.neutral.

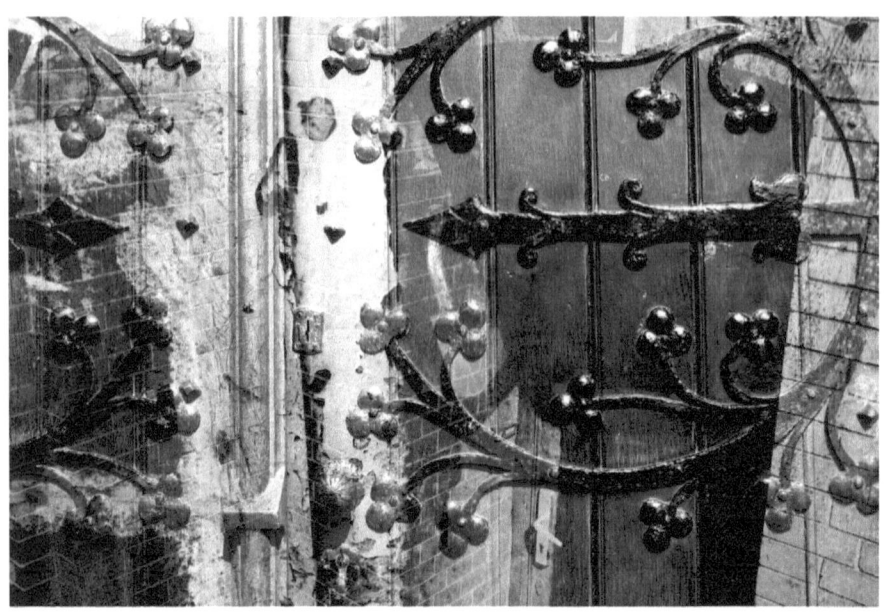

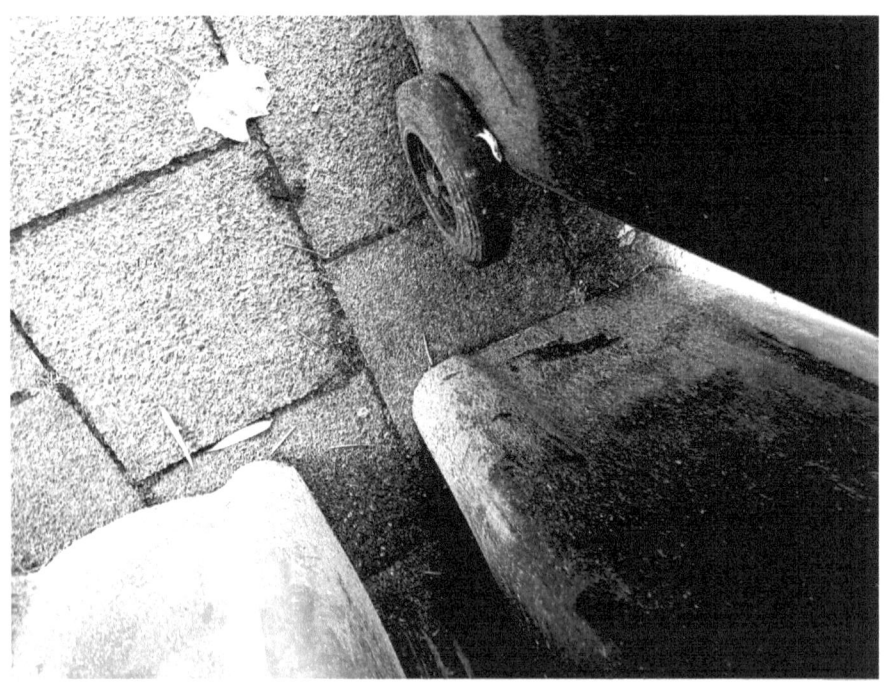

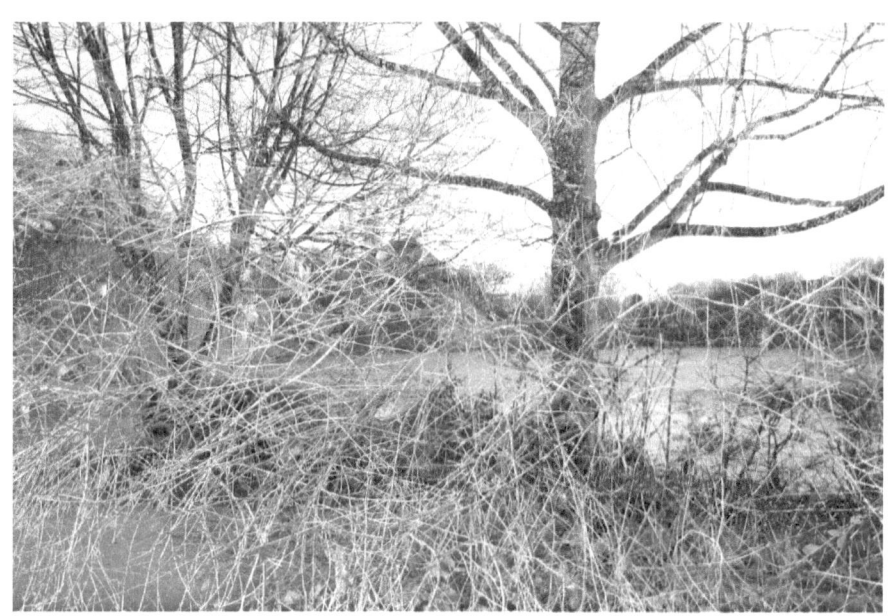

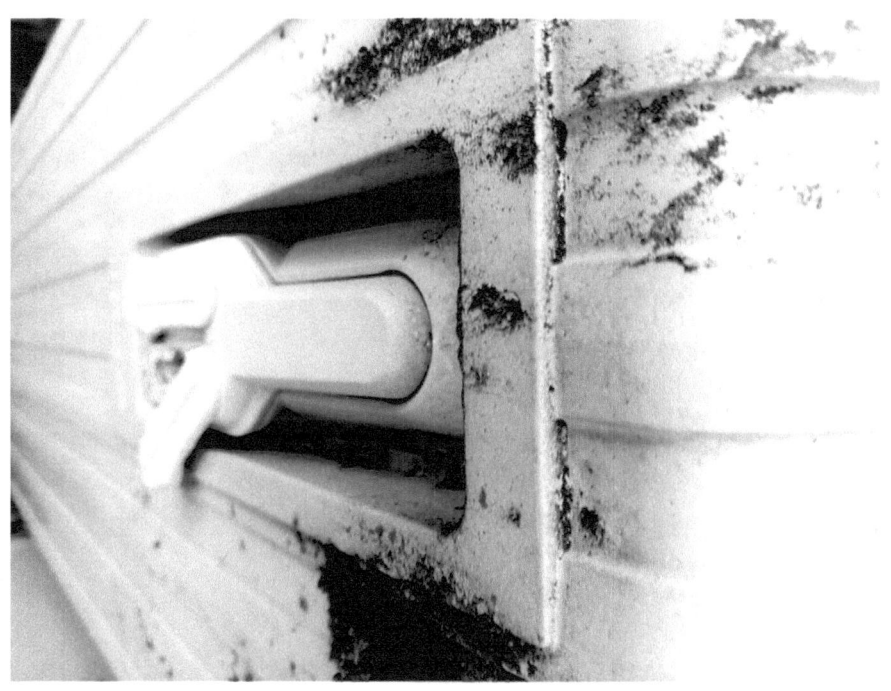

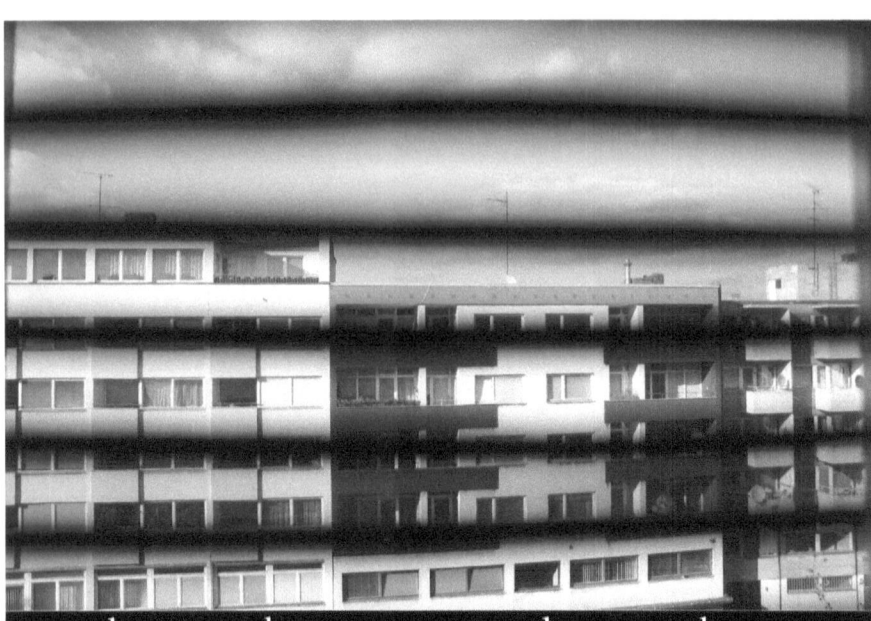

say the words to saysay the words to say
say the words to saysay the words to say
say the words to saysay the words to say
say the words to saysay the words to say
say the words to saysay the words to say
say the words to saysay the words to say
say the words to saysay the words to say
say the words to saysay the words to say
say the words to saysay the words to say
say the words to saysay the words to say
say the words to saysay the words to say
say the words to saysay the words to say
say the words to saysay the words to say
say

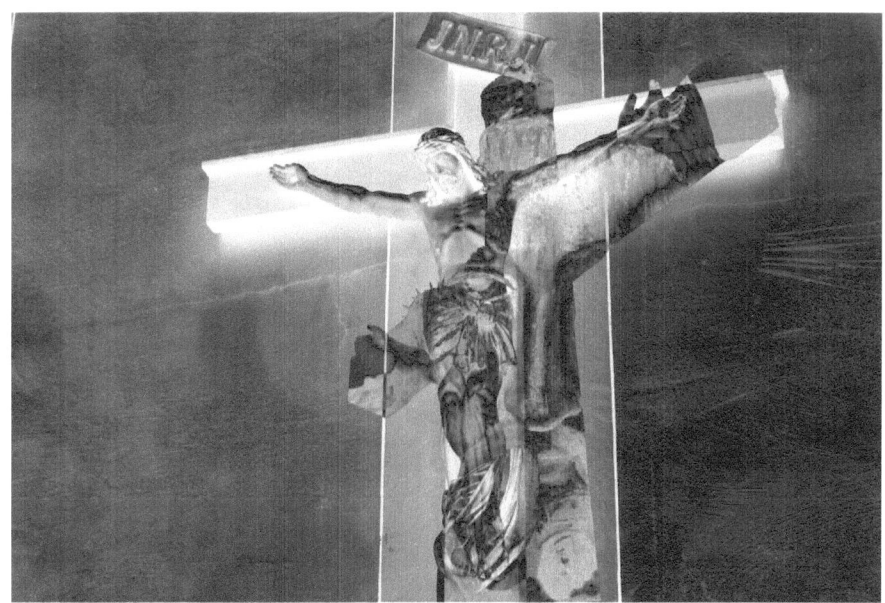

evidence.witness.evidence.witness.evidence.witness.evidence.witn
ess.evidence.witness.evidence.witness.evidence.witness.evide
nce.witness.evidence.witness.evidence.witness.evide
nce.witness.evidence.witness.evidence.witness.evide
nce.witness.evidence.witness.evidence.witness.e
vidence.witness.evidence.witness.evidence.wit
ness.evidence.witness.evidence.witness.evid
ence.witness.evidence.witness.evidence.w
itness.evidence.witness.evidence.witness.
evidence.witness.evidence.witness.evide
nce.witness.evidence.witness.evide
nce.witness.evidence.witness.evide
nce.witness.evidence.witness.evi
dence.witness.evidence.witness.

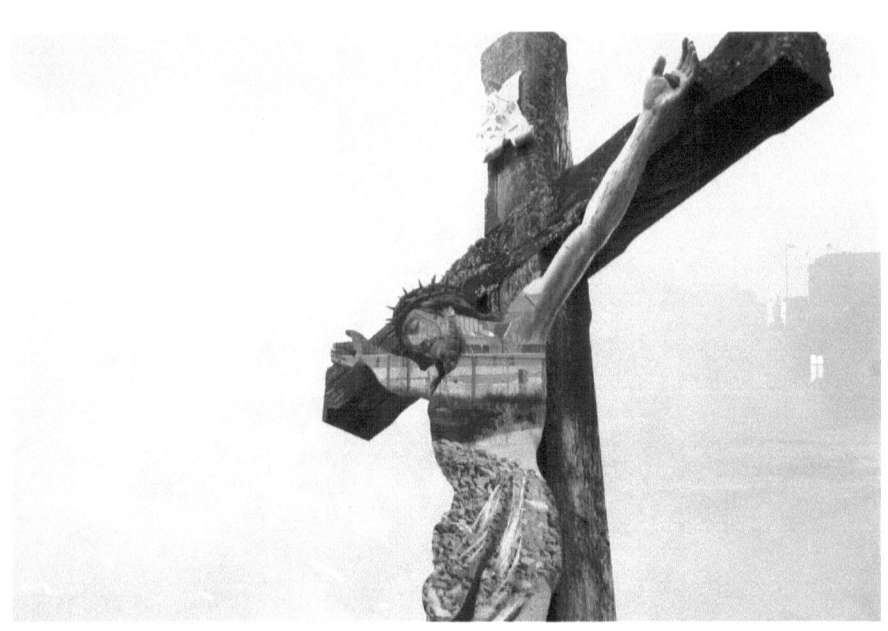

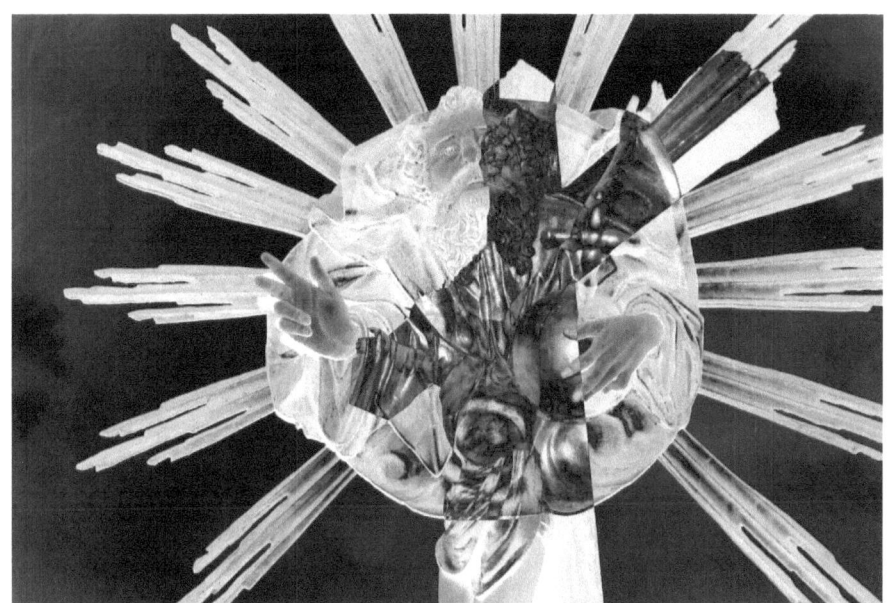

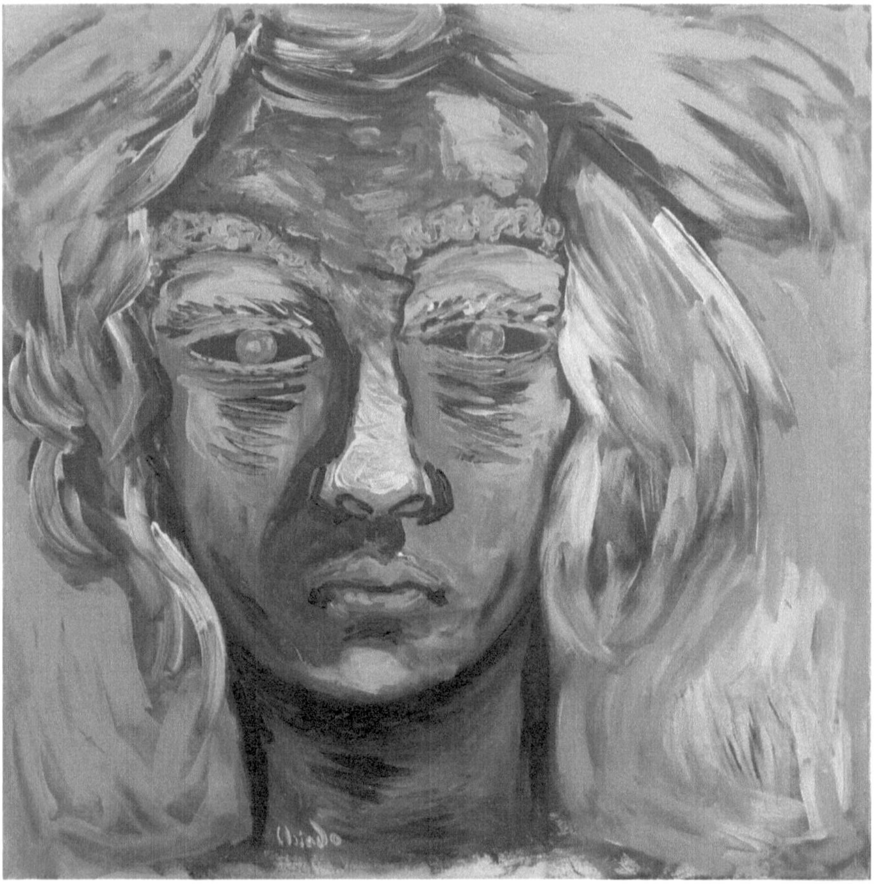

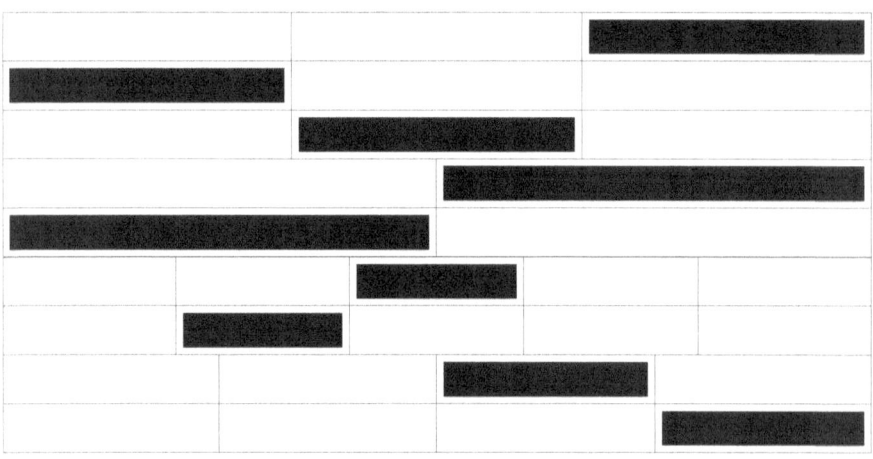

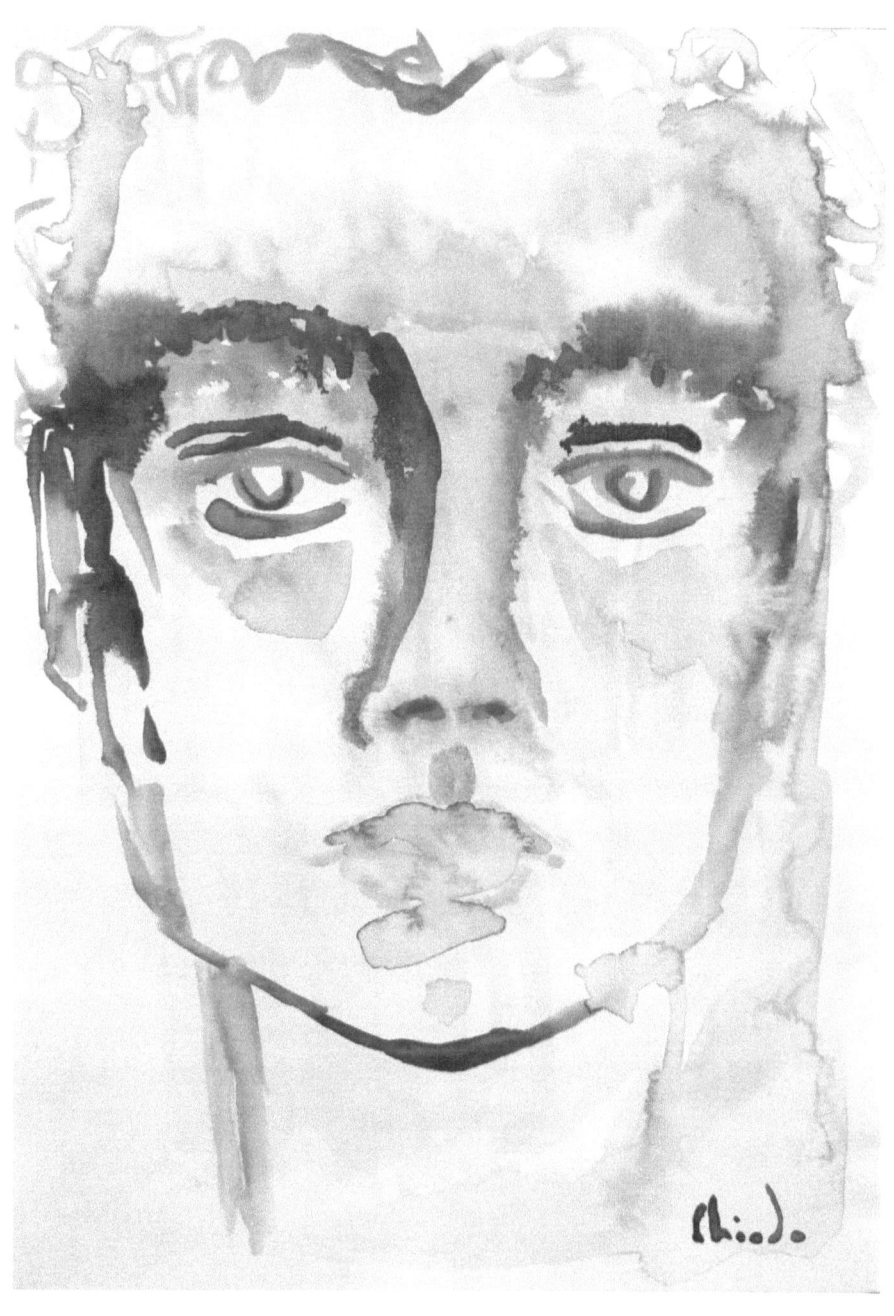

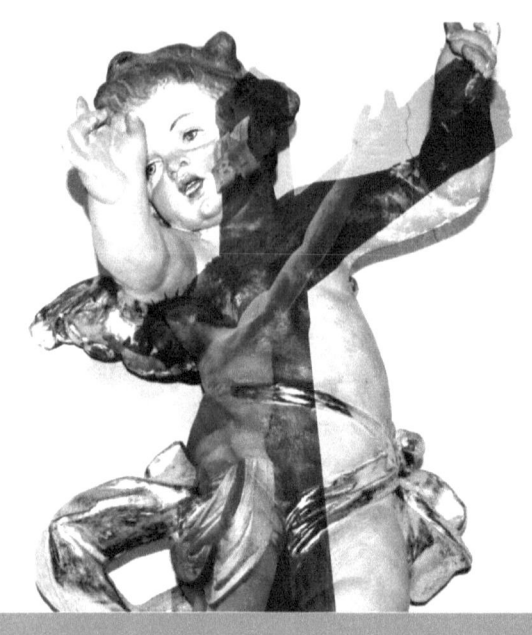

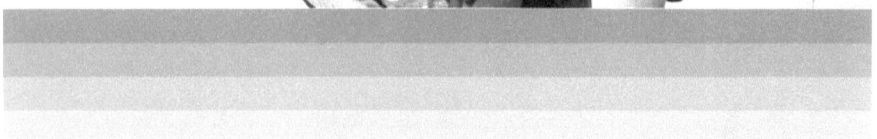

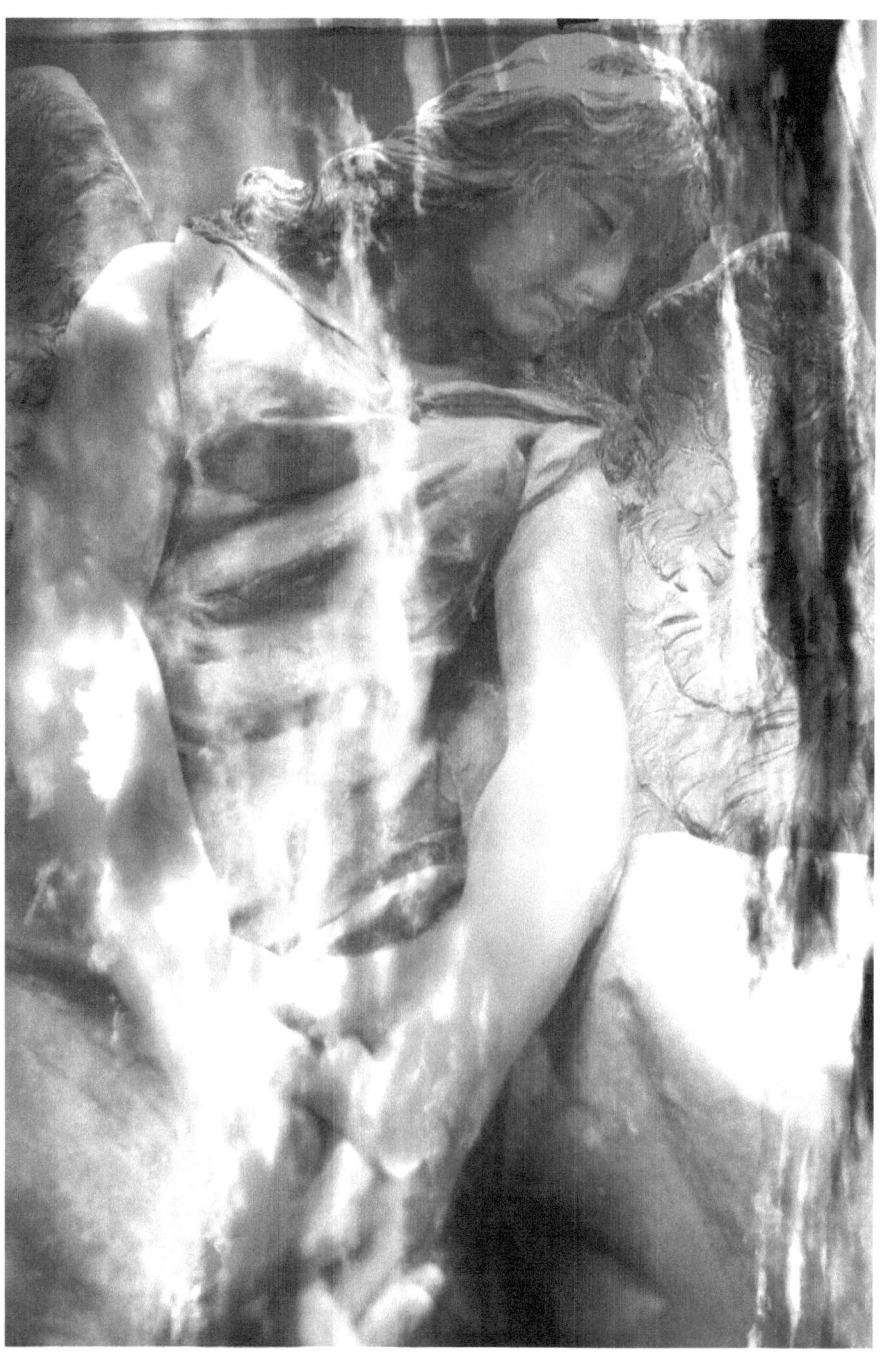

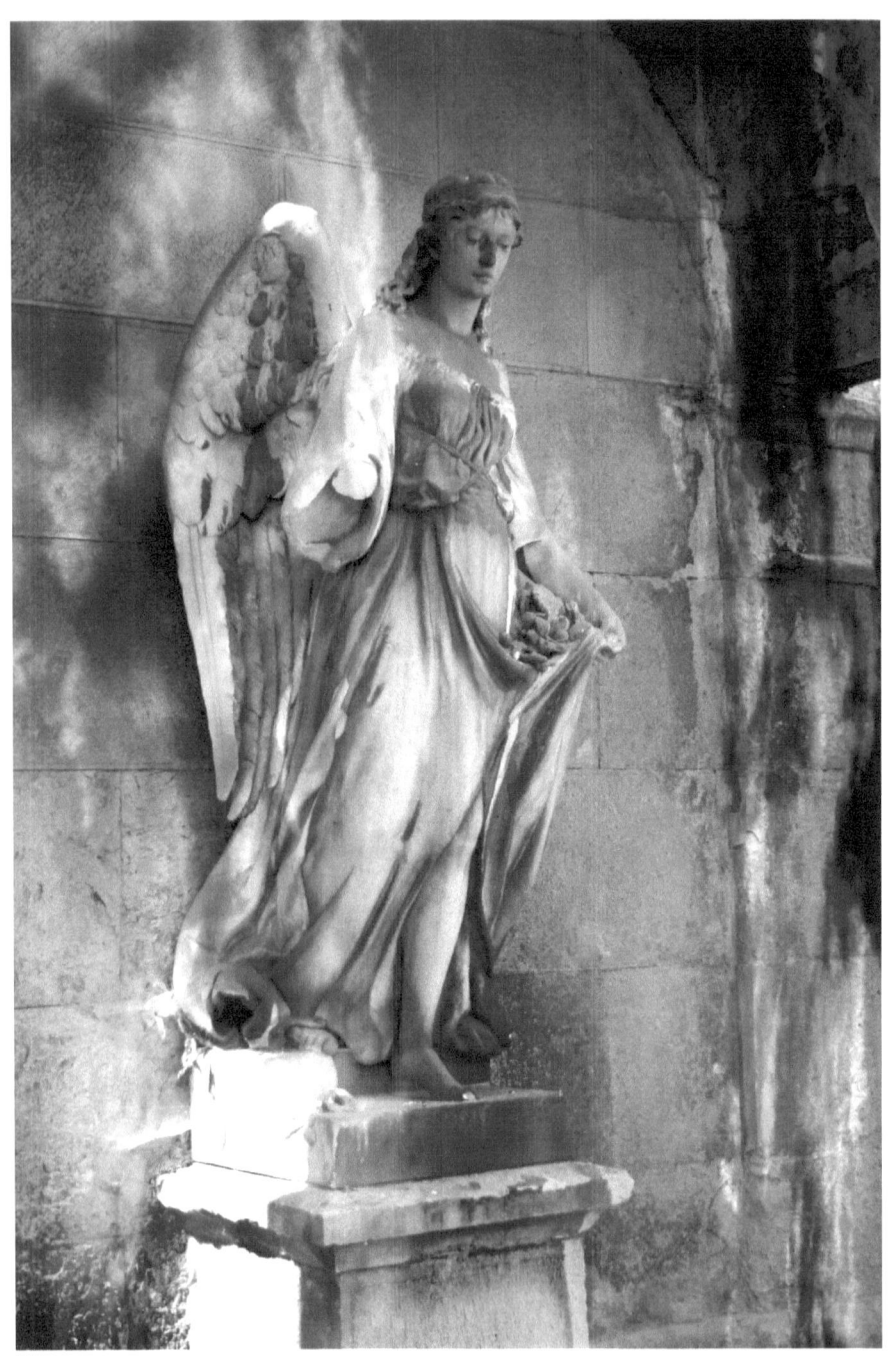

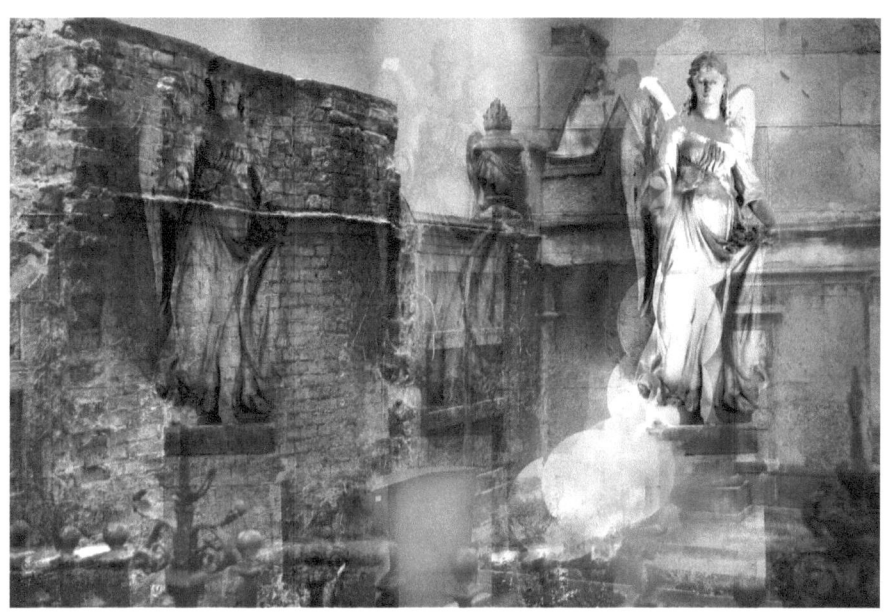

world of **miracles**... and colourful world of miracles... and colourful
world of **miracles**... and colourful world of miracles... and colourful
world of **miracles**... and colourful world of miracles... and colourful
world of miracles... and **colourful** world of miracles... and colourful
world of miracles... and **colourful** world of miracles... and colourful
world of miracles... and **colourful** world of miracles... and colourful
world of miracles... and colourful **world** of miracles... and colourful
world of miracles... and colourful **world** of miracles... and colourful
world of miracles... and colourful **world** of miracles... and colourful
world of miracles... and colourful world of miracles... and colourful
world of miracles... and colourful world of miracles... and colourful
world of miracles... and colourful world of miracles... and colourful
world of miracles... and colourful world of miracles... and colourful
world of miracles... and colourful world of miracles... and colourful
world of miracles... and colourful world of miracles... and colourful
world of miracles... and colourful world of miracles... and colourful
world of miracles... and colourful world of miracles... and colourful
world of miracles... and colourful world of miracles... and colourful
world of miracles... and colourful world of miracles... and colourful
world of miracles... and colourful world of miracles... and colourful
world of miracles... and colourful world of miracles... and colourful

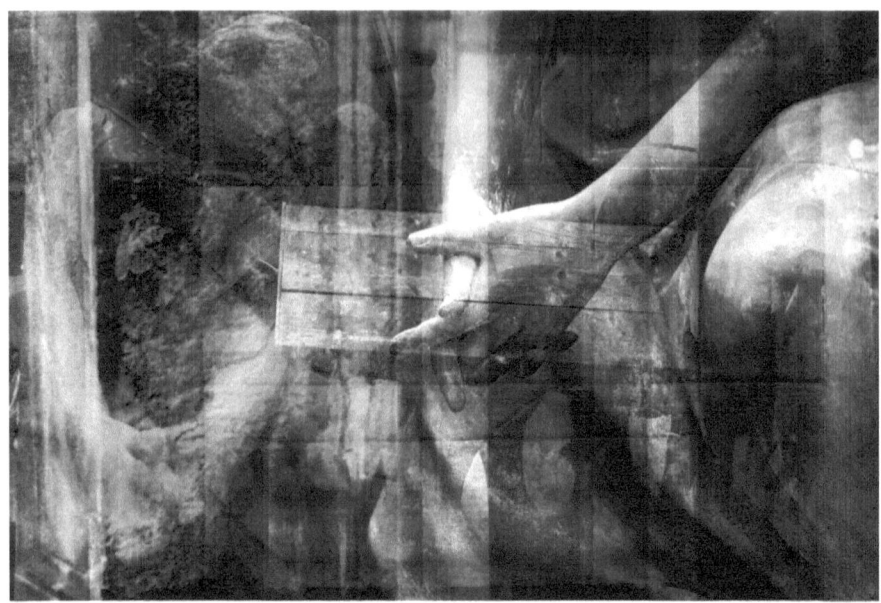

beginning begin the beginning begin the beginning begin the
beginning begin the beginning begin the beginning begin the
beginning begin the beginning begin the beginning begin the
beginning begin the beginning begin the beginning begin the
beginning begin the beginning begin the beginning begin the
beginning begin the beginning begin the beginning begin the
beginning begin the beginning begin the beginning begin the
beginning begin the beginning begin the beginning begin the
beginning begin the beginning begin the beginning begin the
beginning begin the beginning begin the beginning begin the
beginning begin the beginning begin the beginning begin the
beginning begin the beginning begin the beginning begin the
beginning begin the beginning begin the beginning begin the
beginning begin the beginning begin the beginning begin the
beginning begin the beginning begin the beginning begin the
beginning begin the beginning begin the beginning begin the
beginning begin the beginning begin the beginning begin the
beginning begin the beginning begin the beginning begin the
beginning begin the beginning begin the beginning begin the
beginning begin the beginning begin the beginning begin the
beginning begin the beginning begin the beginning begin the
beginning begin the beginning

migrantsare
blessedmigr
antsarebless
edmigrantsa
reblessedmi
grantsareble
ssedmigrant

migrant heart

migrant heart

migrant heart

migrant heart

migrant heart

migrant heart

migrant heart

migrant heart

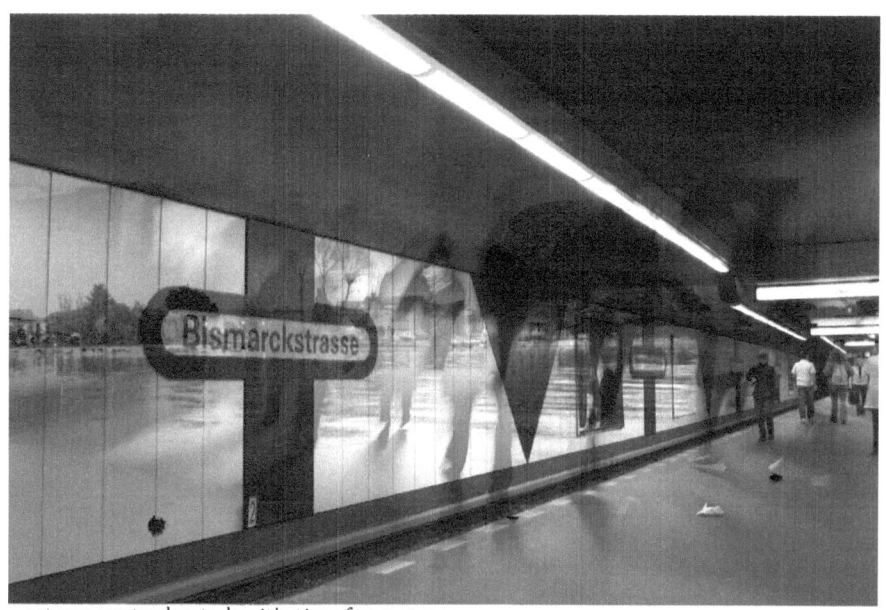

...art was yesterday today it's time for awareness.
...art was yesterday today it's time for awareness.
...art was yesterday today it's time for awareness.
...art was yesterday today it's time for awareness.
...art was yesterday today it's time for awareness.
...art was yesterday today it's time for awareness.
...art was yesterday today it's time for awareness.
...art was yesterday today it's time for awareness.
...art was yesterday today it's time for awareness.
...art was yesterday today it's time for awareness.
...art was yesterday today it's time for awareness.
...art was yesterday today it's time for awareness.
...art was yesterday today it's time for awareness.
...art was yesterday today it's time for awareness.
...art was yesterday today it's time for awareness.
...art was yesterday today it's time for awareness.
...art was yesterday today it's time for awareness.
...art was yesterday today it's time for awareness.
...art was yesterday today it's time for awareness.
...art was yesterday today it's time for awareness.
...art was yesterday today it's time for awareness.
...art was yesterday today it's time for awareness.

art was yesterday today it's time for awareness.
...art was yesterday today it's time for awareness.
...art was yesterday today it's time for awareness.
...art was yesterday today it's time for awareness.
...art was yesterday today it's time for awareness.
...art was yesterday today it's time for awareness.
...art was yesterday today it's time for awareness.
...art was yesterday today it's time for awareness.
...art was yesterday today it's time for awareness.
...art was yesterday today it's time for awareness.
...art was yesterday today it's time for awareness.
...art was yesterday today it's time for awareness.
...art was yesterday today it's time for awareness.
...art was yesterday today it's time for awareness.
...art was yesterday today it's time for awareness.
...art was yesterday today it's time for awareness.
...art was yesterday today it's time for awareness.
...art was yesterday today it's time for awareness.
...art was yesterday today it's time for awareness.
...art was yesterday today it's time for awareness.
...art was yesterday today it's time for awareness.
...art was yesterday today it's time for awareness.

...art was yesterday today it's time for awareness

art was yesterday today it's time for awareness.
...art was yesterday today it's time for awareness.
...art was yesterday today it's time for awareness.
...art was yesterday today it's time for awareness.
...art was yesterday today it's time for awareness.
...art was yesterday today it's time for awareness.
...art was yesterday today it's time for awareness.
...art was yesterday today it's time for awareness.
...art was yesterday today it's time for awareness.
...art was yesterday today it's time for awareness.
...art was yesterday today it's time for awareness.
...art was yesterday today it's time for awareness.
...art was yesterday today it's time for awareness.
...art was yesterday today it's time for awareness.
...art was yesterday today it's time for awareness.
...art was yesterday today it's time for awareness.
...art was yesterday today it's time for awareness.
...art was yesterday today it's time for awareness.
...art was yesterday today it's time for awareness.
...art was yesterday today it's time for awareness.
...art was yesterday today it's time for awareness.

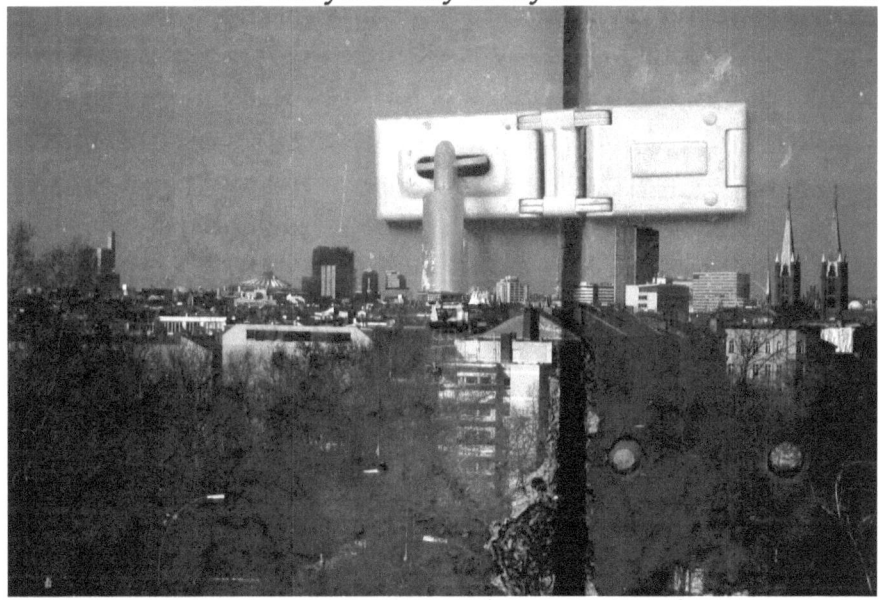

...art was yesterday today it's time for awareness

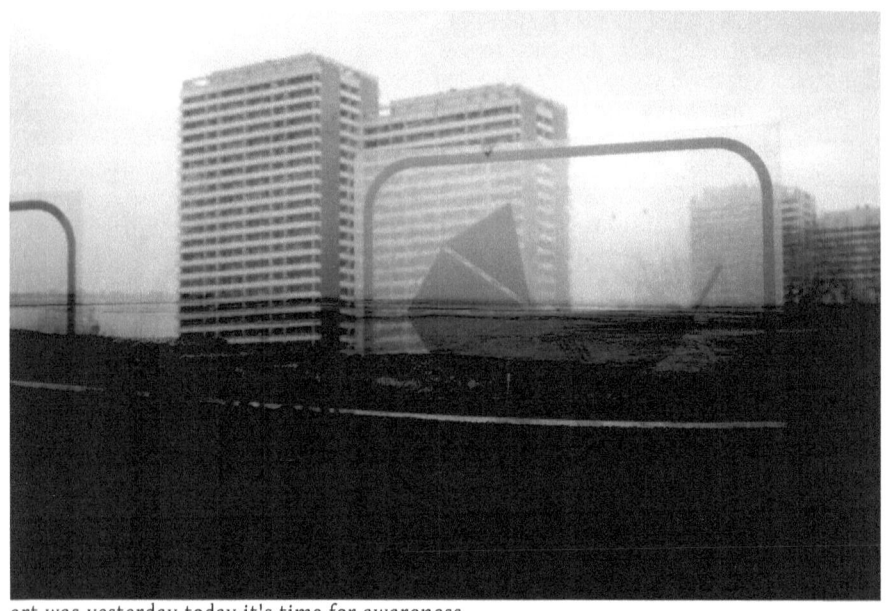

art was yesterday today it's time for awareness.
...art was yesterday today it's time for awareness.
...art was yesterday today it's time for awareness.
...art was yesterday today it's time for awareness.
...art was yesterday today it's time for awareness.
...art was yesterday today it's time for awareness.
...art was yesterday today it's time for awareness.
...art was yesterday today it's time for awareness.
...art was yesterday today it's time for awareness.
...art was yesterday today it's time for awareness.
...art was yesterday today it's time for awareness.
...art was yesterday today it's time for awareness.
...art was yesterday today it's time for awareness.
...art was yesterday today it's time for awareness.
...art was yesterday today it's time for awareness.
...art was yesterday today it's time for awareness.
...art was yesterday today it's time for awareness.

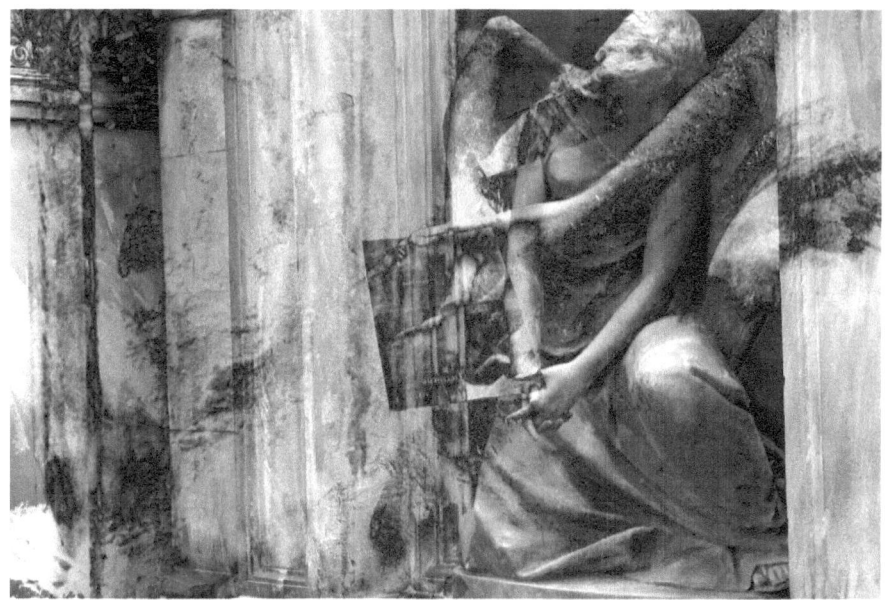

to worry about.
        to worry about.
                to worry about.
                        to worry about.
                                to worry about.
                                        to worry about.
                                                to worry about.
                                        to worry about.
                                to worry about.
                        to worry about.
                to worry about.
        to worry about.
to worry about.
        to worry about.
                to worry about.
                        to worry about.
                                to worry about.
                                        to worry about.
                                                to worry about.
                                        to worry about.
                                to worry about.
                        to worry about.
                to worry about.

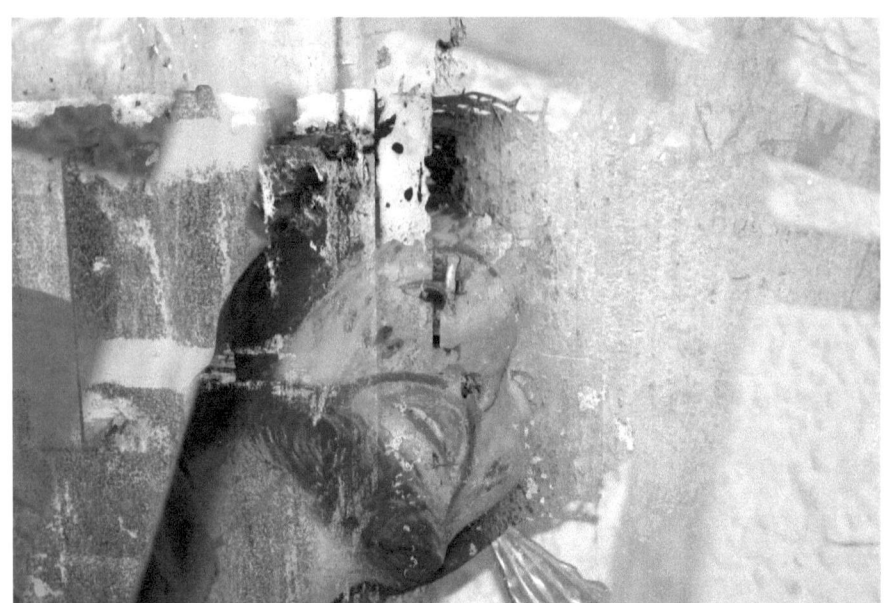

mmmmmmmmmmmmmmmmmmmmmmmmmmmmmmmmmmmmmmmmm
mmmmmmmmmmmmmmmmmmmmmmmmmmmmmmmmmmmmmmmmm
mmmmmmmmmmmmmmmmmmmmmmmmmmmmmmmmmmmmmmmmm
mmmmmmmmmmmmmmmmmmmmmmmmmmmmmmmmmmmmmmmmm
mmmmmmmmmmmmmmmmmmmmmmmmmmmmmmmmmmmmmmmmm
mmmmmmmmmmmmmmmmmmmmmmmmmmmmmmmmmmmmmmmmm
mmmmmmmmmmmmmmmmmmmmmmmmmmmmmmmmmmmmmmmmm
mmmmmmmmmmmmmmmmmmmmmmmmmmmmmmmmmmmmmmmmm
mmmmmmmmmmmmmmmmmmmmmmmmmmmmmmmmmmmmmmmmm
mmmmmmmmmmmmmmmmmmmmmmmmmmmmmmmmmmmmmmmmm
mmmmmmmmmmmmmmmmmmmmmmmmmmmmmmmmmmmmmmmmm
mmmmmmmmmmmmmmmmmmmmmmmmmmmmmmmmmmmmmmmmm
mmmmmmmmmmmmmmmmmmmmmmmmmmmmmmmmmmmmmmmmm
mmmmmmmmmmmmmmmmmmmmmmmmmmmmmmmmmmmmmmmmm
mmmmmmmmmmmmmmmmmmmmmmmmmmmmmmmmmmmmmmmmm
mmmmmmmmmmmmmmmmmmmmmmmmmmmmmmmmmmmmmmmmm
mmmmmmmmmmmmmmmmmmmmmmmmmmmmmmmmmmmmmmmmm
mmmmmmmmmmmmmmmmmmmmmmmmmmmmmmmmmmmmmmmmm
mmmmmmmmmmmmmmmmmmmmmmmmmmmmmmmmmmmmmmmmm
mmmmmmmmmmmmmmmmmmmmmmmmmmmmmmmmmmmmmmmmm
mmmmmmmmmmmmmmmmmmmmmmmmmmmmmmmmmmmmmmmmm
mmmmmmmmmmmmmmmmmmmmmmmmmmmmmmmmmmmmmmmmm

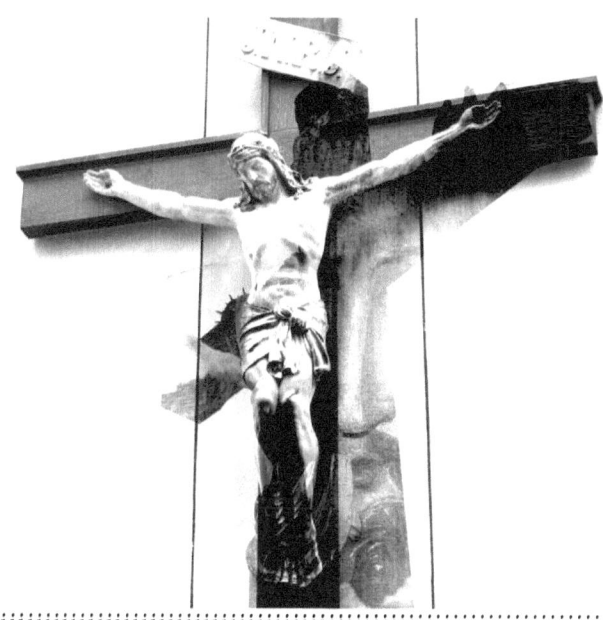

iiiiiiiiiiiiiiiiiiiiiiiiiiiiiiiiiiiiiiiiiiiiiiiiiiiiiiiiiiiiiiiiiiiiiiiiiiiiiiiiiiiiiiiiiiiiiiiii
iiiiiiiiiiiiiiiiiiiiiiiiiiiiiiiiiiiiiiiiiiiiiiiiiiiiiiiiiiiiiiiiiiiiiiiiiiiiiiiiiiiiiiiiiiiiiiiii
iiiiiiiiiiiiiiiiiiiiiiiiiiiiiiiiiiiiiiiiiiiiiiiiiiiiiiiiiiiiiiiiiiiiiiiiiiiiiiiiiiiiiiiiiiiiiiiii
iiiiiiiiiiiiiiiiiiiiiiiiiiiiiiiiiiiiiiiiiiiiiiiiiiiiiiiiiiiiiiiiiiiiiiiiiiiiiiiiiiiiiiiiiiiiiiiii
iiiiiiiiiiiiiiiiiiiiiiiiiiiiiiiiiiiiiiiiiiiiiiiiiiiiiiiiiiiiiiiiiiiiiiiiiiiiiiiiiiiiiiiiiiiiiiiii
iiiiiiiiiiiiiiiiiiiiiiiiiiiiiiiiiiiiiiiiiiiiiiiiiiiiiiiiiiiiiiiiiiiiiiiiiiiiiiiiiiiiiiiiiiiiiiiii
iiiiiiiiiiiiiiiiiiiiiiiiiiiiiiiiiiiiiiiiiiiiiiiiiiiiiiiiiiiiiiiiiiiiiiiiiiiiiiiiiiiiiiiiiiiiiiiii
iiiiiiiiiiiiiiiiiiiiiiiiiiiiiiiiiiiiiiiiiiiiiiiiiiiiiiiiiiiiiiiiiiiiiiiiiiiiiiiiiiiiiiiiiiiiiiiii
iiiiiiiiiiiiiiiiiiiiiiiiiiiiiiiiiiiiiiiiiiiiiiiiiiiiiiiiiiiiiiiiiiiiiiiiiiiiiiiiiiiiiiiiiiiiiiiii
iiiiiiiiiiiiiiiiiiiiiiiiiiiiiiiiiiiiiiiiiiiiiiiiiiiiiiiiiiiiiiiiiiiiiiiiiiiiiiiiiiiiiiiiiiiiiiiii
iiiiiiiiiiiiiiiiiiiiiiiiiiiiiiiiiiiiiiiiiiiiiiiiiiiiiiiiiiiiiiiiiiiiiiiiiiiiiiiiiiiiiiiiiiiiiiiii
iiiiiiiiiiiiiiiiiiiiiiiiiiiiiiiiiiiiiiiiiiiiiiiiiiiiiiiiiiiiiiiiiiiiiiiiiiiiiiiiiiiiiiiiiiiiiiiii
iiiiiiiiiiiiiiiiiiiiiiiiiiiiiiiiiiiiiiiiiiiiiiiiiiiiiiiiiiiiiiiiiiiiiiiiiiiiiiiiiiiiiiiiiiiiiiiii
iiiiiiiiiiiiiiiiiiiiiiiiiiiiiiiiiiiiiiiiiiiiiiiiiiiiiiiiiiiiiiiiiiiiiiiiiiiiiiiiiiiiiiiiiiiiiiiii
iiiiiiiiiiiiiiiiiiiiiiiiiiiiiiiiiiiiiiiiiiiiiiiiiiiiiiiiiiiiiiiiiiiiiiiiiiiiiiiiiiiiiiiiiiiiiiiii
iiiiiiiiiiiiiiiiiiiiiiiiiiiiiiiiiiiiiiiiiiiiiiiiiiiiiiiiiiiiiiiiiiiiiiiiiiiiiiiiiiiiiiiiiiiiiiiii
iiiiiiiiiiiiiiiiiiiiiiiiiiiiiiiiiiiiiiiiiiiiiiiiiiiiiiiiiiiiiiiiiiiiiiiiiiiiiiiiiiiiiiiiiiiiiiiii
iiiiiiiiiiiiiiiiiiiiiiiiiiiiiiiiiiiiiiiiiiiiiiiiiiiiiiiiiiiiiiiiiiiiiiiiiiiiiiiiiiiiiiiiiiiiiiiii
iiiiiiiiiiiiiiiiiiiiiiiiiiiiiiiiiiiiiiiiiiiiiiiiiiiiiiiiiiiiiiiiiiiiiiiiiiiiiiiiiiiiiiiiiiiiiiiii
iiiiiiiiiiiiiiiiiiiiiiiiiiiiiiiiiiiiiiiiiiiiiiiiiiiiiiiiiiiiiiiiiiiiiiiiiiiiiiiiiiiiiiiiiiiiiiiii
iiiiiiiiiiiiiiiiiiiiiiiiiiiiiiiiiiiiiiiiiiiiiiiiiiiiiiiiiiiiiiiiiiiiiiiiiiiiiiiiiiiiiiiiiiiiiiiii
iiiiiiiiiiiiiiiiiiiiiiiiiiiiiiiiiiiiiiiiiiiiiiiiiiiiiiiiiiiiiiiiiiiiiiiiiiiiiiiiiiiiiiiiiiiiiiiii
iiiiiiiiiiiiiiiiiiiiiiiiiiiiiiiiiiiiiiiiiiiiiiiiiiiiiiiiiiiiiiiiiiiiiiiiiiiiiiiiiiiiiiiiiiiiiiiii

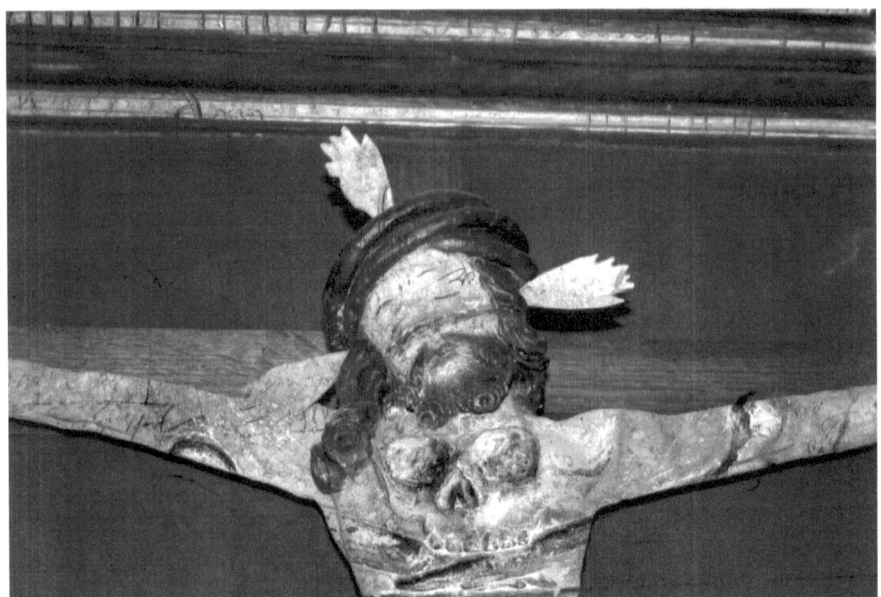

gggggggggggggggggggggggggggggggggggggggggggggggggggggg
gggggggggggggggggggggggggggggggggggggggggggggggggggggg
gggggggggggggggggggggggggggggggggggggggggggggggggggggg
gggggggggggggggggggggggggggggggggggggggggggggggggggggg
gggggggggggggggggggggggggggggggggggggggggggggggggggggg
gggggggggggggggggggggggggggggggggggggggggggggggggggggg
gggggggggggggggggggggggggggggggggggggggggggggggggggggg
gggggggggggggggggggggggggggggggggggggggggggggggggggggg
gggggggggggggggggggggggggggggggggggggggggggggggggggggg
gggggggggggggggggggggggggggggggggggggggggggggggggggggg
gggggggggggggggggggggggggggggggggggggggggggggggggggggg
gggggggggggggggggggggggggggggggggggggggggggggggggggggg
gggggggggggggggggggggggggggggggggggggggggggggggggggggg
gggggggggggggggggggggggggggggggggggggggggggggggggggggg
gggggggggggggggggggggggggggggggggggggggggggggggggggggg
gggggggggggggggggggggggggggggggggggggggggggggggggggggg
gggggggggggggggggggggggggggggggggggggggggggggggggggggg
gggggggggggggggggggggggggggggggggggggggggggggggggggggg
gggggggggggggggggggggggggggggggggggggggggggggggggggggg
gggggggggggggggggggggggggggggggggggggggggggggggggggggg
gggggggggggggggggggggggggggggggggggggggggggggggggggggg
gggggggggggggggggggggggggggggggggggggggggggggggggggggg

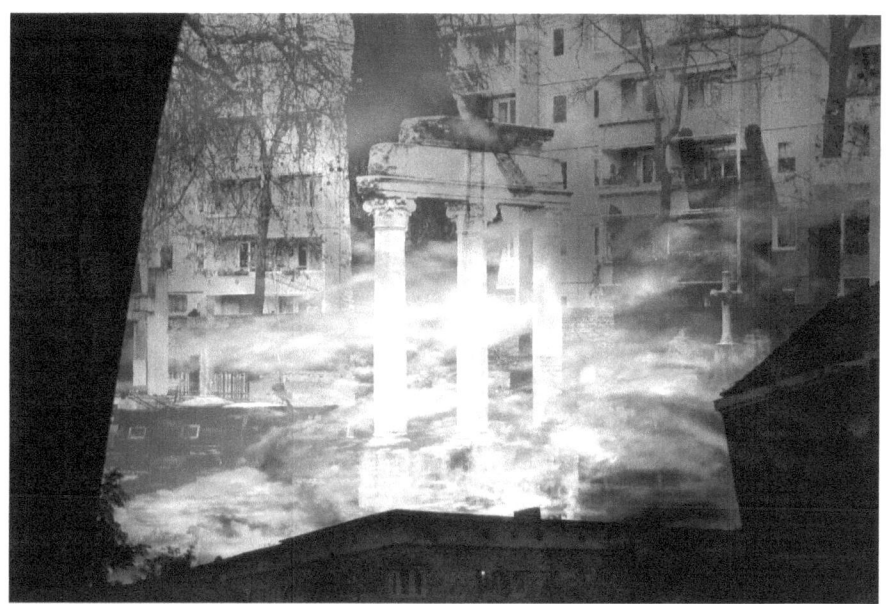

rrrrrrrrrrrrrrrrrrrrrrrrrrrrrrrrrrrrrrrrrrrrrrrrrrrrrrrrrrrrrrrrrrrrrrrrrrrrrr
rrrrrrrrrrrrrrrrrrrrrrrrrrrrrrrrrrrrrrrrrrrrrrrrrrrrrrrrrrrrrrrrrrrrrrrrrrrrrr
rrrrrrrrrrrrrrrrrrrrrrrrrrrrrrrrrrrrrrrrrrrrrrrrrrrrrrrrrrrrrrrrrrrrrrrrrrrrrr
rrrrrrrrrrrrrrrrrrrrrrrrrrrrrrrrrrrrrrrrrrrrrrrrrrrrrrrrrrrrrrrrrrrrrrrrrrrrrr
rrrrrrrrrrrrrrrrrrrrrrrrrrrrrrrrrrrrrrrrrrrrrrrrrrrrrrrrrrrrrrrrrrrrrrrrrrrrrr
rrrrrrrrrrrrrrrrrrrrrrrrrrrrrrrrrrrrrrrrrrrrrrrrrrrrrrrrrrrrrrrrrrrrrrrrrrrrrr
rrrrrrrrrrrrrrrrrrrrrrrrrrrrrrrrrrrrrrrrrrrrrrrrrrrrrrrrrrrrrrrrrrrrrrrrrrrrrr
rrrrrrrrrrrrrrrrrrrrrrrrrrrrrrrrrrrrrrrrrrrrrrrrrrrrrrrrrrrrrrrrrrrrrrrrrrrrrr
rrrrrrrrrrrrrrrrrrrrrrrrrrrrrrrrrrrrrrrrrrrrrrrrrrrrrrrrrrrrrrrrrrrrrrrrrrrrrr
rrrrrrrrrrrrrrrrrrrrrrrrrrrrrrrrrrrrrrrrrrrrrrrrrrrrrrrrrrrrrrrrrrrrrrrrrrrrrr
rrrrrrrrrrrrrrrrrrrrrrrrrrrrrrrrrrrrrrrrrrrrrrrrrrrrrrrrrrrrrrrrrrrrrrrrrrrrrr
rrrrrrrrrrrrrrrrrrrrrrrrrrrrrrrrrrrrrrrrrrrrrrrrrrrrrrrrrrrrrrrrrrrrrrrrrrrrrr
rrrrrrrrrrrrrrrrrrrrrrrrrrrrrrrrrrrrrrrrrrrrrrrrrrrrrrrrrrrrrrrrrrrrrrrrrrrrrr
rrrrrrrrrrrrrrrrrrrrrrrrrrrrrrrrrrrrrrrrrrrrrrrrrrrrrrrrrrrrrrrrrrrrrrrrrrrrrr
rrrrrrrrrrrrrrrrrrrrrrrrrrrrrrrrrrrrrrrrrrrrrrrrrrrrrrrrrrrrrrrrrrrrrrrrrrrrrr
rrrrrrrrrrrrrrrrrrrrrrrrrrrrrrrrrrrrrrrrrrrrrrrrrrrrrrrrrrrrrrrrrrrrrrrrrrrrrr
rrrrrrrrrrrrrrrrrrrrrrrrrrrrrrrrrrrrrrrrrrrrrrrrrrrrrrrrrrrrrrrrrrrrrrrrrrrrrr
rrrrrrrrrrrrrrrrrrrrrrrrrrrrrrrrrrrrrrrrrrrrrrrrrrrrrrrrrrrrrrrrrrrrrrrrrrrrrr
rrrrrrrrrrrrrrrrrrrrrrrrrrrrrrrrrrrrrrrrrrrrrrrrrrrrrrrrrrrrrrrrrrrrrrrrrrrrrr
rrrrrrrrrrrrrrrrrrrrrrrrrrrrrrrrrrrrrrrrrrrrrrrrrrrrrrrrrrrrrrrrrrrrrrrrrrrrrr
rrrrrrrrrrrrrrrrrrrrrrrrrrrrrrrrrrrrrrrrrrrrrrrrrrrrrrrrrrrrrrrrrrrrrrrrrrrrrr
rrrrrrrrrrrrrrrrrrrrrrrrrrrrrrrrrrrrrrrrrrrrrrrrrrrrrrrrrrrrrrrrrrrrrrrrrrrrrr
rrrrrrrrrrrrrrrrrrrrrrrrrrrrrrrrrrrrrrrrrrrrrrrrrrrrrrrrrrrrrrrrrrrrrrrrrrrrrr
rrrrrrrrrrrrrrrrrrrrrrrrrrrrrrrrrrrrrrrrrrrrrrrrrrrrrrrrrrrrrrrrrrrrrrrrrrrrrr

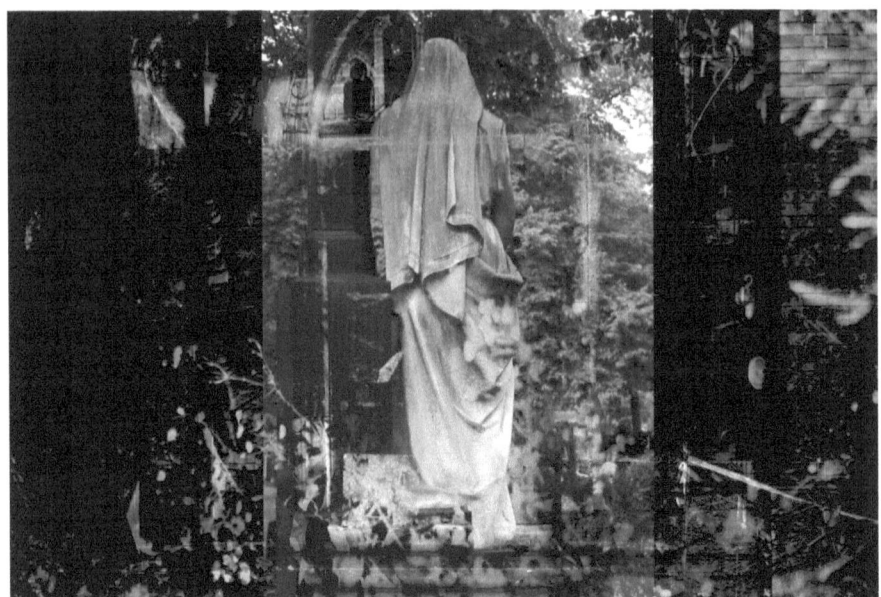

aaaaaaaaaaaaaaaaaaaaaaaaaaaaaaaaaaaaaaaaaaaaaaaaaaaaaaaaaaaaa
aaaaaaaaaaaaaaaaaaaaaaaaaaaaaaaaaaaaaaaaaaaaaaaaaaaaaaaaaaaaa
aaaaaaaaaaaaaaaaaaaaaaaaaaaaaaaaaaaaaaaaaaaaaaaaaaaaaaaaaaaaa
aaaaaaaaaaaaaaaaaaaaaaaaaaaaaaaaaaaaaaaaaaaaaaaaaaaaaaaaaaaaa
aaaaaaaaaaaaaaaaaaaaaaaaaaaaaaaaaaaaaaaaaaaaaaaaaaaaaaaaaaaaa
aaaaaaaaaaaaaaaaaaaaaaaaaaaaaaaaaaaaaaaaaaaaaaaaaaaaaaaaaaaaa
aaaaaaaaaaaaaaaaaaaaaaaaaaaaaaaaaaaaaaaaaaaaaaaaaaaaaaaaaaaaa
aaaaaaaaaaaaaaaaaaaaaaaaaaaaaaaaaaaaaaaaaaaaaaaaaaaaaaaaaaaaa
aaaaaaaaaaaaaaaaaaaaaaaaaaaaaaaaaaaaaaaaaaaaaaaaaaaaaaaaaaaaa
aaaaaaaaaaaaaaaaaaaaaaaaaaaaaaaaaaaaaaaaaaaaaaaaaaaaaaaaaaaaa
aaaaaaaaaaaaaaaaaaaaaaaaaaaaaaaaaaaaaaaaaaaaaaaaaaaaaaaaaaaaa
aaaaaaaaaaaaaaaaaaaaaaaaaaaaaaaaaaaaaaaaaaaaaaaaaaaaaaaaaaaaa
aaaaaaaaaaaaaaaaaaaaaaaaaaaaaaaaaaaaaaaaaaaaaaaaaaaaaaaaaaaaa
aaaaaaaaaaaaaaaaaaaaaaaaaaaaaaaaaaaaaaaaaaaaaaaaaaaaaaaaaaaaa
aaaaaaaaaaaaaaaaaaaaaaaaaaaaaaaaaaaaaaaaaaaaaaaaaaaaaaaaaaaaa
aaaaaaaaaaaaaaaaaaaaaaaaaaaaaaaaaaaaaaaaaaaaaaaaaaaaaaaaaaaaa
aaaaaaaaaaaaaaaaaaaaaaaaaaaaaaaaaaaaaaaaaaaaaaaaaaaaaaaaaaaaa
aaaaaaaaaaaaaaaaaaaaaaaaaaaaaaaaaaaaaaaaaaaaaaaaaaaaaaaaaaaaa
aaaaaaaaaaaaaaaaaaaaaaaaaaaaaaaaaaaaaaaaaaaaaaaaaaaaaaaaaaaaa
aaaaaaaaaaaaaaaaaaaaaaaaaaaaaaaaaaaaaaaaaaaaaaaaaaaaaaaaaaaaa
aaaaaaaaaaaaaaaaaaaaaaaaaaaaaaaaaaaaaaaaaaaaaaaaaaaaaaaaaaaaa
aaaaaaaaaaaaaaaaaaaaaaaaaaaaaaaaaaaaaaaaaaaaaaaaaaaaaaaaaaaaa
aaaaaaaaaaaaaaaaaaaaaaaaaaaaaaaaaaaaaaaaaaaaaaaaaaaaaaaaaaaaa

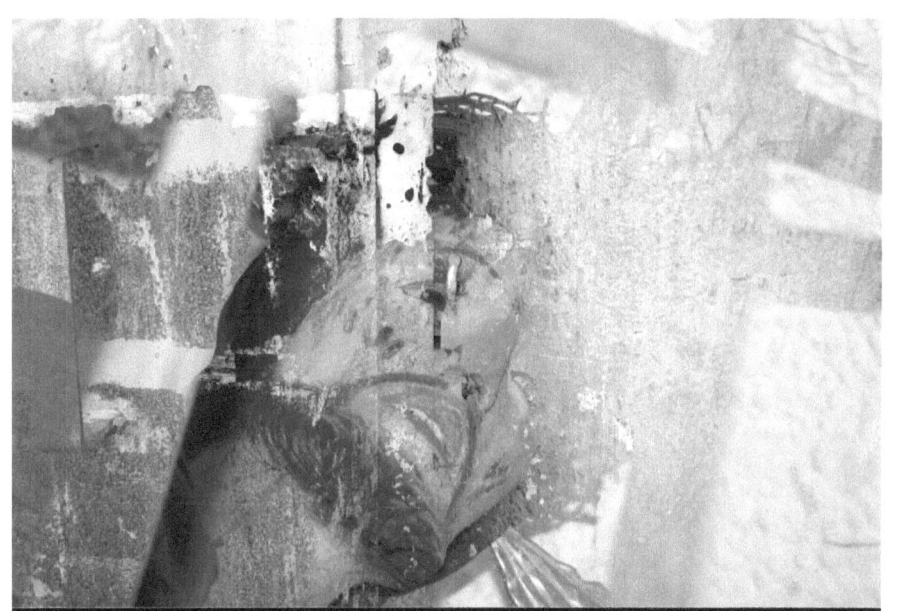

migrantsare
blessedmigr
antsarebless
edmigrantsa

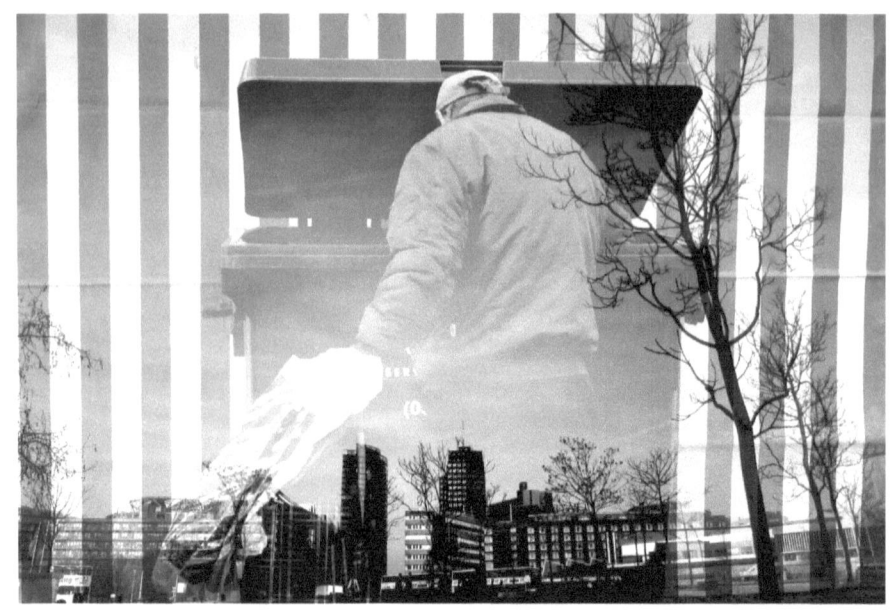

migrantsare
blessedmigr
antsarebless
edmigrantsa

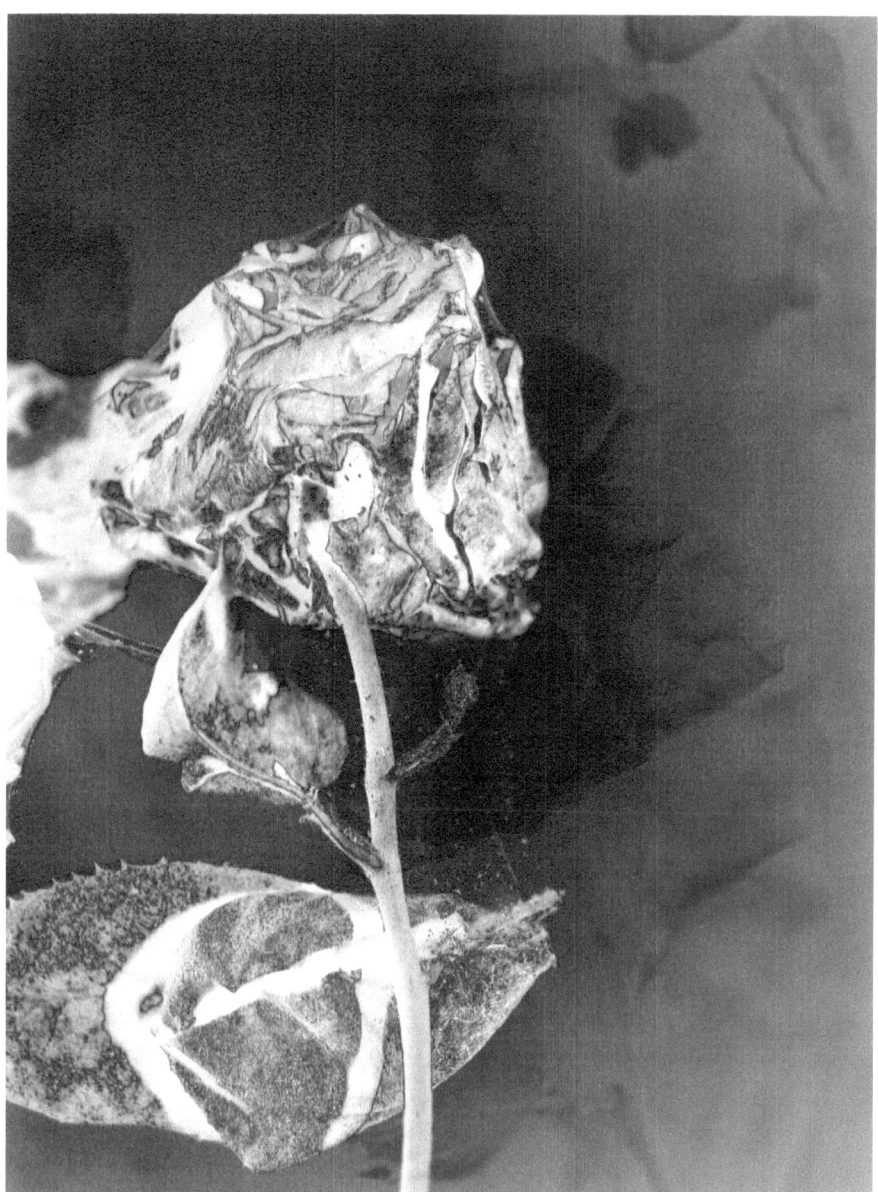

nnnnnnnnnnnnnnnnnnnnnnnnnnnnnnnnnnnnnnnnnnnnnnnnnnnnnnnnn
nnnnnnnnnnnnnnnnnnnnnnnnnnnnnnnnnnnnnnnnnnnnnnnnnnnnnnnnn
nnnnnnnnnnnnnnnnnnnnnnnnnnnnnnnnnnnnnnnnnnnnnnnnnnnnnnnnn
nnnnnnnnnnnnnnnnnnnnnnnnnnnnnnnnnnnnnnnnnnnnnnnnnnnnnnnnn
nnnnnnnnnnnnnnnnnnnnnnnnnnnnnnnnnnnnnnnnnnnnnnnnnnnnnnnnn
nnnnnnnnnnnnnnnnnnnnnnnnnnnnnnnnnnnnnnnnnnnnnnnnnnnnnnnnn

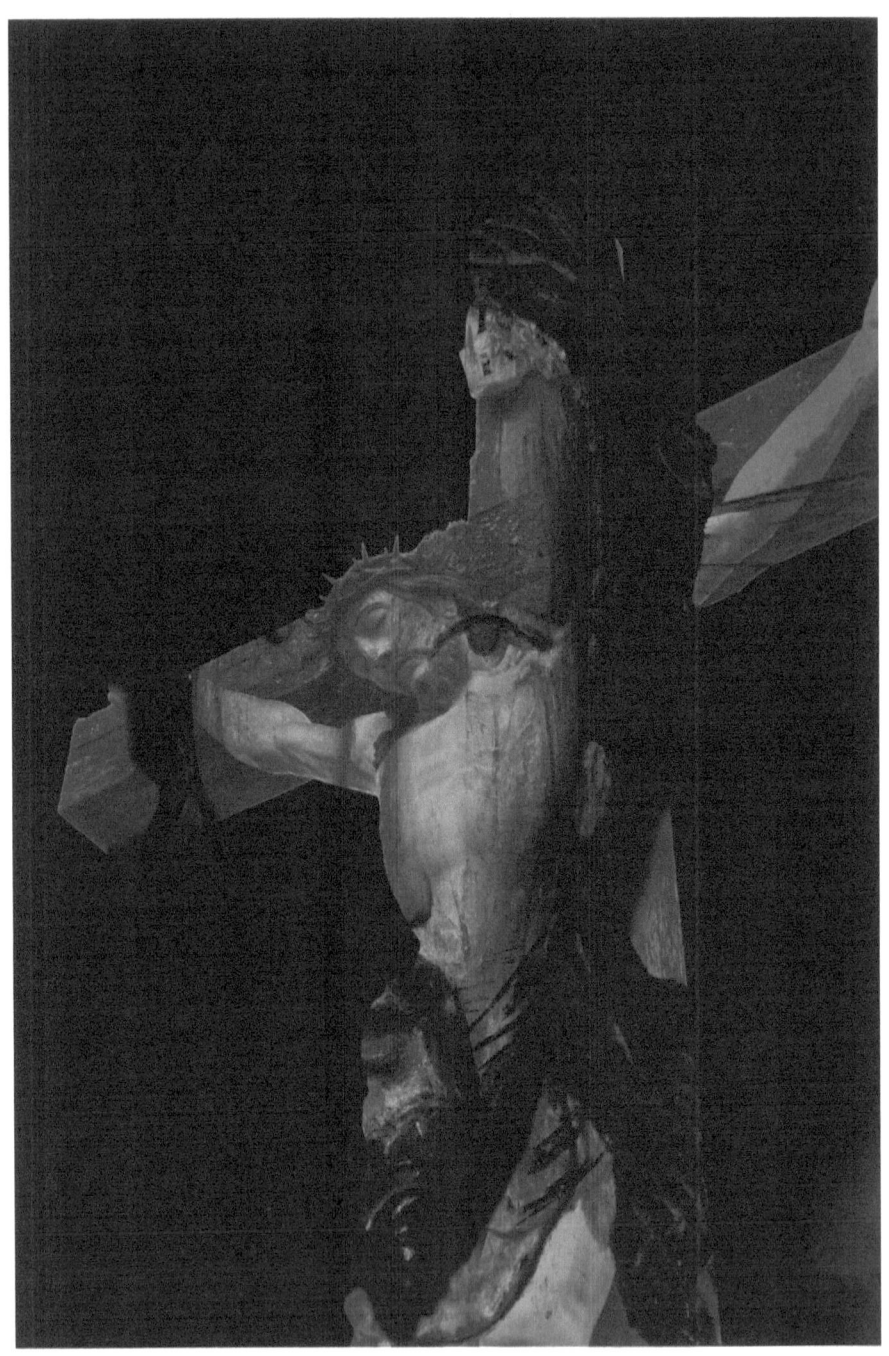

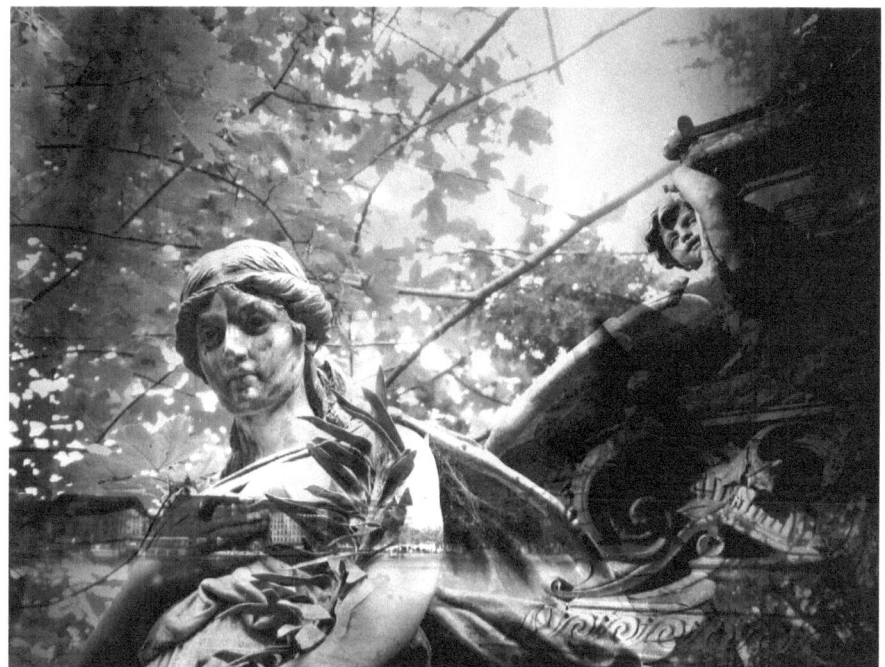

tttttttttttttttttttttttttttttttttttttttttttttttttttttttttttttttttttttttttttttttttttttt
tttttttttttttttttttttttttttttttttttttttttttttttttttttttttttttttttttttttttttttttttttttt
tttttttttttttttttttttttttttttttttttttttttttttttttttttttttttttttttttttttttttttttttttttt
tttttttttttttttttttttttttttttttttttttttttttttttttttttttttttttttttttttttttttttttttttttt
tttttttttttttttttttttttttttttttttttttttttttttttttttttttttttttttttttttttttttttttttttttt
tttttttttttttttttttttttttttttttttttttttttttttttttttttttttttttttttttttttttttttttttttttt
tttttttttttttttttttttttttttttttttttttttttttttttttttttttttttttttttttttttttttttttttttttt
tttttttttttttttttttttttttttttttttttttttttttttttttttttttttttttttttttttttttttttttttttttt
tttttttttttttttttttttttttttttttttttttttttttttttttttttttttttttttttttttttttttttttttttttt
tttttttttttttttttttttttttttttttttttttttttttttttttttttttttttttttttttttttttttttttttttttt
tttttttttttttttttttttttttttttttttttttttttttttttttttttttttttttttttttttttttttttttttttttt
tttttttttttttttttttttttttttttttttttttttttttttttttttttttttttttttttttttttttttttttttttttt
tttttttttttttttttttttttttttttttttttttttttttttttttttttttttttttttttttttttttttttttttttttt
tttttttttttttttttttttttttttttttttttttttttttttttttttttttttttttttttttttttttttttttttttttt
tttttttttttttttttttttttttttttttttttttttttttttttttttttttttttttttttttttttttttttttttttttt
tttttttttttttttttttttttttttttttttttttttttttttttttttttttttttttttttttttttttttttttttttttt
tttttttttttttttttttttttttttttttttttttttttttttttttttttttttttttttttttttttttttttttttttttt
tttttttttttttttttttttttttttttttttttttttttttttttttttttttttttttttttttttttttttttttttttttt
tttttttttttttttttttttttttttttttttttttttttttttttttttttttttttttttttttttttttttttttttttttt
tttttttttttttttttttttttttttttttttttttttttttttttttttttttttttttttttttttttttttttttttttttt
tttttttttttttttttttttttttttttttttttttttttttttttttttttttttttttttttttttttttttttttttttttt
tttttttttttttttttttttttttttttttttttttttttttttttttttttttttttttttttttttttttttttttttttttt

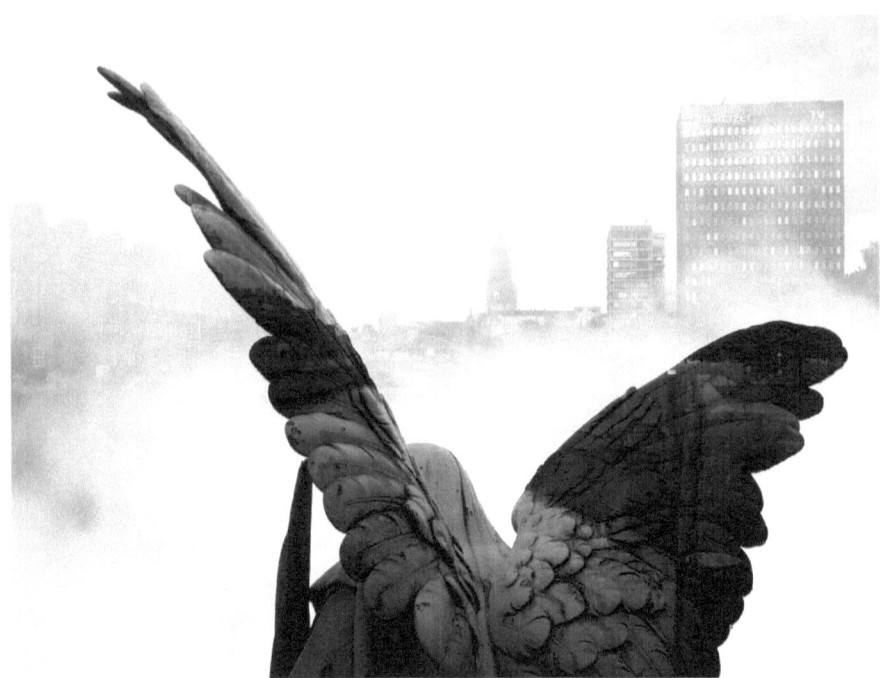

SSSSSSSSSSSSSSSSSSSSSSSSSSSSSSSSSSSSSSSSSSSSSSSSSSSSSSSSSSSSSSSSSSSSSSSSSS
SSSSSSSSSSSSSSSSSSSSSSSSSSSSSSSSSSSSSSSSSSSSSSSSSSSSSSSSSSSSSSSSSSSSSSSSSS
SSSSSSSSSSSSSSSSSSSSSSSSSSSSSSSSSSSSSSSSSSSSSSSSSSSSSSSSSSSSSSSSSSSSSSSSSS
SSSSSSSSSSSSSSSSSSSSSSSSSSSSSSSSSSSSSSSSSSSSSSSSSSSSSSSSSSSSSSSSSSSSSSSSSS
SSSSSSSSSSSSSSSSSSSSSSSSSSSSSSSSSSSSSSSSSSSSSSSSSSSSSSSSSSSSSSSSSSSSSSSSSS
SSSSSSSSSSSSSSSSSSSSSSSSSSSSSSSSSSSSSSSSSSSSSSSSSSSSSSSSSSSSSSSSSSSSSSSSSS
SSSSSSSSSSSSSSSSSSSSSSSSSSSSSSSSSSSSSSSSSSSSSSSSSSSSSSSSSSSSSSSSSSSSSSSSSS
SSSSSSSSSSSSSSSSSSSSSSSSSSSSSSSSSSSSSSSSSSSSSSSSSSSSSSSSSSSSSSSSSSSSSSSSSS
SSSSSSSSSSSSSSSSSSSSSSSSSSSSSSSSSSSSSSSSSSSSSSSSSSSSSSSSSSSSSSSSSSSSSSSSSS
SSSSSSSSSSSSSSSSSSSSSSSSSSSSSSSSSSSSSSSSSSSSSSSSSSSSSSSSSSSSSSSSSSSSSSSSSS
SSSSSSSSSSSSSSSSSSSSSSSSSSSSSSSSSSSSSSSSSSSSSSSSSSSSSSSSSSSSSSSSSSSSSSSSSS
SSSSSSSSSSSSSSSSSSSSSSSSSSSSSSSSSSSSSSSSSSSSSSSSSSSSSSSSSSSSSSSSSSSSSSSSSS
SSSSSSSSSSSSSSSSSSSSSSSSSSSSSSSSSSSSSSSSSSSSSSSSSSSSSSSSSSSSSSSSSSSSSSSSSS
SSSSSSSSSSSSSSSSSSSSSSSSSSSSSSSSSSSSSSSSSSSSSSSSSSSSSSSSSSSSSSSSSSSSSSSSSS
SSSSSSSSSSSSSSSSSSSSSSSSSSSSSSSSSSSSSSSSSSSSSSSSSSSSSSSSSSSSSSSSSSSSSSSSSS
SSSSSSSSSSSSSSSSSSSSSSSSSSSSSSSSSSSSSSSSSSSSSSSSSSSSSSSSSSSSSSSSSSSSSSSSSS
SSSSSSSSSSSSSSSSSSSSSSSSSSSSSSSSSSSSSSSSSSSSSSSSSSSSSSSSSSSSSSSSSSSSSSSSSS
SSSSSSSSSSSSSSSSSSSSSSSSSSSSSSSSSSSSSSSSSSSSSSSSSSSSSSSSSSSSSSSSSSSSSSSSSS
SSSSSSSSSSSSSSSSSSSSSSSSSSSSSSSSSSSSSSSSSSSSSSSSSSSSSSSSSSSSSSSSSSSSSSSSSS
SSSSSSSSSSSSSSSSSSSSSSSSSSSSSSSSSSSSSSSSSSSSSSSSSSSSSSSSSSSSSSSSSSSSSSSSSS
SSSSSSSSSSSSSSSSSSSSSSSSSSSSSSSSSSSSSSSSSSSSSSSSSSSSSSSSSSSSSSSSSSSSSSSSSS
SSSSSSSSSSSSSSSSSSSSSSSSSSSSSSSSSSSSSSSSSSSSSSSSSSSSSSSSSSSSSSSSSSSSSSSSSS
SSSSSSSSSSSSSSSSSSSSSSSSSSSSSSSSSSSSSSSSSSSSSSSSSSSSSSSSSSSSSSSSSSSSSSSSSS
SSSSSSSSSSSSSSSSSSSSSSSSSSSSSSSSSSSSSSSSSSSSSSSSSSSSSSSSSSSSSSSSSSSSSSSSSS
SSSSSSSSSSSSSSSSSSSSSSSSSSSSSSSSSSSSSSSSSSSSSSSSSSSSSSSSSSSSSSSSSSSSSSSSSS

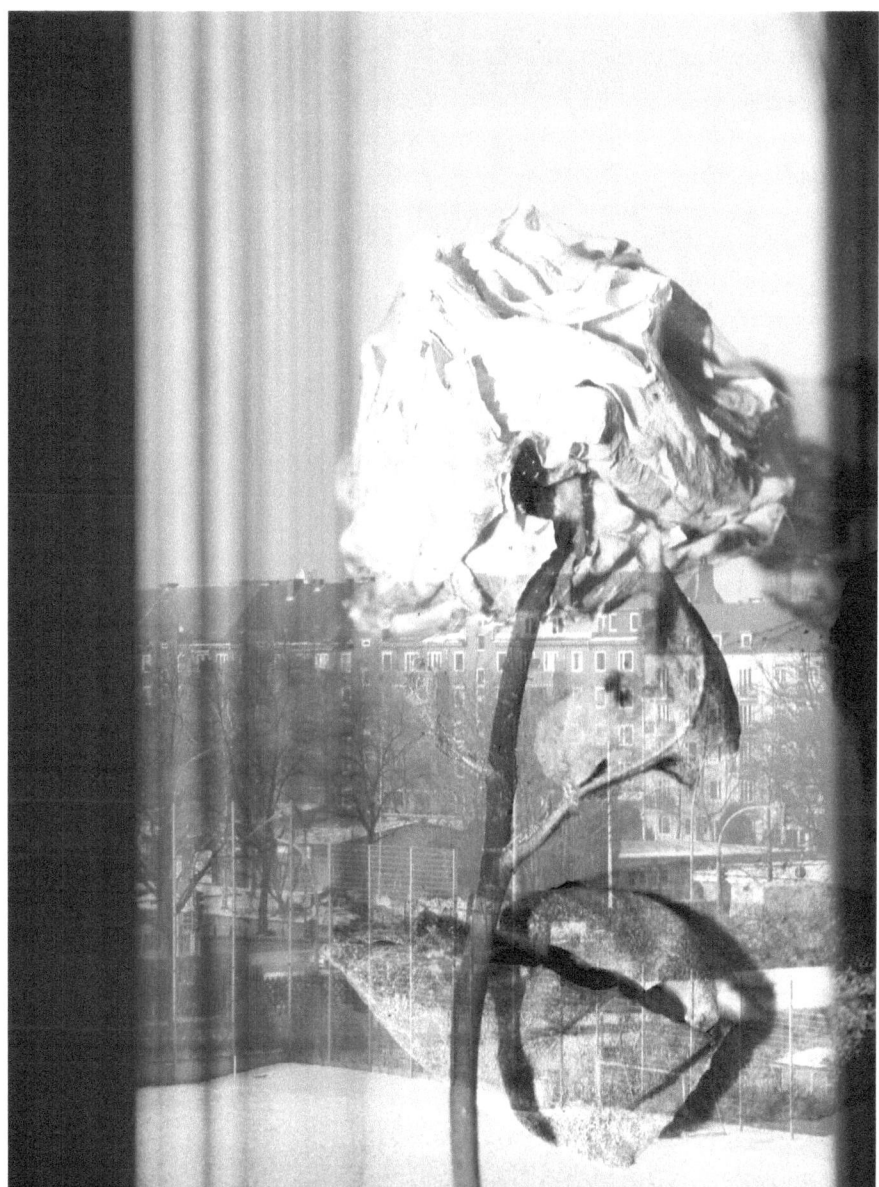

art without life is useless art without life is useless art without life is useless art without life is useless art without life is useless art without life is useless art without life is useless art without life is useless art without life is useless art without life is useless art without life is useless art without life is useless art without life is useless art without life is useless art without life is useless art without life is useless art without life is useless

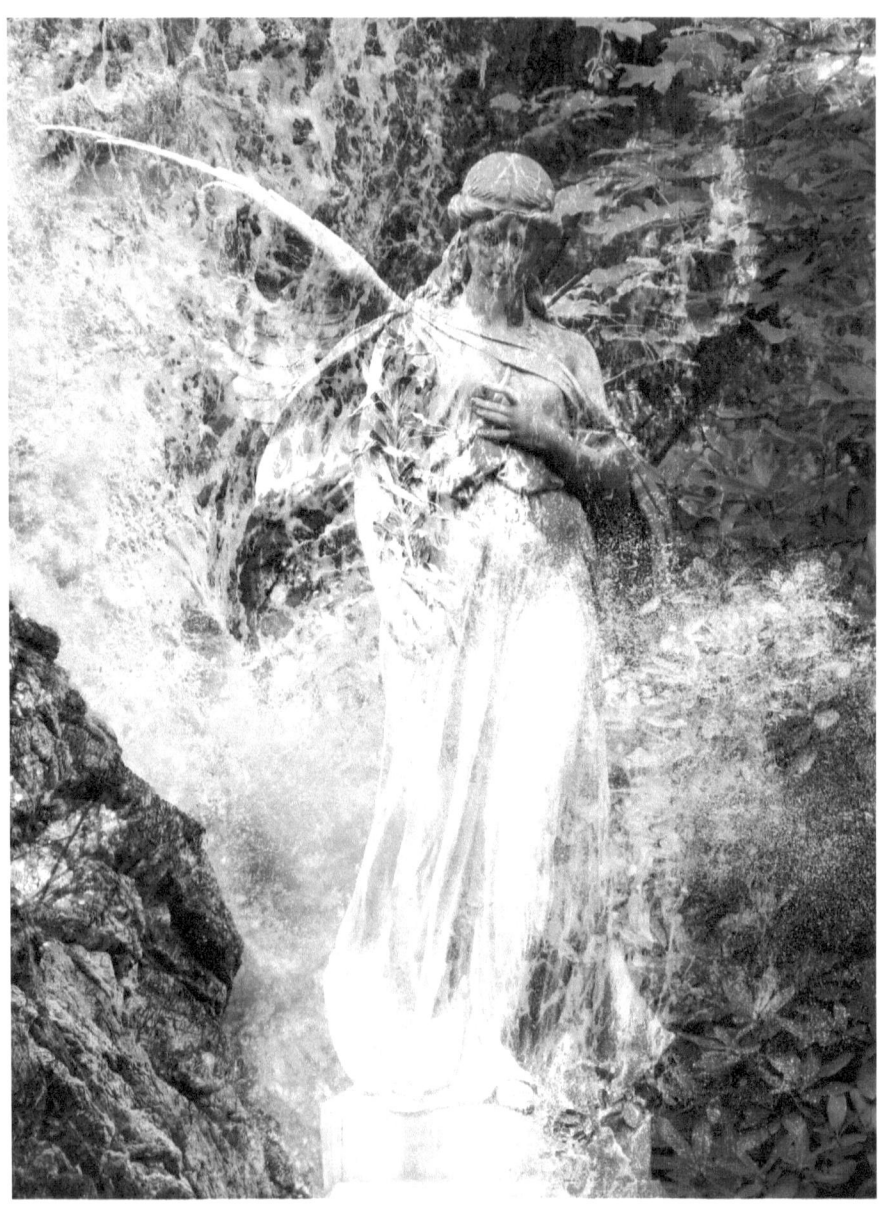

MIGRANTS

powerpowerpowerpowerpowerpo-
werpowerpowerpowerpowerpower
powerpowerpowerpowerpowerpo-
werpowerpowerpowerpowerpower
powerpowerpowerpowerpowerpo-
werpowerpowerpowerpowerpower
powerpowerpowerpowerpowerpo-
werpowerpowerpowerpowerpower
powerpowerpowerpowerpowerpo-
werpowerpowerpowerpowerpower
powerpowerpowerpowerpowerpo-
werpowerpowerpowerpowerpower
powerpowerpowerpowerpowerpo-
werpowerpowerpowerpowerpower
powerpowerpowerpowerpowerpo-
werpowerpowerpowerpowerpower
powerpowerpowerpowerpowerpo..

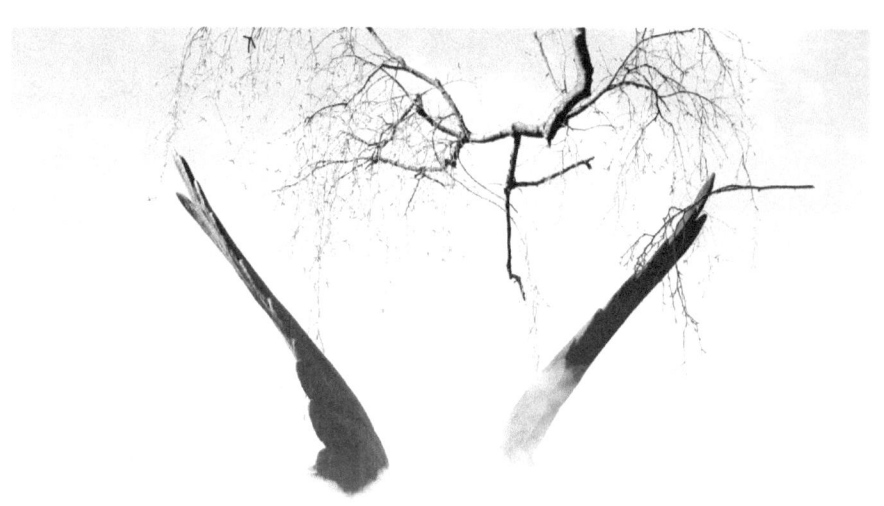

power power power power power power power power power power
power power power power power power power power power power
power power power power power power power power power power
power power power power power power power power power power
power power power power power power power power power power
power power power power power power power power power power
power power power power power power power power power power
power power power power power power power power power power
power power power power power power power power power power
power power power power power power power power power power
power power power power power power power power power power
power power power power power power power power power power
power power power power power power power power power power
power power power power power power power power power power
power power power power power power power power power power
power power power power power power power power power power
power power power power power power power power power power
power power power power power power power power power power
power power power power power power power power power power
power power power power power power power power power power

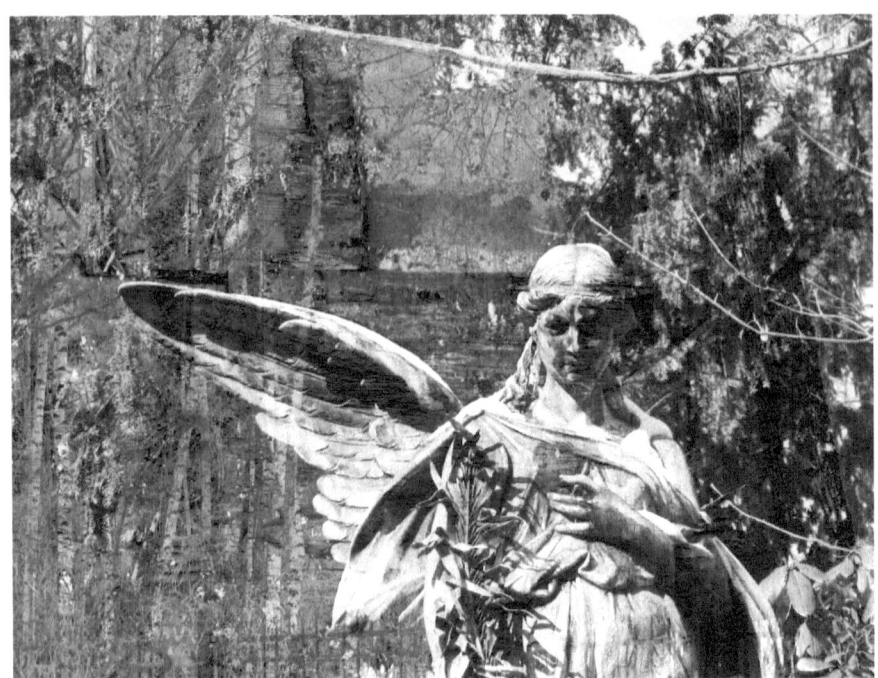

art without life is useless art without life is useless art without life is useless art without life is useless art without life is useless art without **life** is useless art without life is useless art without life is useless **art** without life is useless art without life is useless art without **life** is useless art without life is useless art without life is useless **art** without life is useless art without life is useless art without **life** is useless art without life is useless art without life is useless **art** without life is useless art without life is useless **art**

without life is useless art without life is useless

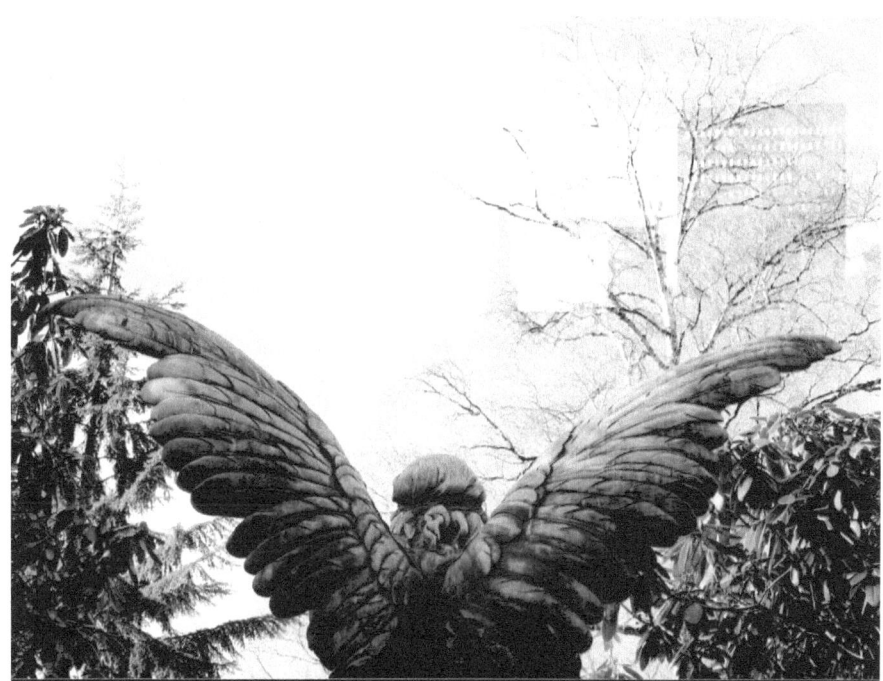

power power power power power power power power power power
power power power power power power power power power power
power power power power power power power power power power
power power power power power power power power power power
power power power power power power power power power power
power power power power power power power power power power
power power power power power power power power power power
power power power power power power power power power power
power power power power power power power power power power
power power power power power power power power power power
power power power power power power power power power power
power power power power power power power power power power
power power power power power power power power power power
power power power power power power power power power power
power power power power power power power power power power
power power power power power power power power power power
power power power power power power power power power power
power power power power power power power power power power
power power power power power power power power power power
power power power power power power power power power power

Art without empathy is useless Art without empathy is useless Art
without empathy is useless Art without empathy is useless Art
without empathy is useless Art without empathy is useless Art
without empathy is useless Art without empathy is useless Art
without empathy is useless Art without empathy is useless Art
without empathy is useless Art without empathy is useless Art
without empathy is useless Art without empathy is useless Art
without empathy is useless Art without empathy is useless Art
without empathy is useless Art without empathy is useless Art
without empathy is useless Art without empathy is useless Art
without empathy is useless Art without empathy is useless Art
without empathy is useless Art without empathy is useless Art
without empathy is useless Art without empathy is useless Art
without empathy is useless Art without empathy is useless Art
without empathy is useless Art without empathy is useless Art
without empathy is useless Art without empathy is useless Art
without empathy is useless Art without empathy is useless Art
without empathy is useless Art without empathy is useless Art
without empathy is useless Art without empathy is useless Art
without empathy is useless Art without empathy is useless Art
without empathy is useless Art without empathy is useless Art
without empathy is useless Art without empathy is useless Art
without empathy is useless Art without empathy is useless Art
without empathy is useless Art without empathy is useless Art
without empathy is useless Art without empathy is useless Art
without empathy is useless Art without empathy is useless Art
without empathy is useless Art without empathy is useless Art
without empathy is useless Art without empathy is useless Art
without empathy is useless Art without empathy is useless Art
without empathy is useless Art without empathy is useless Art
without empathy is useless Art without empathy is useless Art
without empathy is useless Art without empathy is useless Art
without empathy is useless Art without empathy is useless Art
without empathy is useless Art without empathy is useless Art
without empathy is useless Art without empathy is useless Art
without empathy is useless Art without empathy is useless Art
without empathy is useless Art without empathy is useless Art
without empathy is useless Art without empathy is useless Art

beginning is made the beginning is made the
beginning is made the beginning is made the
beginning is made the beginning is made the
beginning is made the beginning is made the
beginning is made the beginning is made the
beginning is made the beginning is made the
beginning is made the beginning is made the
beginning is made the beginning is made the
beginning is made the beginning is made the
beginning is made the beginning is made the
beginning is made the beginning is made the
beginning is made the beginning is made the
beginning is made the beginning is made the
beginning is made the beginning is made the
beginning is made the beginning is made the
beginning is made the beginning is made the
beginning is made the beginning is made

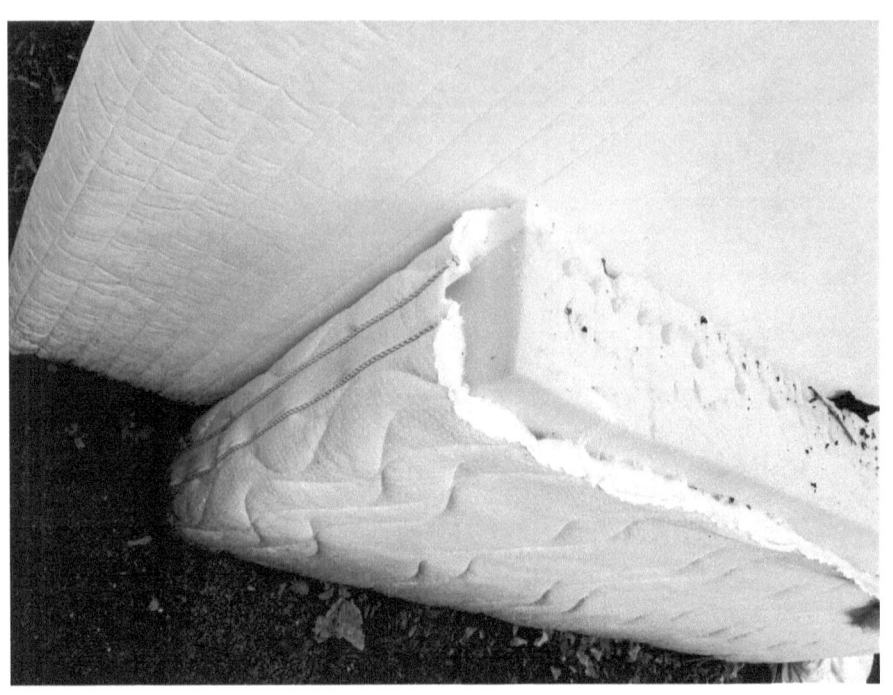

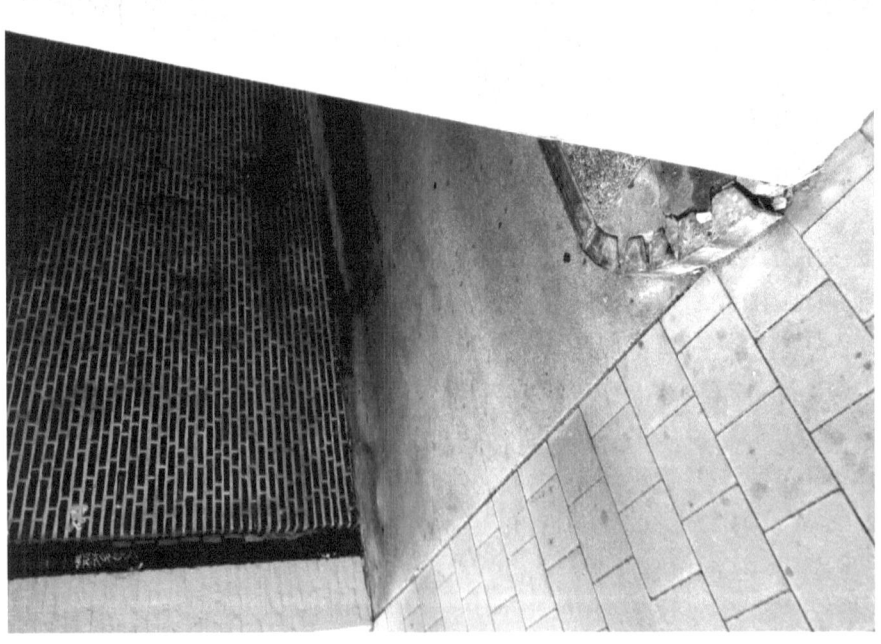

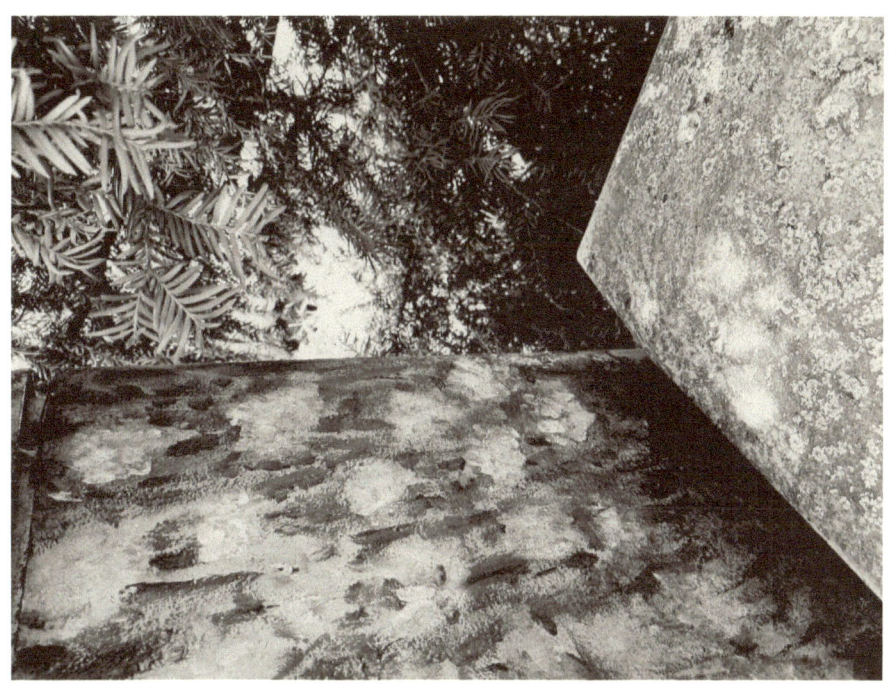

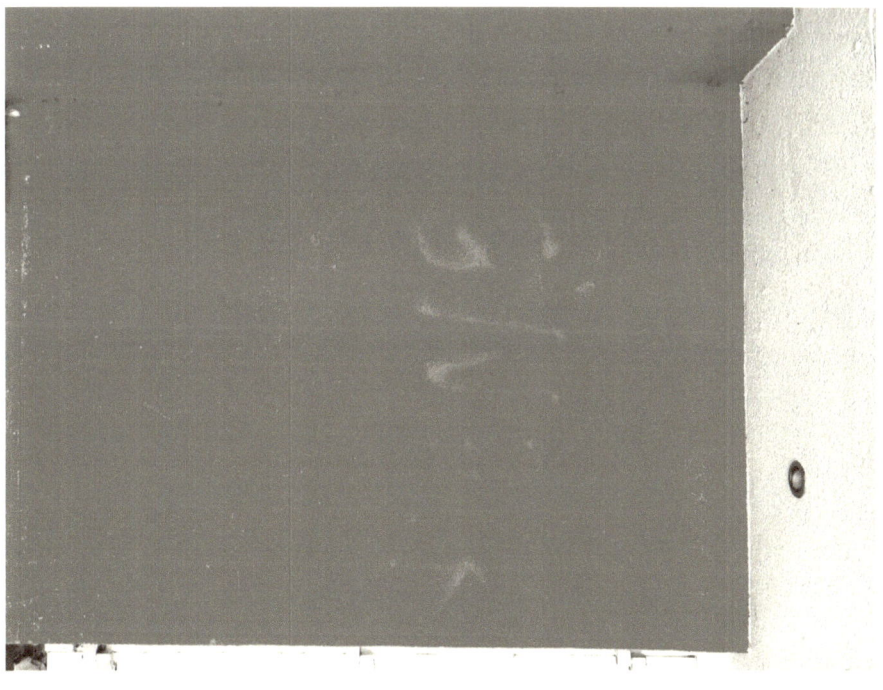

PONDERA VERBORUM art project

ANNO MMXXIII

www.ingramcontent.com/pod-product-compliance
Lightning Source LLC
Chambersburg PA
CBHW050449290526
45786CB00006B/2214